DYNAMICS of GROUP DECISIONS

SAGE FOCUS EDITIONS

DYNAMICS OF GROUP DECISIONS

edited by
Hermann Brandstätter,
James H. Davis, and
Heinz Schuler

 SAGE PUBLICATIONS   Beverly Hills   London

For information address:

SAGE PUBLICATIONS, INC.
275 South Beverly Drive
Beverly Hills, California 90212

SAGE PUBLICATIONS LTD
28 Banner Street
London EC1Y 8QE, England

Printed in the United States of America

Library of Congress Cataloging in Publication Data

Main entry under title:
    Dynamics of group decisions.

    (Sage focus editions ; 5)
    Includes bibliographical references.
    1. Small groups—Congresses. 2. Decision-making,
groups—Congresses. I. Brandstätter, Hermann.
II. Davis, James H., 1932-   III. Schuler, Heinz.
IV. Series.
HM133.D89   301.18'5   78-19143
ISBN 0-8039-0872-5
ISBN 0-8039-0873-3 pbk.

FIRST PRINTING

CONTENTS

ACKNOWLEDGMENTS

We are greatly indebted to several participants, in addition to the authors of the papers, for valuable assistance in the preparation of discussion protocols: Barbara and Hubert Feger, Gerhard Kaminski, and Percy Tannenbaum. We regret their discussion summaries could not be included, but we have tried to summarize their main points in the editorial remarks introducing each of the three sections. In all cases, the authors benefited greatly from the discussion summaries when revising their papers, and we acknowledge our debt to them.

The delightful setting of the symposium contributed greatly to its success. Ottobeuren is a small, idyllic village in the foothills of the Bavarian mountains. The people there are very conscious of the twelve-centuries old Benedictine Monastery and its history. The "Vereinigung der Freunde der Benediktinerabtei" (Society of the Friends of the Benecdictine Abbey) not only supports the renovation and restoration of the marvelous local Rococo church, but has also supported (St. Benedict may bless them on behalf of it) our symposia for several years. We owe special thanks to the chairman of the Society, Regierungspräsident Dr. Frank Sider, the Abbot Vitalis, and Mayor Martin Frehner for their kind support. We are also indebted to the "Gesellschaft der Freunde der Universität Augsburg" (Society of the Friends of the University of Augsburg) and its chairman, Senator Erich Salzmann, who provided financial support for the meeting. The European Association of Experimental Social Psychology advanced the symposium to the status of a "Small Group Meeting of the EAESP," and we are grateful for this opportunity which helped us attract a number of excellent participants from various countries.

Two comparable symposia had already taken place in Ottobeuren, in the course of which the variety of topics and the number of research institutes informally represented gradually increased. Whereas the first meeting (1972) was a workshop of the research group established at the University of Augsburg, Germany, the second (1974) was attended by specialists of the field from German speaking countries. The third in the series (1976) brought together colleagues from eight different countries. It provided the participants with ample opportunity for discussion that often spread beyond the scheduled time to informal chats among three or four people. The fourth symposium (1978) was co-sponsored by the European Association of Experimental Social Psychology and its American counterpart, the Society of Experimental Social Psychologists.

—Hermann Brandstätter
—James H. Davis
—Heinz Schuler

PREFACE

Ivan Steiner commented in the preface to his seminal work, *Group Process and Productivity,* that the group seems to have gone out of fashion. He was referring, of course, to the decline in research activity that took small group interaction and performance as the primary target. Few would disagree with Steiner that by the late 1950s empirical research on groups had simply outrun theory, and the availability of cogent and stimulating theoretical work, perhaps along with other social forces, shifted attention to attitude change and other topics of individual social cognition for more than a decade. However, it is difficult to imagine a social psychology continuing long without a renewed interest developing in interpersonal relations and group action.

Such a renewed interest in small groups now appears to be well underway, but does not appear to be organized around any particular theoretical approach or school of thought. Rather, various practical and social problems ranging from procedural questions of justice to traditional issues of interpersonal conflict have given rise to the increase in research activity. Moreover, group research is not focused in a particular country or a limited geographical region. Such a diversity in problems and approaches is in distinct contrast to the early 1950s, perhaps the high point of small group research activity until now. It is for these reasons that we intend the present book to be a survey of contemporary research on at least some aspects of small groups; the topics range from the predominantly empirical to the primarily theoretical, and cover a number of research areas. The contributors are from various European and North American countries, and the variety of approaches and backgrounds very much reflects the spirit of the survey.

The chapters are grouped into three sections. First, *Cooperative Interaction: Cognitive Aspects,* work dealing with group decisions, problem solving and other aspects of group performance on primarily intellective tasks. Second, *Cooperative Interaction: Social-Emotional Aspects,* research dealing with the social process itself in a more direct way than the preceding section. Third, *Mixed-Motive Interaction,* work dealing with interpersonal behavior in which some element of conflict among members is evident.

This book does not exhaust all topics or research efforts currently underway. However, we hope it reflects some of the major problems currently being studied and the diverse approaches to our perhaps most fundamental research object—the small group.

1

INTRODUCTION: ORIGINS AND CURRENT STATUS OF GROUP DECISION-MAKING

Dennis H. Nagao, David A. Vollrath, and James H. Davis

Small groups serve a variety of purposes in human societies, and the pervasiveness of task-oriented groups has been a salient feature of social life throughout history. Thus, the highly diverse origins of the systematic study of small, task-oriented groups come as no surprise. Widely spaced in time and geography, these origins may be located in several disciplines, although psychology is our primary focus here. Disagreement as to primacy in the scientific study of things is commonplace, but few would disagree that the classic studies by Triplett (1898) were a seminal event in the controlled study of social behavior.

The subjects studied by Triplett were minimally interactive and the primary independent variable was the presence or absence of others, including any interpretation a subject might place on the behavior of the co-actors. The concern with performance facilitation (and decrement) in a social context was continued by Allport (1920, 1924) and Dashiell (1935), among others. It was not until Allport that psychology put to rest the "group mind" concept, and was thus freed to begin the serious empirical study of groups. However, it remained for Zajonc (1965) to perceive an orderliness in the empirical record theretofore judged as inconsistent, if not chaotic. He observed that performance was facilitated by the presence of others on tasks requiring well-learned behaviors but inhibited on those requiring the acquisition of new information. Subsequent researchers (e.g.,

Cottrell, Wack, Sekerak, and Rittle, 1968) have taken exception to some of Zajonc's theoretical assumptions that can be only poorly checked against data at present (e.g., the arousal presumed to infect the observed performer in varying degrees). But, the basic ideas of Zajonc's approach remain viable with only minor reconceptualizations. (See, for example, Cohen and Davis, 1973.)

Another early stimulus for small group study grew out of the practical questions concerning study efficiency posed a half century ago by German educators. Although the major interest was still the individual, albeit in a social context, there was a somewhat greater interest in interaction. Several researchers (e.g., Mayer, 1903; Schmidt, 1904; Meumann, 1914) were interested in performance "together and apart" because of the obvious similarity to classroom work and solitary study at home.

A few years later, Sherif (1935) carried out his classic experiment on norms, using also a minimally interactive social situation and the ambiguity afforded by the autokinetic effect. Again, the focus was on the individual subject as he or she was influenced by others nearby, and the surprising persistence of the norms created by the brief social exchanges with other judges. Several years later, the experimental control and economy in subject hours made variations on this basic experimental paradigm virtually sovereign in experimental social psychology.

Before that happened, however, the small group itself became the major object of inquiry for social psychology. The observation of human groups is as old as recorded history, but the systematic study of small groups under controlled conditions is a relatively recent development. Sociologists, such as Cooley (1902) and Mayo (1933), spurred interest in small groups by their investigations of primary groups and their importance in socialization, the military, and organizations. This early interest in the social-emotional relations between interacting members set the direction for much of the subsequent work in sociology. A landmark study in psychology was that of Marjorie Shaw (1932), who studied the interaction of four-person groups working cooperatively on word puzzles and observed that the proportion of correct solutions they achieved was higher than that of individuals working privately. Her interpretation of this apparent group performance superiority was to go relatively unchallenged for more than two decades (see Lorge and Solomon, 1955; Restle and Davis, 1962; Davis, 1969). Moreover, the primacy of studying *intellective performance* (the whole field was sometimes labeled "group problem solving") in predominantly *cooperative interaction* settings was established for years to come. Although all group situations are to some degree mixtures of cooperation and competition, it would be the late 1950s before substantial research attention would be addressed to task situations involving predominantly a mixture of member motives—mixtures in which positive outcomes for one or more members result in negative outcomes for others, and all the "shades" in between.

Several notable research trends have focused upon social phenomena outside of groups (e.g., opinion polling, culture and personality, communication and persuasion, and so on), but we are concerned here only with the small group of interacting members. Accordingly, the chapters to follow have been divided into three sections, each following from a somewhat separate tradition within the overall umbrella once labeled "group dynamics."

(a) Cooperative Interaction: Cognitive Aspects reflects the area we typically now call "group performance," and illustrates the frequent reliance upon cognitive tasks such as the solution to a problem or the achievement of a decision. Although the emphasis is clearly on the more or less cooperative attainment of the group goal, we see in each chapter a concern with social process, subgroupings that hold different initial positions, group composition, and the like.

(b) Cooperative Interaction: Social-Emotional Aspects takes as its emphasis the social process itself, and a secondary (but not absent) concern with the group task. Like the preceding section, these papers display a primary concern with a cooperative interaction framework, but are concerned with "going inside" the group discussion, to trace out the personal involvements and discover how these mutual activities evolve and persist.

(c) Mixed-Motive Interaction emphasizes those task situations where individual members may not have identical motives to achieve a solution or decision, but rather are in a "game" where one person's objectives are at cross purposes with another's. Of course, there are many kinds and degrees of conflict or disagreement, and the chapters of this section deal with more than one type of mixed-motive situation.

SMALL GROUP RESEARCH TRADITIONS

The study of small groups as a coherent research enterprise has its origins, as mentioned earlier, in various times and places. However, the strong tradition labeled group dynamics was underway by the late 1930s. A rich conceptual basis was provided by Kurt Lewin (1958) who brought a European concern with theoretical issues, especially Gestalt psychology, together with the strong American predilection for empiricism. Lewin's enthusiasm for both theory and experiment was matched by his conviction of the researchability of current social issues or problems.

Lewin's interest in applied problems, guided by theory, led to the founding of the Research Center for Group Dynamics (1945) and the subsequent creation of a workshop (1946) designed to investigate the possible uses of the group as a vehicle for social and personal change. This workshop was the precursor to the National Training Laboratories at Bethel, Maine, and has been recognized (Back, 1972), along with Moreno's work (1953), as the beginning of the sensitivity movement.

Lewin's classic studies (Lewin, Lippitt, and White, 1939) of small group leadership style (autocratic, democratic, laissez-faire) and the group as an agent of changing food attitudes and behavior (Lewin, 1943) were further illustrations of a respect for applied research. For example, one of the findings of the latter set of studies was that group discussion of a persuasive communication followed by individual decision resulted in more women serving less desirable meats to their families than did a lecture presenting the same material.

Lewin's writings reveal a primary concern with the individual and how the group experience effects changes in individual members. Back (1972) suggests that this concern reflects, in part, Lewin's view of the individual as a microcosm of society.

Following Lewin's death, two traditions developed within group dynamics. The first was concerned with the effect of communication, influence, group cohesiveness, etc., on the individual group member, and is closely identified with the work of Lewin's students (e.g., Bavelas, 1948; Deutsch, 1949; Festinger, 1951; Zander, 1958, to name only a few). The second tradition displayed an applied orientation and eventually resulted in the development of sensitivity training methods (e.g., Lippitt, Watson, and Westley, 1958).

A second relevant influence on small group study, Moreno (1953) stimulated a concern with role playing and interpersonal processes conceived as patterned structure. During the early years of his career in Vienna, Moreno developed sociometry as a means of examining the emotional relations among group members. It was intended to be used in conjunction with psychodrama and role playing, which were the foundations of his psychotherapeutic technique. His methodological and conceptual innovations exerted a continuing influence on social research, especially among those concerned more with the sociological than the psychological side of social psychology. However, Moreno's theorizing about psychotherapy and his philosophic concerns had a rather minor impact on research.

A third important influence was the work of Bales, who developed the method of Interaction Process Analysis, a twelve-category checklist of behaviors and an instrument upon which each occurrence of the behavior over time could be coded. Bales' concern was not so much with how the group experience affected the individual, but with how variables (e.g., group size) affected the dynamics of the group process. In general, the emphasis of Bales and his associates has been on the problems that the group faces in establishing a balance between the time spent on the task and the time spent on the social-emotional problems of maintaining group structure. As with Moreno, Bales' work has influenced most those investigators with a primarily sociological orientation.

Despite the dominant position of group dynamics in the early 1950s, small group research as a whole was languishing in the United States by the beginning of the sixties. In retrospect, there are several plausible reasons for this decline. For one thing, there was a new interest in methodology and precise experimentation, and this goal was more easily realized in the study of a single individual than in sets of them freely interacting. For example, attitude change, long a prime substantive problem in social psychology, was studied not within the group after the fashion of Lewin, but in the single individual who, like the persuasive appeals he received, could be more efficiently controlled. Other persons could be efficiently simulated, thus providing a more attractive format than the use of less manageable variable manipulations permitted by interacting subjects. (See Fishbein and Ajzen, 1975, for a discussion of what some have called the Hovland paradigm, and others, the Yale communication research program.) All in all, important features of social phenomena were thus "extracted" from their natural habitat (groups) for study elsewhere, namely, in the solitary laboratory subject.

Another likely reason for the decline of small group research is that the provocative *conceptual* approaches of Lewin had been exhausted. The increasing popularity of *experimental* social psychology was accompanied, and partly caused by, the rise of new theory focusing on the consistency among individual social cognitions. Festinger (1950, 1954) advanced a number of ideas culminating in the theory of cognitive dissonance (Festinger, 1957). Along with a continuing, positive reevaluation of Heider's (1958) proposals, dissonance theory set the stage for much of the North American concern with individual social psychology. A subsequent theoretical development, attribution theory (e.g., Jones and Davis, 1965; Kelley, 1967), was to restore some interest in interpersonal social situations. But there has remained, nonetheless, a preoccupation with *individual inference,* albeit social.

The growth of research on mixed-motive interaction reflected both an increased concern with experimental rigor and the development of new theory. The relatively greater precision and experimental control of a matrix game, such as the Prisoner's Dilemma, proved very attractive to the social psychology developing in the late fifties. Gaming simulations provided concise social situations, into which independent variables were introduced to gauge effects on a simple dependent variable, e.g., the number of cooperative responses. The tremendous popularity of mixed-motive interaction throughout the sixties was in large measure a direct consequence of such a methodological view. Theoretical developments which guided research into mixed-motive interaction arose both within and without social psychology. Deutsch's (1949) theory of cooperation and competition, originally cast at the small group level of analysis, has remained of central importance in mixed-motive interaction studies up to the present. The theory of games (Von Neumann and Morgenstern, 1947), already finding use in economics and political science, came to the attention of psychologists largely through Luce and Raiffa (1957). Bargaining formulations, such as those of Schelling (1960) and Osgood (1962), gained interest not only as stimuli for laboratory research but as prescriptions for international conflict resolution as well. "Mixed motives" were also apparent in theories of exchange (Thibaut and Kelley, 1959; Homans, 1961), of coalitions (Caplow, 1956; Gamson, 1964), and of equity (Adams, 1965; Walster, Berscheid, and Walster, 1973).

Group research, then, was not absent from the 1960s, but sufficiently sparse that Steiner (1974) could accurately entitle the first of the Katz-Newcomb lectures, "Whatever happened to the group in social psychology?" In contrast, a concern with small group behavior was very much alive in Europe during this same period. (See the review by Davis, Laughlin, and Komorita, 1976.) Perhaps it will be useful to consider the current status and preceding developments of what we believe to be a renewed interest in small group research within each of the three areas into which this book is divided.

Recent Developments in Cooperative Interaction: Cognitive Aspects. Much of the work in the recent past has been focused on group decision (as opposed to the earlier emphasis on problem solving), but of a rather limited kind. A decade and a half of intense research activity began with the report by Wallach, Kogan, and Bem (1962) that, on the average, groups were significantly riskier in a task requiring decisions under uncertainty than comparable individuals. Much of the research was motivated by attempts to refute or sustain one or more of the popular explanations of the underlying social process (e.g., diffusion of responsibility; engagement of a social norm and subsequent invidious comparison with others' riskiness; and exchange of task-relevant information, to name only a few), but the importance of the empirical result resided primarily in its counter-intuitive nature (Cartwright, 1973). Conventional wisdom held that groups were moderate decision instruments, and much of their appeal as social mechanisms for accurate and prudent judgments was based on the idea that social processes mollified extreme positions or proposals. Sometimes such constraint was thought to be a liability in group decision; in other cases (e.g., juries, government cabinets, corporate boards, etc.) socially fostered prudence was usually acclaimed. Naturally, surprise and concern followed the spate of research findings (see reviews by Dion, Baron, and Miller, 1970; Vinokur, 1971; Clark, 1971) beginning with a master's thesis by Stoner (1961) that suggested increased risk taking, relative to individuals, was to be expected from groups.

Cautious shifts (e.g., Nordhøy, 1962; Rabow, Fowler, Bradford, Hofeller, and Shibuya, 1966) were discovered later using items of the same "choice dilemma" format as the original investigations (a respondent must select the minimum odds acceptable were he to recommend the riskier of two uncertain courses of action confronting the central figure). This result led to the use of such labels as "extremity shift" or "choice shift" in recognition of the symmetry of possible effects. Myers and Lamm (1976) lamented that too much attention had been devoted to the risk and not enough to the shift, and others (e.g., Davis, Kerr, Sussmann, and Rissman, 1974) expressed regret over the heavy concentration upon a single task, experimental design, and data analysis technique. Nonetheless, the sometimes counterintuitive choice shifts fostered a new attention to group decision-making.

One may speculate that the focus on group decision may have been fostered in a climate of concern about *how* political decisions are made, and not only who makes them. Such concern was particularly evident in the United States during the early 1970s when there developed a substantial public disenchantment with governmental decision-makers and decision-making bodies. The trend may have been strengthened by various governmental scandals involving public figures and official decision-making groups in Asia and Europe about the same time. The perceptive essay by Janis (1972) in fact puts the psychology of group decision-making to work in an analysis of several well-known cases where the supposed "prudence fostering" of decision-making groups did not always prevail. All in all, a number of social forces have encouraged a strong interest in the *mechanics* of group decision—in our terms, an interest in the social processes underlying the decision. (Indeed, the theoretically-oriented papers by Zaleska and by Lambert in this volume reflect just such an emphasis.)

The group "polarization" effect (see Moscovici, 1976), another recent research theme, seems to reflect a similar concern with the social mechanics of interaction among members disparately inclined at the outset. One important side feature of the initial research on polarization (Moscovici and Zavalloni, 1969) was its concern with attitude or opinion items. That is, the reported opinions of French university students were found to be more extreme after discussion than before. No evident risk or problem-solving quality appeared to be involved. Indeed, many of society's most important groups "take positions" on social issues of the day, and much heated debate surrounds the development of a consensus position (e.g., see Kerr, Davis, Meek, and Rissman, 1975). Yet, paradoxically enough, the study of groups working at what are basically opinion-establishing tasks has not been very popular heretofore.

Myers and Lamm (1976: 603) have summarized the growing literature on polarization research (much of which is not concerned with opinion tasks) and provided a clear working definition of polarization—"The average postgroup response will tend to be more extreme in the same direction as the average of the pregroup responses." Observe that the focus is upon the postconsensus individual member. There is here a similarity of a sort to the Lewinian (1958) paradigm, little used since the classic studies in attitude change mentioned above. We thus anticipate a renewed interest in social influence through social interaction, and an accompanying emphasis upon the dynamics of majority-minority relations during the course of group discussion. Indeed, such developments seem to be in prospect (Moscovici and Nemeth, 1974; Moscovici, 1976; Davis, Stasser, Spitzer, and Holt, 1976; Stasser and Davis, 1977; Spitzer and Davis, 1978).

Finally, we might remark upon another current theme in group decision, and one that concentrates once again on the decision at the group level. We noted earlier that current social and practical concerns usually find their way into social research of the period. The renewed interest in groups is no exception. A substantial interest in psychology and the law has recently developed, particularly in Canada, Great Britain, and the United States. A variety of relevant research problems have claimed attention (Tapp and Levine, 1977; Sales, in press), and the jury, a research focus for several years (Kalven and Zeisel, 1966), has recently become a special focus (Simon, 1975; Gerbasi, Zuckerman, and Reis, 1977; Davis, Bray, and Holt, 1977).

Many legal systems make no provision at all for a citizen jury of peers (e.g., Israel), have abandoned it as unworkable (e.g., India), or use a mixture of judges and laymen (e.g., France). However, the jury as an example of one kind of group decision institution has counterparts of one sort or another perhaps everywhere. The kinds of questions currently being asked involve optimum jury size (e.g., Kessler, 1973; Bermant and Coppock, 1973), assigned working procedures or decision rule (e.g., Broeder, 1958; Simon, 1975), and assigned performance criteria (e.g., Simon, 1970; Kerr, Atkin, Stasser, Meek, Holt, and Davis, 1976), to name only a few. One kind of problem, rarely studied in recent years, has become particularly salient in legal systems providing for juries of citizens: group composition. Quotas, representative sampling, bias, and so on, are among the issues newly salient in group performance research. In many countries, the appropriate representation of subpopulations in decision-making bodies of all kinds is a problem of keen political interest, and substantial practical import. The formation of a jury is an interesting realization of this general representation problem; the paper by Davis, Spitzer, Nagao, and Stasser in this volume considers this issue and reports some experimental data on some aspects of it.

Recent Developments in Cooperative Interaction: Social-Emotional Aspects. The seminal works of Lewin, Moreno, and Bales marked the beginning of a very active period of research into various aspects of interpersonal processes per se. However, unlike the other two areas of group dynamics (Cooperative Interaction: Cognitive Aspects, and Mixed-Motive Interaction), interest in the social-emotional aspects of the group process has shown few signs of a resurgence since its heyday in the late 1950s. There is virtually no recent history in the direct study of the interaction process within groups, but at the moment there appears to be some activity developing (e.g., Hackman and Morris, 1975; Bakeman and Dabbs, 1976; Brandstätter's summary of the Augsburg research project on discussion in this volume).

The study of group processes requires the examination of the pattern of interpersonal relations in a group at a particular moment in time. Group structure is thus "frozen process." In one approach, selected structures may be imposed upon a group under controlled conditions and their effect, with regard to interpersonal reactions of group members, group performance, and the like, observed. The latter research strategy, in which structure is considered an independent variable, is well illustrated by the communication network studies of Bavelas (1948, 1950, 1952) and Shaw (1954, 1955, 1956). However, by the late 1960s this trend was all but finished and current research with an imposed structure of any sort is apparently at an end.

A second research strategy regards group structure as an emergent phenomenon, resulting from the interpersonal reactions of the group members over a period of time. Hence, group structure is viewed as a dependent variable, apparently related to such variables as group size, member composition, and the like. The work of Moreno and Bales, as noted earlier, provided the major impetus for this approach. However, by the late 1960s and early 1970s there was relatively little empirical research involving the direct, observational study of the interaction process within a group setting.

Perhaps one reason for this decrease can be attributed to the rise of the group sensitivity movement and the "shift" of concern of some investigators (Bales, for example) towards the development of a more applied, therapeutic use of group processes (e.g., Bales, 1970). Other reasons surely include the measurement difficulties and conceptual problems attendant upon managing such complex data sets.

Sociometric *techniques* in and of themselves have, on the other hand, continued to enjoy a certain popularity. The classic studies by Sherif (1951, 1956) involving the development, and later reduction, of tensions in boys camp groups exemplify the way in which sociometry has been commonly used. Further evidence of their popularity is indicated by their inclusion, usually rather perfunctorily, on the postgroup questionnaire of many current group investigations in which the main focus is on other phenomena.

A major stimulus to the current research in social process may have originated, oddly enough, with Steiner (1966, 1973) whose major interest was in group productivity. Steiner conceptualized group performance in terms of the idea: Actual Productivity = Potential Productivity − Process Losses. Moreover, he developed a partial typology of tasks, based upon his analysis of the interrelations among task demands, member resources, and group process, which lends itself rather nicely to the generation of testable hypotheses (e.g., Laughlin and Bitz, 1975; Laughlin, Kerr, Munch, and Haggarty, 1976).

More recently, Hackman and his associates (e.g., Hackman, Weiss, and Brousseau, 1974; Hackman and Morris, 1975) have used Steiner's formulations in their efforts to show that direct interventions into the group process (such as instructions to discuss performance strategies) can lead to more efficient group performance, and hence engineer process gains rather than process losses.

Another recent trend has been in the development and use of mathematical models, embodying certain social process assumptions, to predict group performance on a given task (Lorge and Solomon, 1955; Smoke and Zajonc, 1962; Restle and Davis, 1962; Davis, 1973). Generally such models only consider the performance preferences, etc., of individual members at one or two points in time. However, models more dynamic in character have recently been proposed (e.g., Godwin and Restle, 1974; Stasser and Davis, 1977). These latter developments, though giving more attention to the unfolding social process, still address social interaction indirectly. Perhaps somewhat closer in its concern for the social-emotional aspects of the group process is the recent work examining the relative influence of majorities and minorities within a group (e.g., Moscovici and Faucheux, 1972; Moscovici and Nemeth, 1974).

However, the direct study of social-emotional aspects in the group process appears to be in the hands of (a) Bakeman and Dabbs (1976), who have proposed ways of representing observational data leading to the analysis of behavior streams, and (b) the Augsburg Research Project on Group Discussion. The investigations of the latter have been concerned with the effects that expected (or perceived) and friendly (or hostile) discussant behavior would have upon both participants and observers of that discussion. Several papers representative of this research (i.e., Brandstätter; Schuler and Peltzer; Von Rosenstiel and Stocker-Kreichgauer) and a chapter by Verhagen investigating the transfer of "expert" power into influence in dyads and triads of interacting expert and nonexpert members are included in this volume.

Recent Developments in Mixed-Motive Interaction. Gaming studies predominate in the large body of research which has accumulated over the last twenty years. By the count of Rubin and Brown (1976), for example, the Prisoner's Dilemma alone comprises 300 of the over 1000 investigations since 1960. Although the vigorous growth of experimental gaming seems to have crested, recent research continues, especially into such topics as individual perceptions and strategies, sex and cultural differences, payoff and other situational factors, and n-person games (Davis, Laughlin, and Komorita, 1976). At the same time, publications addressing mixed-motive interaction have increasingly been occupied with review, integration, and criticism.

Criticism of experimental gaming has usually centered on issues of external validity and on the paucity of theoretical developments. For example, Pruitt and Kimmel (1977) argue that investigators fail to extrapolate their findings to real life, both because of unwillingness and because of confusion about how such speculation ought to be made. (In this volume, Morley suggests some steps toward a fair application of gaming research.) The lack of guiding theory is a result of the historical overreliance on a limited paradigm such as the Prisoner's Dilemma. Moreover, the theoretical ideas that are in use suggest a basically functionalist approach to the last decade of mixed-motive research.

Recent work in bargaining and negotiation has investigated the effects of concession-making, in particular work testing earlier formulations of Siegel and Fouraker (1960) and Osgood (1962). A related topic of current research interest is the impact of third parties in which mutual concessions to a third party avoid signs of weakness that might otherwise complicate bargaining and negotiation. Studies of representative negotiation continue to delineate conditions under which delegates are accountable and competitive (Davis, Laughlin, and Komorita, 1976). (See the chapter by Müller and Crott for a study of longitudinal bargaining behavior, and the chapter by Stephenson for an investigation of problems facing a representative on a negotiation team.)

Coalition research of late continues to rely on three-person groups or triads. As Komorita and Chertkoff (1973) have indicated, more sensitive tests of the several theories of coalition formation and reward allocation require groups of more than three members. The older conceptual notions which have guided past research in this area (e.g., Caplow, 1956; Gamson, 1964) are gradually being augmented and replaced by new theory (e.g., Komorita and Chertkoff, 1973). Not since the social process work on intragroup, mutual support of members (e.g., Mills, 1953, 1954; Bales, 1954; Strodtbeck, 1954) was dismissed as beyond the proper limit of coalition research by Gamson (1964) has mixed-motive interaction been extended to nonmonetary motives of small group members. The recent investigations of Moscovici and his colleagues (e.g., Moscovici and Nemeth, 1974) on majority-minority relations and influence present an exciting possibility of reintegration. (See also the chapter by Mikula and Schwinger in this volume.)

Of course, distinctions such as those implied here among the terms bargaining, coalition formation, gaming, and negotiation are by no means commonly held by investigators. For example, both Morley and Stephenson (1976) and Rubin and Brown (1976) consider many experimental gaming situations as instances of bargaining. While Morley and Stephenson define bargaining as a subset of negotiation, Rubin and Brown make no distinction between the terms. On the other hand, much of bargaining and negotiation might alternatively come under the label of "n-person games." The picture becomes more confusing still if one accepts the "bargaining" theory of "coalitions" offered by Komorita and Chertkoff (1973). Thus, there is some disagreement and confusion over the very topics of mixed-motive interaction and the relationships among them—posing an interesting challenge for future conceptual work.

CONCLUDING REMARKS

There seems to be something of a renaissance in small group research, especially group decision processes. This resurgence is hardly an immediate threat to the continuing preeminence of the social psychology of the individual, but it does imply the emergence of a more balanced set of research topics in the near future. We have suggested above that current work has clear roots in the problems, theories, and methods of earlier years. However, we have also suggested that the current social climate and development of group-oriented theory have contributed to the salience of the general topic.

This volume contains a sample of current thought on group decision and related topics. Most of the contributors are European, reflecting the trends emerging in various European countries. However, group decision-making seems to be an inescapable property of modern societies everywhere.

REFERENCES

Adams, J.S. Inequity in social exchange. In L. Berkowitz (Ed.), *Advances in Experimental Social Psychology,* Vol. 2. New York: Academic Press, 1965.

Allport, F.H. *Social Psychology.* Boston: Houghton Mifflin, 1924.

–––. The influence of the group upon association and thought. *Journal of Experimental Psychology,* 1920, *3,* 159-182.

Back, K.W. *Beyond Words: The Story of Sensitivity Training and the Encounter Movement.* New York: Russell Sage Foundation, 1972.

Bakeman, R., and J.M. Dabbs. Social interaction observed: Some approaches to the analysis of behavior streams. *Personality and Social Psychology Bulletin,* 1976, *2,* 335-345.

Bales, R.F. *Personality and Interpersonal Behavior.* New York: Holt, Rinehart and Winston, 1970.

–––. In conference. *Harvard Business Review,* 1954, *32,* 44-50.

–––. *Interaction Process Analysis: A Method for the Study of Small Groups.* Cambridge, Mass.: Addison-Wesley, 1950.

Bavelas, A. Communication patterns in problem-solving groups. In H. von Foerster et al. (Eds.), *Cybernetics: Circular Causal and Feedback Mechanisms in Biological and Social Systems.* New York: Josiah Macy, Jr., Foundation, 1952.

–––. Communication patterns in task oriented groups. *Journal of the Accoustical Society of America,* 1950, *22,* 725-730.

–––. A mathematical model for group structures. *Applied Anthropology,* 1948, *7,* 16-30.

Bermant, G., and R. Coppock. Outcomes of six- and twelve-member jury trials: An analysis of 128 civil cases in the State of Washington. *Washington Law Review,* 1973, *48,* 593-596.

Broeder, D.W. The University of Chicago jury project. *Nebraska Law Review,* 1958, *38,* 744-761.

Caplow, T. A theory of coalitions in the triad. *American Sociological Review,* 1956, *21,* 489-493.

Cartwright, D. Determinants of scientific progress: The case of research on the risky shift. *American Psychologist,* 1973, *28,* 222-231.

Clark, R.D. Group-induced shift toward risk: A critical appraisal. *Psychological Bulletin,* 1971, *76,* 251-270.

Cohen, J.L., and J.H. Davis. Effects of audience status, evaluation, and time of action on performance with hidden-word problems. *Journal of Personality and Social Psychology,* 1973, *27,* 74-85.

Cooley, C.H. *Human Nature and the Social Order.* New York: Scribner, 1902.

Cottrell, N.B., D.L. Wack, G.J. Sekerak, and R.H. Rittle. Social facilitation of dominant responses by the presence of an audience and the mere presence of others. *Journal of Personality and Social Psychology,* 1968, *9,* 245-250.

Dashiell, J.F. Experimental studies of the influence of social situations on the behavior of individual human adults. In C. Murchison (Ed.), *A Handbook of Social Psychology*. Worcester, Mass.: Clark University Press, 1935.

Davis, J.H. Group decision and social interaction: A theory of social decision schemes. *Psychological Review,* 1973, *80,* 97-125.

———. *Group Performance.* Reading, Mass.: Addison-Wesley, 1969.

Davis, J.H., R.M. Bray, and R.W. Holt. The empirical study of decision processes in juries; A critical review. In J.L. Tapp and F.J. Levine (Eds.), *Law, Justice, and the Individual in Society: Psychological and Legal Issues.* New York: Holt, Rinehart and Winston, 1977.

Davis, J.H., N. Kerr, M. Sussmann, and A.K. Rissman. Social decision schemes under risk. *Journal of Personality and Social Psychology,* 1974, *30,* 248-271.

Davis, J.H., P.R. Laughlin, and S.S. Komorita. The social psychology of small groups: Cooperative and mixed-motive interaction. *Annual Review of Psychology*, 1976, *27,* 501-541.

Davis, J.H., G. Stasser, C.E. Spitzer, and R.W. Holt. Changes in group members' decision preferences during discussion: An illustration with mock juries. *Journal of Personality and Social Psychology,* 1976, *34* 1177-1187.

Deutsch, M. A theory of cooperation and competition. *Human Relations,* 1949, *2,* 129-152.

Dion, K.L., R.S. Baron, and N. Miller. Why do groups make riskier decisions than individuals? In L. Berkowitz (Ed.), *Advances in Experimental Social Psychology,* Vol. 5. New York: Academic Press, 1970.

Festinger, L. *A Theory of Cognitive Dissonance.* Evanston, Ill.: Row, Peterson, 1957.

———. Theory of social comparison processes. *Human Relations,* 1954, *7,* 117-140.

———. Informal communications in small groups. In H. Guetzkow (Ed.), *Groups, Leadership and Men: Research in Human Relations.* Pittsburgh: Carnegie, 1951.

———. Informal social communication. *Psychological Review,* 1950, *57,* 271-292.

Fishbein, M., and I. Ajzen. *Belief, Attitude, Intention and Behavior: An Introduction to Theory and Research.* Reading, Mass.: Addison-Wesley, 1975.

Gamson, W.A. Experimental studies of coalition formation. In L. Berkowitz (Ed.), *Advances in Experimental Social Psychology,* Vol. 1. New York: Academic Press, 1964.

Gerbasi, K.C., M. Zuckerman, and H.T. Reis. Justice needs a new blindfold: A review of mock jury research. *Psychological Bulletin,* 1977, *84,* 323-345.

Godwin, W.F., and F. Restle. The road to agreement: Subgroup pressures in small group consensus processes. *Journal of Personality and Social Psychology,* 1974, *30,* 500-509.

Hackman, J.R., and C.G. Morris. Group tasks, group interaction process, and group performance effectiveness: A review and proposed integration. In L. Berkowitz (Ed.), *Advances in Experimental Social Psychology,* Vol. 8. New York: Academic Press, 1975.

Hackman, J.R., J.A. Weiss, and K. Brousseau. *Effects of Task Performance Strategies on Group Performance Effectiveness.* Technical Report No. 5. New Haven, Conn.: Department of Administrative Sciences, Yale University, 1974.

Heider, F. *The Psychology of Interpersonal Relations.* New York: Wiley, 1958.

Homans, G.C. *Social Behavior: Its Elementary Forms.* New York: Harcourt, Brace, 1961.

Janis, I.L. *Victims of Groupthink.* Boston, Mass.: Houghton Mifflin, 1972.

Jones, E.E., and K.E. Davis. From acts to dispositions. In L. Berkowitz (Ed.),

Advances in Experimental Social Psychology, Vol. 2. New York: Academic Press, 1965.

Kalven, J., Jr., and H. Zeisel. *The American Jury.* Boston, Mass.: Little, Brown, 1966.

Kelley, H.H. Attribution theory in social psychology. In D. Levine (Ed.), *Nebraska Symposium on Motivation: 1967.* Lincoln, Nebr.: University of Nebraska Press, 1967.

Kerr, N.L., R.S. Atkin, G. Stasser, D. Meek, R.W. Holt, and J.H. Davis. Guilt beyond a reasonable doubt: Effects of concept definition and assigned decision rule on the judgments of mock jurors. *Journal of Personality and Social Psychology,* 1976, *34,* 282-294.

Kerr, N.L., J.H. Davis, D. Meek, and A.K. Rissman. Group position as a function of member attitudes: Choice shift effects from the perspective of social decision scheme theory. *Journal of Personality and Social Psychology,* 1975, *31,* 574-593.

Kessler, J.B. An empirical study of six- and twelve-member jury decision-making processes. *University of Michigan Journal of Law Reform,* 1973, *6,* 712-734.

Komorita, S.S., and J.M. Chertkoff. A bargaining theory of coalition formation. *Psychological Review,* 1973, *80,* 149-162.

Laughlin, P.R., and D.S. Bitz. Individual versus dyadic performance on a disjunctive task as a function of initial ability level. *Journal of Personality and Social Psychology,* 1975, *31,* 487-496.

Laughlin, P.R., N.L. Kerr, M.M. Munch, and C.A. Haggarty. Social decision schemes of the same four-person groups on two different intellective tasks. *Journal of Personality and Social Psychology,* 1976, *33,* 80-88.

Lewin, K. Group decision and social change. In E.E. Maccoby, T.M. Newcomb, and R.L. Hartley (Eds.), *Readings in Social Psychology.* New York: Holt, Rinehart and Winston, 1958.

–––. Forces behind food habits and methods of change. *Bulletin of the National Research Council,* 1943, *108,* 35-65.

Lewin, K., R. Lippitt, and R.K. White. Patterns of aggressive behavior in experimentally created "social climates." *Journal of Social Psychology,* 1939, *10,* 271-299.

Lippitt, R., J. Watson, and B. Westley. *The Dynamics of Planned Change: A Comparative Study of Principles and Techniques.* New York: Harcourt, Brace, 1958.

Lorge, I., and H. Solomon. Two models of group behavior in the solution of Eureka-type problems. *Psychometrika,* 1955, *20,* 139-148.

Luce, R.D., and H. Raiffa. *Games and Decisions: Introduction and Critical Survey.* New York: Wiley, 1958.

Mayer, A. On the schoolchild's work alone and in the group. *Archiv für die Gesamte Psychologie,* 1903, *1,* 276-416.

Mayo, E. *The Human Problems of an Industrial Civilization.* New York: Macmillan, 1933.

Meumann, E. *Haus- und Schularbeit* [*Home and School Work*], 1914. [Cited in G. Murphy and L.B. Murphy, *Experimental Social Psychology.* New York: Harper, 1931.]

Mills, T.M. The coalition pattern in three-person groups. *American Sociological Review,* 1954, *19,* 657-667.

–––. Power relations in three-person groups. *American Sociological Review,* 1953, *18,* 351-357.

Moreno, J.L. *Who Shall Survive?* Rev. ed. Beacon, New York: Beacon House, 1953.

26 DYNAMICS OF GROUP DECISIONS

Morley, I.E., and G.M. Stephenson. *The Social Psychology of Bargaining.* London: George Allen and Unwin, 1976.

Moscovici, S. *Social Influence and Social Change.* London: Academic Press, 1976.

Moscovici, S., and C. Faucheux. Social influence, conformity, bias, and the study of active minorities. In L. Berkowitz (Ed.), *Advances in Experimental Social Psychology,* Vol. 6. New York: Academic Press, 1972.

Moscovici, S., and C. Nemeth. Social influence II: Minority influence. In C. Nemeth (Ed.), *Social Psychology: Classic and Contemporary Integrations.* Chicago: Rand McNally, 1974.

Moscovici, S., and M. Zavalloni. The group as a polarizer of attitudes. *Journal of Personality and Social Psychology,* 1969, *12,* 125-135.

Myers, D.G., and H. Lamm. The group polarization phenomenon. *Psychological Bulletin,* 1976, *83,* 602-627.

Nordhøy, F. Group interaction in decision-making under risk. Unpublished Master's thesis, Massachusetts Institute of Technology, 1962.

Osgood, C.E. *An Alternative to War or Surrender.* Urbana, Ill.: University of Illinois Press, 1962.

Pruitt, D.G., and M.J. Kimmel. Twenty years of experimental gaming: Critique, synthesis, and suggestions for the future. *Annual Review of Psychology,* 1977, *28,* 363-392.

Rabow, J., F.J. Fowler, D.L. Bradford, M.A. Hoefeller, and Y. Shibuya. The role of social norms and leadership in risk-taking. *Sociometry,* 1966, *29,* 16-27.

Restle, F., and J.H. Davis. Success and speed of problem solving by individuals and groups. *Psychological Review,* 1962, *69,* 520-536.

Rubin, J.Z., and B.R. Brown. *The Social Psychology of Bargaining and Negotiation.* New York: Academic Press, 1976.

Sales, B.D. (Ed.) *Perspectives in Law and Psychology. Volume I: The Criminal Justice System.* New York: Plenum, in press.

Schelling, T.C. *The Strategy of Conflict.* New York: Harvard University, 1960.

Schmidt, F. Experimental studies of the schoolchild's homework. *Archive für die Gesamte Psychologie,* 1904, *3,* 33-152.

Shaw, Margaret E. A comparison of individuals and small groups in the rational solution of complex problems. *American Journal of Psychology,* 1931, *44,* 491-504.

Shaw, M.E. Random versus systematic distribution of information in communication nets. *Journal of Personality,* 1956, *25,* 59-69.

———. A comparison of two types of leadership in various communication nets. *Journal of Abnormal and Social Psychology,* 1955, *50,* 127-134.

———. Some effects of problem complexity upon problem solution efficiency in different communication nets. *Journal of Experimental Psychology,* 1954, *48* 211-217.

Sherif, M. Experiments in group conflict. *Scientific American,* 1956, *195,* 54-58.

———. A preliminary study of inter-group relations. In J.H. Rohrer and M. Sherif (Eds.), *Social Psychology at the Crossroads: The University of Oklahoma Lectures in Social Psychology.* New York: Harper, 1951.

———. A study of some social factors in perception. *Archives of Psychology,* 1935, *27,* No. 187.

Siegel, S., and L.E. Fouraker. *Bargaining and Group Decision Making: Experiments in Bilateral Monopoly.* New York: McGraw-Hill, 1960.

Simon, R.J. (Ed.). *The Jury System in America: A Critical Overview.* Beverly Hills, Calif.: Sage, 1975.

–––. "Beyond a reasonable doubt"–An experimental attempt at quantification. *Journal of Applied Behavioral Science,* 1970, *6,* 203-209.

Smoke, W.H., and R.B. Zajonc. On the reliability of group judgments and decisions. In J.H. Criswell, H. Solomon, and P. Suppes (Eds.), *Mathematical Methods in Small Group Processes.* Stanford, Calif.: Stanford University Press, 1962.

Spitzer, C.E., and J.H. Davis. Mutual social influence in dynamic groups. *Sociometry,* 1978, *41,* 24-33.

Stasser, G., and J.H. Davis. Opinion change during group discussion. *Personality and Social Psychology Bulletin,* 1977, *3,* 252-256.

Steiner, I.D. Whatever happened to the group in social psychology? *Journal of Experimental Social Psychology,* 1974, *10,* 94-108.

–––. *Group Process and Productivity.* New York: Academic Press, 1972.

–––. Models for inferring relationships between group size and potential group productivity. *Behavioral Science,* 1966, *11,* 273-283.

Stoner, J.A.F. A comparison of individual and group decisions involving risk. Unpublished Master's thesis, Massachusetts Institute of Technology, 1961.

Strodtbeck, F.L. The family as a three-person group. *American Sociological Review,* 1954, *19,* 23-29.

Tapp, J.L., and F.J. Levine (Eds.). *Law Justice, and the Individual in Society: Psychological and Legal Issues.* New York: Holt, Rinehart & Winston, 1977.

Thibaut, J.W., and H.H. Kelley. *The Social Psychology of Groups.* New York: Wiley, 1959.

Triplett, N. The dynamogenic factors in pacemaking and competition. *American Journal of Psychology,* 1898, *9,* 507-533.

Vinokur, A. Review and theoretical analysis of the effects of group processes upon individual and group decisions involving risk. *Psychological Bulletin,* 1971, *76,* 231-250.

Von Neumann, J., and O. Morgenstern. *Theory of Games and Economic Behavior.* Princeton, N.J.: Princeton University Press, 1947.

Wallach, M.A., Kogan, N., and D.J. Bem. Group influence on individual risk taking. *Journal of Abnormal and Social Psychology,* 1962, *65,* 75-86.

Walster, E., E. Berscheid, and G.W. Walster. New directions in equity research. *Journal of Personality and Social Psychology,* 1973, *25,* 151-176.

Zajonc, R.B. Social facilitation. *Science,* 1965, *149,* 269-274.

Zander, A. Group membership and individual security. *Human Relations,* 1958, *11,* 99-111.

PART I

COOPERATIVE INTERACTION:
COGNITIVE ASPECTS

Introduction by David A. Vollrath and James H. Davis

As the introductory chapter indicates, the cognitive aspects of cooperative interaction have often been labeled "group performance." Recent investigations in this area have often employed cognitive tasks of decision-making and, to a considerably lesser extent, problem-solving. As suggested earlier, recent studies may be seen as addressing three general themes: group choice shifts, changes in ex-member preference or response, and application of group performance findings, especially to legal issues. The reader will note that the papers in this section relate to one or another of these themes. The relation, however, is often modest—the theme may better serve as a beginning point or as a general perspective. Each article, nonetheless, engages questions of substantial interest and importance and illustrates recent research in cognitive aspects of group interaction current in Europe and North America.

Davis, Spitzer, Nagao, and Stasser explore the nature of bias in social decision, focusing illustratively upon the jury as found in the United States. The notion of a biased statistical estimator, the expected value of which differs from some true value, is presented as a guide to the analysis of bias in group decision. Turning to the jury, for example, Davis et al. remark upon the frequent difficulties of determining either a "true" value to be sought or an exact point in procedure where bias occurs. Possible loci of bias in the juror's cognitive processes, the underrepresentation of

relevant subgroup members seated on a jury, and the jury's deliberation
process are considered.

Using an empirical example of locating bias in a mock trial with
students, Davis, Spitzer, Nagao, and Stasser show that *general* belief, held
prior to presentation of evidence, affect and bias both juror predelibera-
tion opinion and jury verdicts. Further analysis narrows the plausible loci
of the bias effect. In conclusion, the authors argue for attaching increased
significance to the composition of groups from variously inclined populations.

Research of group choice shifts has occupied a dominant position in the
social psychology of groups for the last fifteen years. Lambert's explora-
tion of "Situations of Uncertainty: Social Influence and Decision Processes" moves beyond a majority-rule account of such shifts, examining
other explanations in some situations where a majority model may not
always fit. The author describes a study which shows the potential value of
multiple group tasks and develops specific measures of influence to investigate these alternative accounts. Results suggesting possible cross-task influence of certain individuals are related to the discussion dynamics of group
choice shift.

Both Lambert's and Zaleska's papers address social influence in situations where group choice shifts cannot be accounted for by a majority-rule
model. While the former examines the influence of certain individuals
upon group performance, the latter deals with the effect of subgroups of
individuals, or minorities. Zaleska summarizes some data showing exceptions to the predictions of majority and of averaging models. Since a
majority model does not always describe group choice shifts, the author
reasons, *minorities* must have a more influential role than that of simple
acquiescence. Further, it is noted that the high frequency of a particular
response in the underlying population affects the success of both minorities and majorities in small groups, and an informal model reflecting these
considerations is presented.

Doise's discussion of "Actions and Judgments: Collective and Individual Structuring" addresses the cognitive aspects of group interaction
directly. The first part of this paper establishes that, for a variety of tasks
where consensus is required, groups structure or organize materials and
responses more singularly than individuals. Doise's analysis features statis-
tics of variability, an important step in freeing choice shift research from
historical devotion to measures of central tendency. The author then
relates this group-level phenomenon to Piaget's ideas on social processes of
cognitive development, focusing in turn on the effects of interaction on
subsequent individual responses. Similar interest in postdiscussion individ-

uals marks a theme of recent research which is likely to be important in the future.

Despite the diverse backgrounds of the authors, the chapters of this section show a distinct convergence in problem conception and approach to understanding the social processes at work. The international flavor of such a convergence only serves to enhance our optimism for the immediate future of research on the cognitive aspects of cooperative interaction.

2

BIAS IN SOCIAL DECISIONS BY INDIVIDUALS AND GROUPS: AN EXAMPLE FROM MOCK JURIES[1]

James H. Davis, Craig E. Spitzer,
Dennis H. Nagao, and Garold Stasser

The use of decision-making bodies has been a prominent feature in many cultures throughout history. Democratic and autocratic societies alike have depended upon small groups whether for executive decisions or advisory judgments to be used later by others. There appear to be two particularly prominent classes of reasons for the appeal of small groups in this capacity. First, there is the question of accuracy and/or moderation of extreme opinions, depending upon the task and outcome. There is a strong intuitive feeling, even among the statistically naive, that in the long run collective errors should in some fashion be mutually cancelling and that collective judgments should be closer to the solution, optimum, or true value, if one exists. For more ambiguous tasks not explicitly possessing the feature of correctness or response accuracy, groups have the virtue of compromise, whereby imprudent or rash proposals can be muted. That is, there may in some cases be a region of choices better than those on either side, and a sample of several persons seems intuitively more likely to achieve consensus there than at the extremes.

A second class of reasons for the appeal of group decisions is again most closely related to those ambiguous tasks possessing no compellingly correct or best answer—tasks for which there are perhaps no responses rendered unarguable by logic, or the "psychologic" of a common value system. In such a case, there arises the question of "appropriate" *representation* for those coming from populations holding *different* "true" values, or favoring different "best decision" regions along the response continuum or over the set of discrete choice alternatives. Even though the group members may be in an essentially cooperative relationship in that all benefit from performing a common task, conflict over perhaps widely disparate views is possible, and sometimes intense. Prior to disagreement arising in the discussion of differing goals, conflict may develop over what proportion of the membership is to represent what constituency, and/or how they are to be selected.

In a sense, we may summarize the foregoing by saying that group, as opposed to individual, decision-making is often a mechanism to avoid or minimize *bias* in reaching judgments, especially in situations of some social importance. The purpose of this paper is to consider bias in social decisions, note various kinds and "locations" of bias, and illustrate some of the associated problems in a mock jury study. The jury is a highly respected institution in the United States, and much of this respect rests on the jury's reputation for fairness (unbiasedness) in reaching verdicts.

BIAS

Dictionary definitions stress bias as an inclination, tendency, bent, prejudice, or inclination of a line, process, perception, and so on, away from a true value, appropriate goal, or the like. For our purposes, the definition consists of two important ingredients: (a) a true value or goal that should or would "normally" be attained, and (b) the process or procedure for reaching or approximating the true value. The biasing entity is the latter, but controversy or conflict can and does surround both. (In fact, evaluation of bias is difficult in many instances because of disagreement over what constitutes the true value.) In general then, bias is present in a process or procedure when it produces a consistent deviation from the true value.

The true value may be implicit in a widely shared social convention or norm, or it may be explicitly stated in law or the governing code of a social body. The true value may be numerically valued, and originate as a feature of an actual physical entity such as the mean value of some trait in a well-defined population, or arise as a mathematical constant in a formal theoretical expression ("law"). Whether cultural, physical, or logical in origin, the true value definition is as important as its estimation under the fixed conditions at issue. The estimation mechanism with which we shall be concerned is the small group whose estimate (decision) is achieved by consensus of some sort.

The analogy of the foregoing with formal statistical estimation is clear. Groups are like samples and their task performance is the estimate of a true value or parameter. However, the analogy is not perfect and as we shall see later holds some problems if followed rigidly. In any event, we can imagine there exists a parameter (true value), θ, whatever its origin, and a group response, $\hat{\theta}$, that estimates it. In general, one would be surprised if always $\hat{\theta} = \theta$, but apprehensive if replications of the process would routinely and consistently produce $\hat{\theta} \neq \theta$. A statistical estimator is said to be biased if its expectation does not equal the true value, i.e., $\theta - E(\hat{\theta}) \neq 0$. According to the same reasoning, we might regard groups as biased when the expected value of the decision is different from the true value. Unfortunately, for the purity of the analogy, group members interact and cannot be regarded in the same way as a sample of marbles from an urn. We require an example at this point.

THE JURY

Recall the jury mentioned earlier. The true value in which we are most interested is the defendant's guilt or innocence. The defendant in a criminal trial (the only kind of courtroom trial we shall consider here) is either guilty or not guilty, but in principle this "value" is unknowable (excluding ritualistic trials of confessed criminals, or some clear a priori guilt determination). However, we can redefine the situation to a more practical end, and say there exists a parameter, θ, which is the *conditional probability* of a guilty verdict, *given the evidence, trial procedure,* etc. (See Gelfand and Solomon, 1973, 1974, 1975, for a more comprehensive discussion of this line of reasoning.) We should thus like to evaluate trial procedures, etc., on the basis of their *promise* in coming as close to this ideal and unknowable parameter as possible. In other words, if P_G is the probability of a jury convicting the defendant under some set of conditions, and $\hat{P}_G$ is its estimate from a sample of juries under those conditions, is it likely that $E(\hat{P}_G) = P_G$?

Few social institutions excite as much emotion or so many charges of bias as do juries and the courtroom trial in general. (See reviews by Gerbasi, Zuckerman, and Reis, 1977, and Davis, Bray, and Holt, 1977.) Part of the emotion may be due to the important place of the jury trial in the affections of citizens, but part probably stems from the very reason that the jury is entrusted with the decision: the improbability of ever knowing (convincingly and decisively) whether the defendant is guilty or not guilty. We will not be concerned here with the question of bias that may be associated with particular trial procedures, but will concentrate instead on the jury. At least three possible locations of bias are rather easily identified, and we consider these below.

The Individual Juror. Jurors may deviate systematically from the true value by virtue of imperfections in perception, memory, recall, reasoning, and many other features of the information-processing apparatus of humans. However, these are irreducible and the whole point of using a group rather than a single individual is that fluctuations in cognition may be muted in the former. Yet, the law recognizes the possibility that bias in the jury might be reduced by a careful choice of jurors eligible to serve.

Thus, there is a special mechanism, the voir dire examination, designed to filter out prospective jurors who display what the presiding judge believes to be legally unacceptable bias. (Such jurors are "excused for cause" and should not be confused with those who are peremptorily challenged by defense or prosecution. Only a limited number of peremptory challenges are permitted defense and prosecution lawyers, and no cause need be shown in order for these prospective jurors to be excused.) The kind of bias we are essentially considering here is attitudinal in nature, or at least a disposition apart from that associated with limited intellective ability. A defense or prosecution lawyer's own "implicit personality theory" may lead him or her to challenge peremptorily members of certain social classes, ethnic populations, or other "types," he believes might be biased for or against the defendant. But an important basis for challenging for cause is the detection of an opinion or belief that seems prima facie to imply a possible bias in judgment, recall information, etc., that can somehow be publicly argued.

Voir dire examinations vary considerably from jurisdiction to jurisdiction, but generally the presiding judge has an astonishing degree of leeway in conducting the proceedings and reaching a decision to excuse or retain a juror. The examination may be long and expensive. It is quite possible that, when a juror displays a pro or con attitude that may ostensibly be related to a consistent preference, and thus constitute potential bias, the judge will simply further inquire whether or not the subject feels he can be fair and impartial. If the answer is affirmative, the juror may very well be retained.[2] What is the effect of opinions pro or con the defendant either at the level of the individual juror or at the level of the jury? Do such general opinions as might be detected at voir dire result in bias, or are they related in any sense to juror guilt preferences and jury verdicts? There are after all very strong exhortations, and implicit norms, encouraging impartiality and fairness.

Answers to these questions are not clearly evident from the small group research literature. Personality measures and general attitude scale responses have in the past not been closely related to overall group perfor-mance (Mann, 1959; Heslin, 1964; McGrath and Altman, 1966; Davis, Bray, and Holt, 1977), although such general dispositions as authoritari-anism have sometimes been related to guilt preferences or harsh punish-ment inclinations (e.g., Mitchell and Byrne, 1973; Bray and Noble, 1977). However, there has been little study of the relationship between juror guilt preferences (or subsequent verdicts) and simple pretrial opinions about the defendant, alleged crime, and the like. In actual trials, the opportunity for empirical inquiry is usually limited; the administration of justice is too important to permit the usual interventions associated with social research. (See Diamond and Zeisel, 1974, for a rare exception.) Furthermore, bias cannot easily be assessed (i.e., the extent to which jurors' initial disposi-tions, pro or con, influence their verdict preferences) if the voir dire has eliminated those most likely to display the effect.

Representativeness of Members. The representation of various popu-lations among group members has provided a second site where bias may arise, and indeed has been the occasion for substantial criticism of jury selection methods (e.g., Kairys, 1972; Kairys, Schulman, and Harring, 1975). Concern with the representation of various minorities, males/females, and so on, is a tacit admission that not only may the voir dire examination be imperfect in filtering out the biased individual, but that populations exist which simply have different true values! That is to say, some groups of "unbiased" individuals will ordinarily arrive at different estimates (verdicts), in the long run, than other groups com-posed of individuals from some different population. For example, Davis, Kerr, Atkin, Holt, and Meek (1975) observed that males and females differed significantly in their guilt preferences after seeing a video record-ing of a mock trial in which the defendant was accused of rape. Are such differences "genuine" or "permissible" in the sense that the problem should be regarded as $E(\hat{\theta}_{males}) = \theta_{males}$, and $E(\hat{\theta}_{females}) = \theta_{females}$, but $\theta \neq \theta_{females}$?

Indeed, if samples of males and samples of females are regarded as *legitimately* estimating different population parameters, then the single, appropriately *mixed* group offers a means of avoiding a confrontation by the simple expedient of "representing" all parties in some way within the decision process. The deliberation and subsequent decision are thus re-garded as "having worked the matter out," even though the logical properties of the social production process may be largely a mystery. The jury is a kind of balancing mechanism which at least offers the important comfort of involvement to recognized segments of a society, and at best some kind of informal balancing of legitimate opinions.

Deliberation and Verdict. A third general location for bias is at the level of the group decision. Deliberation and polling constitute a means of aggregating preferences such that the many wishes of the members are transformed into a single response. Bias would arise if this aggregation process were to depart from that prescribed, such that the expectation of the estimate was not the true value. (A vexing logical dilemma would arise if the prescribed social decision scheme did not yield a decision as close to the true value as one that was not allowed.) One example would be where females always deferred to males under conditions where the two sexes consistently preferred different verdicts.

In any event, Davis et al. (1975) have observed that mock juries seem to operate on a somewhat strong majority social decision scheme, a result subsequently confirmed by Davis, Kerr, Stasser, Meek, and Holt (1977), and substantially in agreement with Kalven and Zeisel (1966). It is not at all clear that a majority social decision scheme constitutes bias, even though the jury has received a charge that unanimity is required; unanimity is actually a criterion to which all may have subscribed but have reached that criterion by a majority rule. Perhaps a more serious question is to what extent the form of the social decision process itself depends upon the preponderance of pretrial opinion against or for a defendant. In other words, if there is anti- or pro-defendant opinion represented in the group, does this produce a "bandwagon" effect or some similar accumulating influence on the social process beyond what we would expect in groups having moderate or diverse opinions among the members?

In summary, we have proposed that a desirable property of statistical estimators, unbiasedness, is by analogy also a useful notion for clarifying and analyzing bias in social decisions. However, it is important not only to detect and assess bias in individual and group decisions, but to seek the location of the biasing process. In the following section, we are concerned with a specific empirical example. We will report research exploring how general opinions about guilt (solicited *before* the trial) relate, if at all, to mock juror guilt preferences and/or jury verdicts.

GENERAL OPINIONS, PREFERENCES, AND GROUP DECISIONS

In a sense, the whole need for a voir dire examination is predicated upon the idea that there exist pretrial opinions likely to prevent an assessment of the evidence and subsequent decision such as would occur if no opinion (i.e., neither pro nor con) were held on the matter. However, there are very general opinions that could escape scrutiny and admit the holder to jury duty, but still result perhaps in that inclination we have come to call bias. Moreover, if a potential juror were to disclose a preconceived opinion that appeared relevant to guilt preference, the court probably would not excuse him or her for cause unless he or she also believed it impossible to reach a fair and impartial decision.

Whether or not the general opinions or prejudices as we are implying above would be effective in determining the outcome is not clear from the general literature dealing with pregroup assessment of individual members-to-be, as we mentioned. It would seem that the normative pressures for playing the role of "fair juror" must be considerable, and direct admonishments from the judge (and perhaps defense and prosecution as well) are specifically designed to instill seriousness of purpose and appropriate role performance. Such strictures are routine in jury trials, and carefully followed in mock trial studies as well. Our own informal observations (Davis et al., 1975; Kerr, Atkin, Stasser, Meek, Holt, and Davis, 1976; Davis, Stasser, Spitzer, and Holt, 1976; Davis, Kerr, Stasser, Meek, and Holt, 1977) of mock jurors suggest a substantial seriousness of purpose and a close adherence to the role.

However, using a mock rape trial, Spitzer and Davis (1976) have reported a significant relationship between *juror* guilt preferences and pretrial responses to items soliciting (a) a judgment concerning the difficulty of committing rape, and (b) an opinion as to the justification of rape charges in general. A similar relationship was observed between these predictors and mock *jury* verdicts. Neither question would necessarily become salient in challenging a prospective juror for cause. In any event, neither the role strictures on the individual juror, nor the presumed balancing and filtering action of jury deliberation were apparently sufficient to prevent preconceived notions from affecting the outcome.

However, the Spitzer-Davis findings were retrospective in that they represented an analysis of data that had been collected earlier in connection with studies undertaken for different purposes. The mock juries they studied had been randomly formed, without regard to any personal features of members. Thus, questions about patterns of pretrial beliefs (i.e., patterns of pro-con opinions), juries of like-believing jurors (i.e., all members similar in relevant opinions), and so on, remained unanswered. Group composition issues are particularly interesting (e.g., Kairys, 1972) in that it is easy to imagine the selection of a preponderance of jurors favoring or attitudinally predisposed to one side or the other (i.e., pro or con). Thus, in the study reported below the general guilt belief was an independent variable. Three kinds of juries were constructed (pro-defense, moderate, and pro-prosecution) by roughly trichotomizing the pretrial response distribution to a question soliciting a judgment as to the likelihood that rape defendants are generally guilty.

METHOD

Subjects. A total of 828 subjects (475 male, 348 female, and five uncoded) participated for two hours each as part of a class exercise in an introductory social psychology course. Of the total, 708 were assigned to six-person juries and the remainder to individual conditions.

Design and Procedure. The independent variable in this study was the pretrial opinion of the potential jurors with regard to the likelihood that rape trial defendants are in general actually guilty. Three types of jurors were identified (pro-prosecution, moderate, and pro-defense) by trichotomizing the distribution of responses, along a six-point rating scale, to the question, "What is the likelihood that a rape trial defendant is actually guilty?" Three kinds of six-person juries were randomly composed of subjects from the three regions of the distribution.

The subjects defined as pro-prosecution believed 80% or more of defendants in rape trials were actually guilty; the moderates believed 60% to 80% of such defendants were guilty; and pro-defense subjects thought less than 60% of the defendants were guilty as charged. (A moderate juror was occasionally assigned to one of the extreme juries to maintain all juries at six persons.) There were forty-one, forty and thirty-nine juries in the pro-prosecution, moderate and pro-defense conditions, respectively.

The first part of the experiment took place in a large classroom and in advance of any discussion or information about crime, trials, juries, and so on. Upon arrival, subjects were seated before response consoles by means of which they subsequently responded to the bias question along with other items soliciting general preliminary information. Their responses were transmitted to a computer, which randomly assigned individuals to juries subject to the constraints discussed above.

Subjects next viewed a mock trial, which had been prerecorded on videotape, in which the defendant had been accused of rape. The defendant admitted that intercourse had taken place. However, he argued that the alleged victim not only had clearly consented, but had initiated the whole affair. The victim argued the defendant had misrepresented himself as a police officer, and had subsequently raped her. (See further Kerr et al., 1976, and Davis, Kerr, Stasser, Meek, and Holt, 1977.) Summaries of the testimony of minor witnesses, the concluding arguments of the prosecution and defense, and the judge's charge to the jury were presented on audiotape. At the conclusion of the trial, all subjects indicated their *personal* opinions about the guilt or innocence of the defendant, and answered several other questions about the trial. Jurors then joined their juries and went to smaller rooms. Individuals remaining after the maximum number of six-person juries had been formed participated alone and interacted with no one during subsequent portions of the experiment.

Juries then elected a foreman and deliberated until they reached a verdict or thirty minutes had elapsed (in which case they were declared hung). Unassigned individuals spent this time reflecting and writing brief summaries of the evidence favoring the prosecution and the defense. Following the verdict, all subjects again gave their personal opinion as to the defendant's guilt, and completed a questionnaire soliciting their opinions about a number of trial- and deliberation-related issues; several items also tested their recall of information presented at the trial. Everyone was then debriefed and much later participated in class discussions of the exercise.

RESULTS

Pre-deliberation Jurors. We assessed the effects of the experimental conditions representing three levels of initial guilt belief on the proportion of guilty sayers, $\hat{p}_G$, among the individual jurors-to-be across the three conditions: $(167/240) = .695$, $(158/234) = .675$, and $(122/234) = .521$ for the pro-prosecution, moderate, and pro-defense conditions, respectively. A significant contingency between a guilty decision and experimental condition (χ^2 (2) = 18.383, p < .001) was due to the leniency of the pro-defense subjects; the other two conditions yielded quite similar values of $\hat{p}_G$.

The overall proportion of individual guilty verdict preferences, $\hat{p}_G = .631 = (447/708)$, compared rather closely (no significant difference) with the value of .650 observed in recent research (Davis et al., 1976) using the same version of the rape trial and subjects from essentially the same population. Subjects in the three conditions did not differ significantly in responses to other items soliciting the certainty of their decisions, the "extent" of guilt (i.e., a nine-point guilt scale), or the length of sentence the defendant should receive if actually found guilty.

We thus seem to have evidence that the population of jurors can be partitioned into subpopulations based on a rather general belief about the guilt of defendants and that this general belief can influence a personal opinion about a particular defendant's guilt. That is to say, we have observed a biasing effect of a belief at the level of the individual juror. The bias prevails despite the trial format with its procedural guidelines and social pressures designed to eliminate or at least minimize such biases.

Juries (Verdicts). Group discussion is an important instrument, according to conventional wisdom, for achieving prudent decisions by minimizing such things as personal biases through a number of processes such as a cancelling effect from extremes, or the elimination of ignorance by sharing information. Thus, we can inspect the verdicts from juries in the three conditions to ascertain the extent to which the differential input (showing individual bias) observed above has been dampened through deliberation. First, however, recall that for whatever reason the relative frequency of juror verdict preferences in the pro-prosecution and moderate conditions were very similar, and thus unless the social processes differed in the two conditions we should not be surprised if the verdicts (output) from these two conditions were quite similar as well. Indeed, the pro-prosecution and moderate conditions were quite similar in their verdict distributions, $\hat{P}_G = .49$ and $.48$, respectively, but the pro-defense juries rendered relatively fewer guilty verdicts, $\hat{P}_G = .28$. From the standpoint of the original three conditions, the verdict-bias association is a moderate one, $\chi^2(2) = 4.32$, $p < .12$; but, if the pro-prosecution and moderate conditions had been pooled on the evidence presented earlier (viz., that the bias composition variable was not sufficiently varied at the outset for the pro-defense/moderate regions of the bias continuum), a stronger association may be indexed, $z = 2.13$, $p < .04$.

Social Decision Processes. The deliberation-verdict process may be conceptualized as a social decision scheme (Davis, 1973). The social decision scheme in turn may be represented as a $m \times n$ stochastic matrix, D, with entries $[d_{ij}]$, the conditional probability that the ith intragroup opinion distribution (corresponding to the ith of m rows) is followed by the jth outcome (corresponding to the jth of n columns). The social decision scheme matrix, D, is then 7×3, since juries are composed of six persons, and there are three possible outcomes of deliberation (guilty, not guilty, and hung).

The observed social decision scheme matrices, $\hat{D}$, for each condition are given in Table 2-1. Moderate and pro-prosecution matrices are rather similar, but the pro-defense matrix is somewhat different from the first two. However, the row subsamples are *very* small, and a single case can make the relative frequencies appear quite different. We lack a standard, straightforward means of assessing the intercondition agreement among the matrices, $\hat{D}$, but inspection of Table 2-1 offers no clear evidence that group decision processes differ with condition—at least as summarized by social decision schemes. At this point, it thus seems likely that the biasing process resides in the individual juror. We turn now to consider further this problem.

Postverdict Juror Responses. Actual court trials are, of course, not affected by the postverdict opinions of jurors. Nonetheless, we examined the guilt inclinations of individuals (postverdict jurors) after they had been

TABLE 2-1

Observed frequencies (and relative frequencies) with which mock juries having the (guilty, not guilty) distribution listed along the rows yielded the outcome noted over the columns, providing estimates, $\hat{D}$, for each experimental condition

Member Distribution		Experimental condition											
		Pro-prosecution				Moderate				Pro-defense			
G	NG	G	NG	H	Total	G	NG	H	Total	G	NG	H	Total
6	0	7 (1.00)	0 (.00)	0 (.00)	7	5 (1.00)	0 (.00)	0 (.00)	5				0
5	1	7 (.78)	2 (.22)	0 (.00)	9	7 (.70)	1 (.10)	2 (.20)	10	6 (1.00)	0 (.00)	0 (.00)	6
4	2	6 (.50)	1 (.08)	5 (.42)	12	5 (.46)	3 (.27)	3 (.27)	11	4 (.29)	5 (.36)	5 (.36)	14
3	3	0 (.00)	6 (.75)	2 (.25)	8	1 (.11)	4 (.44)	4 (.44)	9	1 (.14)	1 (.14)	5 (.71)	7
2	4	0 (.00)	2 (.50)	2 (.50)	4	0 (.00)	3 (1.00)	0 (.00)	3	0 (.00)	5 (1.00)	0 (.00)	5
1	5				0	0 (.00)	1 (1.00)	0 (.00)	1	0 (.00)	5 (1.00)	0 (.00)	5
0	6				0				0	0 (.00)	2 (1.00)	0 (.00)	2

TABLE 2-2

Relative frequency of guilty/not guilty preferences of individual,
postverdict jurors as a function of verdict and bias condition

| | Preferences of subjects who were in juries rendering a: | | | | | |
| | Guilty verdict | | | Not guilty verdict | | |
Bias condition	Guilty pref.	Not guilty pref.	N	Guilty pref.	Not guilty pref.	N
Pro-defense	.86	.14	65	.24	.76	166
Moderate	.92	.08	113	.38	.62	126
Pro-prosecution	.97	.03	114	.37	.63	124

"filtered" through whatever social processes (conformity, consensus pressures, etc.) that marked deliberation and decision, and which we have summarized overall as a social decision scheme (Table 2-1). The postgroup verdict preferences retained by subjects are given in Table 2-2 as a function of both bias condition and verdict of the preceding jury of which they had been a member. (The former jury outcomes of not guilty and hung have been combined into a single "not guilty" category for convenience.) The contingency between juror guilt preference and previous verdict is obviously quite large, and hardly surprising. Consequently, we elected to analyze separately the two sides of Table 2-2. The association between bias condition and ex-juror opinion, our primary interest, was significant for both the subjects who had been in the juries rendering guilty verdicts $(\chi^2(2) = 7.97, p < .02)$, and those from juries not reaching a guilty verdict $(\chi^2(2) = 8.36, p < .02)$.

The preceding relationship between bias and personal opinions was further confirmed by the significant effect of bias on mean "likelihood of guilt" judgments; the pro-defense jurors were inclined to regard the defendant as significantly less likely to be guilty, $F(2,355) = 3.176, p < .05$.

TABLE 2-3

Means and variances of likelihood of guilt judgments by jurors,
following deliberation, by experimental condition

Experimental condition	Males			Females			Total		
	N	Mean	Var.	N	Mean	Var.	N	Mean	Var.
Pro-prosecution	136	5.05	7.160	71	5.45	7.594	207	5.18	7.309
Moderate	122	6.13	8.247	103	6.34	5.991	225	6.23	7.194
Pro-defense	113	6.24	7.148	118	6.89	6.013	231	6.57	6.646

(Recall that judgments on this scale had not been significantly affected in this way prior to deliberation.) The bias factor significantly interacted with sex, $F(2,355) = 3.547$, $p < .03$, but served to intensify rather than reverse the direction of the relationship. (See Table 2-3.)

Overall, guilt preferences of postdeliberation jurors continued to be biased according to the general disposition observed at the outset. The extent of the bias is perhaps best documented from a slightly different perspective, and we turn now to that assessment.

Regression Analyses. Product moment correlation coefficients were calculated to describe the association between the initial guilt belief, and both the guilty/not guilty verdict and the likelihood of guilt decisions (not available for groups due to time limitations). These results are displayed in Table 2-4. All correlation coefficients were significant, and approximately equal in magnitude. There is little reduction in size, if any, between pre- and postdeliberation coefficients, suggesting that the bias thus indexed is relatively stable over the experiences in such a context. Moreover, these values are quite similar to those reported by Spitzer and Davis (1976).

Despite the enduring quality of the bias as again displayed in Table 2-4, it is tempting to take some comfort in the apparently small magnitude of the correlations reported there. For example, the average correlation, $\bar{r}$, in Table 2-4 is .20, and $\bar{r}^2 = .04$, a relatively small proportion of the total variance.

TABLE 2-4

Product moment correlation coefficients between initial guilt belief ratings and two criteria: the guilty/not guilty verdict and the likelihood of guilt decisions

	Criterion variables			
	G, NG decision		Guilt likelihood decision	
	r	F	r	F
Juror predeliberation (N = 609)	.21	27.97[**]	.20	24.30[**]
Jury verdict (N = 75)	.25	6.19[*]	—	—
Juror post deliberation (n = 609)	.14	12.44[**]	.20	24.93[**]

[*]$p < .025$, [**]$p < .001$

Note: Juries rendered only a guilty/not guilty decision and only those reaching a decision were included. The pre- and postdeliberation likelihood of guilt scales differed by one alternative and differed slightly in labeling.

Trial Perceptions and Recall. We inferred earlier that the locus of the bias seemed to be with the individual juror rather than the group decision. That is to say, there did not seem to be changes in verdict beyond those we could attribute to the individual juror at the time of input. However, we might now ask, what is the biasing process in the individual? Differently biased subjects might distort initial perceptions of information or selectively recall crucial testimony or simply weigh the available facts according to their biases. The postverdict questionnaires provide some informal evidence to aid in roughly localizing the bias.

Twelve multiple choice items tested recall of information designed to sample essential trial details. The content of these items ranged from the precise nature of the victim's injuries to the occupations of participants. Table 2-5 contains the proportion of correct responses on each of the twelve items (abbreviated along the left side of Table 2-5). It is evident by inspection that not only was there little contingency between the general initial belief ratings and the correctness of response, but there was a very high level of overall recall accuracy. The case was not especially complicated, but such uniformly excellent recall was not anticipated. It thus appears that initial perceptions and stored information were not an obvious source of bias; the "test" results of Table 2-5 suggest that the information needed for action was probably present during deliberations.

Subjects also made judgments concerning the believability of testimony by the principals and persuasiveness of arguments by the opposing attor-

TABLE 2-5

Relative frequency of correct answers to each of twelve recall test items as a function of initial guilt belief response (N=512)

| | Initial guilt (likelihood) belief | | | | | | |
| | Not guilty | | | | Guilty | | |
Test item	1	2	3	4	5	6	Total
Victim's employer	.89	.94	.95	.92	.93	.84	.93
Victim's clothing	1.00	.97	.95	.95	.98	.95	.96
Victim's injuries (1)	.96	.99	.99	.97	.99	1.00	.98
Defendant's "beers"	.96	.99	.95	.97	.99	1.00	.97
Defendant's remarks	.82	.87	.85	.89	.86	.95	.87
Defendant's record	.91	.97	.92	.94	.92	.74	.93
Victim's religion	.89	.88	.90	.86	.88	.95	.88
Victim's spouse	.87	.82	.89	.90	.82	.83	.87
Defendant's license	.98	1.00	1.00	1.00	1.00	1.00	.99
Defendant's occupation	.80	.91	.87	.89	.92	.84	.89
Victim's injuries (2)	.91	.87	.86	.90	.80	.79	.87
Defendant's marriage	.93	.91	.90	.93	.88	.82	.91

neys. The means of these judgments appear in Table 2-6. The average ratings are in a direction consistent with the respondents' initial general guilt belief. A sex x condition analysis of variance revealed a significant effect of experimental condition on three items. More specifically, for victim believability, $F(2,674) = 2.863$, p = .058; for prosecution persuasiveness, $F(2,674) = 3.569$, p = .029; for defendant believability, $F(2,674) = 2.236$, p = .108; and $F(2,674) = .529$, n.s., for defense persuasiveness. The main effect of sex and the interaction were not significant on all four items. (Taken as independent tests of the same basic hypothesis, the preceding set of four probabilities were combined according to— $2\Sigma_i \ln(p_i) = \chi^2(8) = 17.42$, p $<$ .05; see Winer, 1971.)

[1] On the average, the perceived credibility or "quality" of the testimony seems to be the site of the difference rather than the actual content of memory. That is to say, acquisition and/or recall accuracy do not appear to be the source of bias so much as the evaluation or weight given the information. Moreover, it has been evident from the outset that the bias first reported by Spitzer and Davis (1976) and documented more thoroughly here is at best a subtle effect. We now have some evidence as to its location (individual decision preferences) and its origin (the evaluation of testimony).

TABLE 2-6
Means and standard deviations of postverdict believability and persuasiveness ratings for each experimental condition (N=242)

	Experimental condition					
	Pro-defense		Moderate		Pro-prosecution	
Judgment	Mean	SD	Mean	SD	Mean	SD
Victim believability [**]	3.47	1.70	3.01	1.50	2.87	1.68
Prosecution persuasivenss [***]	3.21	1.34	2.83	1.47	2.61	1.39
Defendant believability [*]	3.67	1.48	4.11	1.48	4.16	1.43
Defense persuasiveness	3.40	1.38	3.61	1.42	3.49	1.43

[*]p ≃ .10, [**]p ≃ .05, [***]p ≃ .03
Note: Response scale ranged from 0, extremely believable/persuasive, to 7, extremely unbelievable/unpersuasive.

DISCUSSION

The relationship between the pretrial guilt belief and subsequent individual and group verdicts indexes one role of bias, even though we cannot complete the earlier analogy with statistical estimation by calculating a numerically valued true value. The relationship is fairly robust; it obtained both before and after deliberation, as well as in the jury verdict itself, although social interaction did attenuate the effect somewhat. As mentioned earlier, research evidence has not offered much support for the compelling intuition of a close relationship between individual traits, opinions, etc., and group level performance. The results of this study, along with the earlier findings of Spitzer and Davis (1976), provide some evidence at the group level, perhaps because the group task itself engages social content to a substantial degree.

Bray and Noble (1977) have just reported the effects of an even more general individual pretrial disposition, authoritarianism, upon the group level decision. Uniformly high or low juries judged guilt and punishment following a mock murder trial. High authoritarian jurors and juries preferred and rendered harsher verdicts and punishments than did those low in authoritarianism. Bray and Nobel point out that their

> . . . results offer support for the widely held, but generally untested notion that high authoritarian *juries* [emphasis added] are more inclined than low authoritarian juries to find a defendant guilty (see Davis et al., 1977; Elwork and Sales, in press). (pp. 14-15.)

(See also related research on mock *jurors* by Boehm, 1968; Jurow, 1971; Mitchell and Byrne, 1973; Berg and Vidmar, 1975.)

Bray and Noble also point out that one implication of the general harshness associated with the highly authoritarian is that they are more likely than low authoritarians to agree publicly that the death penalty is acceptable punishment. Thus, it is the latter who are likely to be excused from jury duty in capital cases, and the resulting "death-qualified" jury stands to be "biased" toward a guilty verdict. Yet, a jury composed of the other extreme, those low in authoritarianism, is similarly biased, but in the opposite direction. We have in this instance the ingredients of a generally unrecognized dilemma, but one which emphasizes certain important problems which we will consider more fully in a later section.

Bias Location. We noted earlier that groups seem to offer the special protection of the cancellation of extremes, discussion-stimulated moderation, and normative pressures to guard against the error-prone or biased. That social interaction does not routinely serve this function has been observed in studies of choice shifts, group polarization, among others (see further Janis, 1972; Davis, 1973; Myers and Lamm, 1976; Davis, Bray, and

Holt, 1977). With regard to juries per se, the findings of Spitzer and Davis from randomly formed groups suggested that the give and take in deliberation did not mute entirely the effects of biased members. The results of the present study along with those of Bray and Noble suggest similar conclusions when the biasing belief or personal disposition is controlled as an independent variable.

However, there is the additional problem that a preponderance of like-minded (biased) subjects might create an atmosphere that amplifies or pushes the bias further than would be anticipated from considering only the input level of individual bias. The results were encouraging in that we obtained no evidence of further biasing effects from social interaction; the social decision scheme summarizing the group decision process did not appear to vary with composition in the way we had feared. Of course, in other contexts, and with different compositions (including certain mixtures) we might find a contingency between bias and the observed social decision scheme.

Bias in the individual juror might originate with information acquisition, memory, or the interpretation of recalled material. The uniformly accurate recall by all types of subjects suggested that the biasing process resided with the interpretation of evidence—differential weight was perhaps placed upon exonerating and incriminating testimony. Such a result might be expected more often in the general population than from college student subjects who were probably more intelligent, detached, idealistic, and experienced in analytic problem-solving than the general population. Of course, ours was a mock trial and participants were not responsible for an actual verdict.

Apparently, we must consider different populations of persons as having different "true values," and move away from a single true value for all subjects. Well-meaning and in many ways similar persons see the same world differently—hardly a new finding. If the situational constraints do not serve to keep bias effects to an acceptable minimum (and those we have observed are relatively small), new attention to the composition of juries and other such formal groups is necessary.

CONCLUDING REMARKS

The *idea* of bias in statistical estimators provided a useful metaphor for the analysis of bias in group decisions. Given imperfections in membership filtering mechanisms, and given the inefficacy of procedural/situational constraints, such as observed in the empirical example we reported earlier, balancing member predilections may offer the best hope for muting unwanted bias. At some point, moreover, it is not even clear that we should refer to different guilt preferences, given the evidence, as bias. We may find it necessary to recognize legitimate differences in true values for different populations. However, identifying and agreeing upon "legitimate differences" in true values for persons from different populations may prove to be a difficult social decision task in its own right.

An example may serve to illustrate the dilemma. We have consistently observed differences in the guilt preferences of males and females observing the same case in which the defendant was charged with rape (Davis et al., 1975, 1976; Davis, Kerr, Stasser, Meek, and Holt, 1977). Such differences in inclination are fairly small, but apparently represent definite differences in perspectives (i.e., population true values/parameters). It is difficult to imagine any but the most extreme members of these populations being identified during voir dire examinations and excused for this cause. It is very easy to imagine, however, situations and/or communities in which the initial call for jurors as well as the remaining selection apparatus, yields a jury quite imbalanced with respect to sex. Random sampling from a sex-balanced roll might still yield (by virtue of sampling error) a jury imbalanced by sex; neither the defense nor prosecution will necessarily be impressed by the argument for equal expected values, since this is the only time they will be engaged in this contest. Other disturbing examples come easily to mind. One example could be constructed from the findings of Bray and Noble who not only demonstrated the outcome to be expected from heavily authoritarian juries, but proposed a likely way in which imbalances could come about—dismissals of low authoritarians in capital cases during voir dire. Still others could be constructed from highly complicated cases (especially likely to arise in certain civil trials), and the possibility of obtaining jurors with limited education, intelligence, etc.— only a special case of the more general dilemma which democracies must repeatedly engage.

Fortunately, we do not deal with such political issues. Our goal has only been to document some features of bias in group decision. An important future task will be the study of various group compositions (i.e., subjects from differently parameterized populations) and their consequences.

NOTES

1. This research at the University of Illinois was supported by Grant BNS 76-21326 from the National Science Foundation, for which the first author is

principal investigator. We would like to express our thanks to Robert Holt and David Vollrath for their assistance at various stages of the project and our appreciation to Professor Elaine Shoben for informal advice on legal questions.

2. This view reflects the opinion of several trial-experienced attorneys who were contacted by the authors.

REFERENCES

Berg, K.S., and N. Vidmar. Authoritarianism and recall of evidence about criminal behavior. *Journal of Research in Personality*, 1975, *9*, 147-157.

Boehm, V. Mr. Prejudice, Miss Sympathy, and the authoritarian personality: An application of psychological measuring techniques to the problem of jury bias. *Wisconsin Law Review*, 1968, 734-750.

Bray, R.M., and A. Noble. Authoritarianism and decisions of mock juries: Evidence of jury bias and group polarization. Unpublished manuscript, University of Kentucky, Lexington, Kentucky, 1977.

Davis, J.H. Group decision and social interaction: A theory of social decision schemes. *Psychological Review*, 1973, *80*, 97-125.

Davis, J.H., R.M. Bray, and R.W. Holt. The empirical study of decision processes in juries: A critical review. In J. Tapp and F. Levine (Eds.), *Law, Justice, and the Individual in Society: Psychological and Legal Issues*. New York: Holt, Rinehart & Winston, 1977.

Davis, J.H., N.L. Kerr, R.S. Atkin, R.W. Holt, and D. Meek. The decision processes of 6- and 12-person juries assigned unanimous and two-thirds majority rules. *Journal of Personality and Social Psychology*, 1975, *32*, 1-14.

Davis, J.H., N.L. Kerr, G. Stasser, D. Meek, and R. Holt. Victim consequences, sentence severity, and decision processes in mock juries. *Organizational Behavior and Human Performance*, 1977, *18*, 346-365.

Davis, J.H., G. Stasser, C.E. Spitzer, and R.W. Holt. Changes in group members' decision preferences during discussion: An illustration with mock juries. *Journal of Personality and Social Psychology*, 1976, *34*, 1177-1187.

Diamond, S.S., and H. Zeisel. A courtroom experiment on juror selection and decision making. Presented at the American Psychological Association, New Orleans, 1974.

Gelfand, A.E., and H. Solomon. Analyzing the decision-making process of the American jury. *Journal of the American Statistical Association*, 1975, *70*, 305-310.

–––. Modeling jury verdicts in the American legal system. *Journal of the American Statistical Association*, 1974, *69*, 32-37.

–––. A study of Poisson's models for jury verdicts in criminal and civil trials. *Journal of the American Statistical Association*, 1973, *68*, 271-278.

Gerbasi, K.C., M. Zuckerman, and H.T. Reis. Justice needs a new blindfold: A review of mock jury research. *Psychological Bulletin*, 1977, *84*, 323-345.

Heslin, R. Predicting group task effectiveness from member characteristics. *Psychological Bulletin*, 1964, *62*, 248-256.

Janis, I.L. *Victims of Groupthink*. Boston, Mass.: Houghton Mifflin, 1972.

Jurow, G.L. New data on the effect of a "death-qualified" jury on the guilt determination process. *Harvard Law Review,* 1971, *84,* 567-611.

Kairys, D. (Ed.), J. Schulman, and S. Harring (Co-Eds.). *The Jury System: New Methods for Reducing Prejudice.* Philadelphia, Penn.: Philadelphia Resistance Print Shop, 1975.

———. Juror selection: The law, a mathematical method of analysis, and a case study. *American Criminal Law Review,* 1972, *10,* 771.

Kalven, H., Jr., and H. Zeisel, *The American Jury.* Boston, Mass.: Little, Brown, 1966.

Kerr, N.L., R.S. Atkin, G. Stasser, D. Meek, R.W. Holt, and J.H. Davis. Guilt beyond a reasonable doubt: Effects of concept definition and assigned decision rule on the judgments of mock jurors. *Journal of Personality and Social Psychology,* 1976, *34,* 282-294.

Mann, R.D. A review of the relationships between personality and performance in small groups. *Psychological Bulletin,* 1959, *56,* 241-270.

McGrath, J.E., and I. Altman. *Small Group Research: A Synthesis and Critique of the Field.* New York: Holt, Rinehart and Winston, 1966.

Mitchell, H.E., and D. Byrne. The defendant's dilemma: Effects of jurors' attitudes and authoritarianism on judicial decisions. *Journal of Personality and Social Psychology,* 1973, *25,* 123-129.

Myers, D.G., and H. Lamm. The group polarization phenomenon. *Psychological Bulletin,* 1976, *83,* 602-627.

Spitzer, C.E., and J.H. Davis. The effects of juror bias on judicial decisions. Paper presented at the Rocky Mountain Psychological Association meeting, Phoenix, 1976.

Winer, B.J. *Statistical Principles in Experimental Design.* New York: McGraw-Hill, 1971.

3

SITUATIONS OF UNCERTAINTY: SOCIAL INFLUENCE AND DECISION PROCESSES[1]

Roger Lambert

I. THEORETICAL PRESENTATION OF THE PROBLEM

It has been demonstrated that in every situation involving a finite number of events ordered on a unidimensional continuum, any group decision process leading to unanimous agreement necessarily implies a shift of the group mean relative to the individual mean choices, provided that the group adopts the majority position. The direction and the size of this shift depend on the initial distribution of individual choices on the continuum (Lambert, 1969, 1971).

It is thus undeniable that in risk-taking situations, if the choice structure (distribution of member response preferences) makes it possible to adopt the majority-rule, and if this rule is strictly followed by groups, risky as well as conservative shifts may be observed. The former would occur if initial individual choices are risky, and the latter if they are conservative. The notions of risk and conservatism are defined here only in relation to the range of proposed choices and not in reference to any absolute values.

For example, let us take five persons who choose individually, and then collectively with consensus, a choice more or less risky among the following:

Winnings :	40	14	8	6	4
Probabilities :	0.1	0.3	0.5	0.7	0.9

and let us consider two examples.

In the first example, the mean, m_I, of individual probability choices is 0.38. Observing a majority-rule, the group chooses the probability 0.30 = m_G. The positive difference ($m_I - m_G$) between these two values indicates a risky shift. In the second example the choice structure is the same (3-1-1) but the choice distribution is symmetrically inverted. The difference ($m_I - m_G$) is negative and indicates a conservative shift.

The majority effect is not a question of reducing group risk-taking behavior to an artifact; it is genuine effect. Though in larger groups the relative majority and its importance can vary considerably, the majority effect is generalizable to groups of any size.

When there is no discussion, decision-making by majority-rule is relatively frequent, and our majority-rule model satisfactorily accounts for the observed group risk shift (Lambert, 1969, 1971). However, when group members are allowed to exchange arguments in favor of their respective positions, the resulting risky shift is generally greater than that predicted by the model, while the conservative shift most often proves smaller than prediction (Zaleska, 1974, 1976).

Only in the case of deviations from model predictions can an increase in the risk level taken by groups be considered genuine. We may then attempt to account for this increase by referring to various explanatory theories, such as those based on the diffusion of responsibility, on the social value of risk, or on the predominant influence of the more risk-prone individuals, to mention only the most frequently cited proposals. These theories are not mutually exclusive in that the underlying social processes they imply may sometimes concur to produce the same phenomenon.

Thus, a positive relation between the propensity to take risks and the influence exercised within decision-making groups in situations of uncertainty may well be explained by a certain valorization of risk. It is possible that risk-taking individuals are more influential, not because of their personality, but because their position is more likely to be adopted by the group if risk is a social value.

However, when observing individual and group behavior on a single task such as a series of choices among several monetary bets which are, or appear to be, more or less risky, it is difficult to decide which of the alternative explanations is correct. In order to settle this question it would be necessary to observe the behavior of the same individuals on several group tasks involving decisions on issues of which some are associated with

TABLE 3-1

Examples of majority-rule shifts (risky and conservative) in groups of five persons

	Response alternatives (probabilities)												Shift
	Individual choices						Group choices						
	0.1	0.3	0.5	0.7	0.9	m_I	0.1	0.3	0.5	0.7	0.9	m_G	$m_I - m_G$
Example 1	1	3			1	0.38		1				0.30	0.08
Example 2	1			3	1	0.62				1		0.70	−0.08

social values and some are not. Comparison of the observed behavior would then offer the possibility of a better interpretation of the underlying influence process.

The experiment presented here has been devised with this theoretical perspective in mind.

II. EXPERIMENTAL PROCEDURE

Groups of six members were involved in three experimental tasks. The first was a manual task. It consisted of collectively maneuvering a mobile cbject as rapidly as possible through a maze without touching any of the baffles (utilization of cybernometer). The task was of the speed-accuracy type and learning it was easy. The influence exerted by each individual was measured by the systematic elimination of each subject when a plateau in the learning performance in the group was achieved. The most influential individual was that group member whose absence from a series of trials brought about the greatest decline of group performance in terms either of speed or of accuracy (Lambert, 1965, p. 77).

During the second task, ten choices among monetary bets were proposed to subjects. Each choice involved five bets which were more or less

TABLE 3-2
Monetary bets: payoff matrix (in French francs)

Bet number		1	2	3	4	5
Fixed stake		0.2	0.4	0.8	1.6	3.2
	1/2	0.25	0.5	1	2	4
	1/4	0.5	1	2	4	8
Probability	1/8	1	2	4	8	16
	1/16	2	4	8	16	32
	1/32	4	8	16	32	64
Bet number		6	7	8	9	10
Fixed probability		1/2	1/4	1/8	1/16	1/32
	0.2	0.25	0.5	1	2	4
	0.4	0.5	1	2	4	8
Stake	0.8	1	2	4	8	16
	1.6	2	4	8	16	32
	3.2	4	8	16	32	64

risky (see Table 3-2). For the first five choices the stake was fixed and each subject was to select the probability of winning he preferred. For the other five, the probability of winning was imposed, while each participant was to choose the stake he wanted to bet. The group situation was the same but all group members had to agree on one bet for each of the ten choices.

From the start subjects were informed that one bet only was to be played for money and that it would be designated by a random device at the end of the experimental session. The extent to which each individual yielded to influence during this task was measured by calculating the sum of the differences, expressed in absolute values, between each of his initial choices and the corresponding group choice.

The third task was perceptual in nature. It consisted of making two estimates: one of the length of a sinuous line, and the other, of the number of points on a rectangular board. A written estimate was made by subjects exposed to each stimulus for three seconds. After the second presentation, all group members had to agree on a single estimate for each of the two stimuli.

A measurement of the extent to which individuals responded to influence was based on the difference between their own initial estimate and that made by their group. These differences were expressed in absolute values.

Finally, a personality questionnaire (CDR) was given to all subjects in order to compare their behavior in everyday situations with the behavior adopted during the three tasks. It contained thirty questions bearing on self-confidence, dominance and risk-taking (see Appendix 1).

The experiment was carried out with thirty-two groups of six subjects, half of which were male and half female, who were attending the first and the second class of a high school near Paris.[2] They ranged in age from fifteen to seventeen years. Groups were formed at random.

The manual task (cybernometer) was presented as a competition between all groups, with a prize of 120 francs to be awarded the winning group.

At the beginning of the experimental session, each participant was alloted 3.20 francs for betting. The amount each participant bet on the single wager actually played at the end of the experiment was deducted from this sum. The payoff matrices presented in Table 1 show that a subject could possibly win as much as 64 francs in the betting. The order of task presentation was counterbalanced.

III. DATA ANALYSIS

1. VERIFICATION OF THE MAJORITY-RULE MODEL

Of the three tasks described above, only the one involving choices among monetary bets, permitted a valid study of the risk shift. Consequently, we shall examine the results observed in the betting task in order to test in the first place whether group choices become more extreme following discussion and in the second, whether the majority-rule model provides a satisfactory explanation of this phenomenon. It is only if the adjustment of this model to the data does not prove satisfactory that one may turn to other explanatory theories, as said before.

But in that case what metrics should one use? How should probabilities and stakes be transformed so that they correspond to the exact perception of the subjects? In the course of a differential study of the behavior of individuals and groups in risk-taking (Lambert, 1971), the author showed that the conclusions concerning risk shift in group betting were not substantially modified by a transformation of p into log p, excepting a strait zone within which the sense of the risk shift was reversed (Lambert, 1972).

The systematic application of several metrics concerning the risk manipulated in this task shows large correlations between them. But the one selected here consists of using risk scales on which the values of the successive points are proportional either to the denominator of the probabilities, or to the stake, as shown below:

Points	1	2	4	8	16	
Probabilities	1/2	1/4	1/8	1/16	1/32	
Stakes	.2	.4	.8	1.6	3.2	(in French francs)

The mean level of risk taken by individuals and groups is calculated using this metric. As shown in Table 3-3, it appears that groups shift towards choices riskier than the initial individual positions.

It should, however, be noted that the size of this shift tends to decrease as the risk associated with the proposed bets increases. A more detailed examination of collective choices shows that a group may even become more conservative than its members are when betting individually. (See Table 3-4.)

Those results, apparently contradictory to those in Table 3-2 for bets 4, 5, 9, and 10, are due to the fact that those groups which shifted towards risk shifted further than those which shifted towards caution.

Such reversal of change in risk level may be brought about by groups which are making decisions by majority-rule. The question is whether the

TABLE 3-3
Differences observed between mean risk level
taken by individuals and groups

Bet number	Fixed stake					Fixed probability				
	1	2	3	4	5	6	7	8	9	10
Group mean	11.3	8.1	5.1	3.5	3.8	10.8	7.9	6.2	4.4	4.4
Individual mean	6.1	4.3	4.1	3.2	3.6	8.0	5.5	4.7	4.3	4.0
Mean Difference	5.2	3.8	1.0	0.3	0.2	2.8	2.4	1.5	0.1	0.4

model of decision-making based on this rule proves sufficient to account for the size of the observed phenomenon. In order to answer this question it is necessary to examine group decisions in relation to the structure of initial individual choices within groups.

Since, for each item, each of the six group members has to choose among five bets, ten different classes of choice structures may be observed. In some of these structures there is a majority or a plurality choice (6, 5-1, 4-2, 4-1-1, 3-2-1, 3-1-1-1, 2-1-1-1-1); in others, different positions are taken by subgroups of equal size (3-3, 2-2-1-1, 2-2-2).

Of the 320 observed choice structures (32 groups each making 10 bets), 237 are of the majority or plurality type (see Table 3-5). However, for only 102 of them was the choice of the majority or of the largest subgroup adopted. The corresponding percentage is 43%. When this decision-making rule was not observed, group choice appeared to be riskier than predicted by our model in 46% of the cases, and less risky in 11% of them.

TABLE 3-4
Monetary bets: direction of shift of risk level in groups

Bet number	Fixed stake					Fixed probability				
	1	2	3	4	5	6	7	8	9	10
Shift towards risk	28	27	18	14	10	21	26	20	14	12
No shift	1	3	3	1	1	2	1	1	1	2
Shift towards conservatism	3	2	11	17	21	9	5	11	17	18

Note: The entries of this table represent the number of groups shifting towards risk, towards conservatism, and without any change in risk level.

TABLE 3-5

Monetary bets: the distribution of choice structures
(members' initial choices) observed within groups over all bets

Choice structures	Observed group consensus on a bet, that was:			
Majorities and pluralities	Less risky than initial majority	Same as initial majority	More risky than initial majority	Total
6	0	3	0	3
5-1	3	14	13	30
4-2	4	17	16	37
4-1-1	3	19	22	44
3-2-1	11	41	37	89
3-1-1-1	3	7	17	27
2-1-1-1-1	3	1	3	7
Total	27	102	108	237
Other structures	Less risky than initial mean	Same as initial mean	More risky than initial mean	
3-3	6		11	17
2-2-1-1	21	1	31	53
2-2-2	4		9	13
Total	31	1	51	83

This tendency is confirmed in choice structures where different positions were defended by subgroups of equal size. When such was the case, groups chose riskier bets with a significantly higher frequency than would be predicted on the basis of the distribution of the initial individual choices.

Discussion seems to be necessary in order that the consensus becomes riskier than the answer predicted by the majority-rule model. However, in a betting situation discussion seems to be very limited. Nevertheless, arguments are proposed such as: "The stake is so small so what is the risk we take?" These arguments, although few, seem to be very powerful.

Thus, it appears that in groups making decisions by unanimous agreement after discussion, the resulting risky shift is generally greater than that predicted by the model, while conservative shift most often proves less. Our majority-rule model does not fully account for this phenomenon. Under these conditions it is necessary to inquire into the deeper causes of the observed phenomenon by examining more closely the underlying influence processes which may eventually justify behavior of groups in this type of situation.

2. EXAMINATION OF INFLUENCE PROCESSES

The measurement of the extent to which individuals have yielded to influence or of the influence exercised by them within their group has been operationally defined for each of the three tasks.

However, contrary to the two other tasks, influence in the manual task (cybernometer) was not measured by comparing each individual decision to the corresponding group decision. The earlier approach in this case produced a measure of influence of a positive or negative value which is the result of the impact of each individual's action on the total group performance. Consequently such a measure could not be used for examining the risk shift.

The procedure can be used for the perception task, which does not involve risk, but it does not permit a study of the majority-rule model as it does for the betting task. When a variable comprises a great number of possible values on the continuum, it is difficult to find a distribution of values of a type similar to that found when the number of values is limited.[3] In this case, should one arbitrarily define a small number of classes each comprising a more or less restricted range of values?

This problem concerning the number of response alternatives, which refers to the perception of differences, is of great importance because it often arises. The questions involved here are those of discrimination, which is a function of the partition of a continuum into more or less small units as perceived by each individual, and of assimilation, which is a function of the tolerance to change when seeking a consensus.

In the perception task, values of estimates have not been regrouped arbitrarily into classes. Results show a convergence of individual estimates, not on their mean, but on the average estimate of the total population

TABLE 3-6
Perception task: means of individual and group estimates

Response	Actual stimulus value	Mean estimate	
		Individuals	Groups
Estimate of the number of dots	64	56.2	57.3
Estimate of the length (in cm) of the line	56	42.7	43.4

($p < .05$). The slight improvement of group estimates relative to the true stimulus value is not significant (see Table 3-6).

Is it possible to deduce from the three measures of influence that there is a transfer of influence from task to task, corresponding to a possible generalization of influential behavior? If such is the case the rank of each individual's influence should remain the same, or be only slightly modified in the course of the three tasks.

A correlational study of these ranks (see Table 3-7) does not reveal any significant relation between the influence exercised in the manual and the betting tasks.

On the other hand, the individuals who were the least influenced in their estimates during the perception task tend to be significantly the least influential with respect to the accuracy of performance during the manual task (cybernometer) and also the least influenced in their betting behavior. They take higher risks when they make individual choices of bets, and they claim to have more self-confidence, to take more risks and to be more dominant. Furthermore, when calculations were made using scores instead

TABLE 3-7
Correlations Φ between variables

	V	P/V	R	I_r	P/L	CDR
P	.06	.56 ($p < .001$)	.02	−.02	−.15 ($p < .05$)	−.06
V		.46 ($p < .001$)	.06	−.06	−.02	−.06
P/V			.06	.02	.00	−.17 ($p < .02$)
R				.06	.17 ($p < .02$)	−.08
I_r					.17 ($p < .02$)	−.02
P/L						.19 ($p < .01$)

Manual task (cybernometer): P = influence on accuracy
                             V = influence on speed
                             P/V = overall influence

Monetary bets: R = risk level
                             I_r = influence on betting behavior

Perception task: P/L = influence on the both estimates
                             CDR = rank in the group on the CDR questionnaire

of ranks,[4] it appears that these individuals exercised more influence than others on the speed of performance in the manual task.

Though there seemed at first to be no correlation between scores on the CDR questionnaire and risk-taking behavior, a more detailed examination of the data showed that individuals whose responses to Questions 7, 9, 26, and 29 were risk oriented (n = 50) took, on the average, higher risks in betting than others.

It may be concluded that, although the transfer of influence is not systematic, there is a certain relation between actual risk-taking or verbal indication of preference for risk, on one hand, and actual influence, on the other hand, since to modify to a lesser extent than others one's position in relation to group decision can generally be interpreted as a manifestation of a certain influence exercised within the group.

Groups achieving the highest speed when performing on the cybernometer, and groups composed of individuals who declared themselves oriented towards risk, also take more risks than others. Groups as well as individuals attributing more importance to accuracy are more conservative in betting. It would then seem that risk is to a certain extent related to a dynamogenic factor operationalized by a trend to act rapidly and to assert oneself vigorously.

IV. CONCLUSION

Thus, it appears that in this experiment the individuals most inclined to take risks and least influenced in group decisions were the more dynamic. This permitted them, if not to impose their choice, at least to orient the choice of the group towards risk when discussing a bet. The result is that the majority-rule is less often followed when there is a discussion (only 43% of the majority and plurality structures were predictive; see Table 3-5), a result to be compared with that of another experiment without discussion (where 74% followed a majority and plurality structure; Lambert 1969, 1971). Nevertheless, one should not eliminate the possibility that there exists a diffusion of responsibility in the group, or a valorization of risk due to the arguments presented during the discussion, which would explain shifts towards risk or a decrease in conservatism, such as observed in a large number of experiments of this type.

APPENDIX 1
CDR QUESTIONNAIRE

Factors*	Question		Percentage** of responses
C +	1. Do you have difficulty in admitting that you are wrong?	yes	46%
C −	2. Do you launch out into a discussion only when you are entirely sure of yourself?	no	56%
D −	3. Do you find it difficult to speak in public?	no	40%
R +	4. Do you have the impression that you are generally lucky?	yes	48%
R −	5. Do you worry about possible misfortunes?	no	57%
D −	6. Do you avoid all quarrels?	no	29%
R +	7. Do you seek out activities giving you strong emotions?	yes	40%
C −	8. Do you prefer to know other persons' points of view before making a decision?	no	20%
R −	9. Do you fear perilous situations?	no	63%
D +	10. Have you already, on your own initiative, formed groups of your playmates or school friends?	yes	48%
C +	11. Do you prefer to make your decisions all by yourself?	yes	52%
D +	12. Are you ambitious?	yes	62%
C −	13. Do you often lose your head in a dangerous situation?	no	80%
R −	14. When your friends plan to undertake a dangerous action, do you recommend carefulness?	no	19%

APPENDIX 1 (Continued)   CDR Questionnaire

Factors[*]		Question		Percentage[**] of responses
D +	15.	Do you seek competition and struggle?	yes	39%
C −	16.	Are you susceptible to influence?	no	46%
C +	17.	Do you have confidence in your ability to cope in an emergency?	yes	70%
D −	18.	When you participate in an activity, do you prefer someone else to be the leader?	no	50%
R −	19.	Are you anxious about the idea of engaging in an operation of uncertain consequences?	no	45%
D −	20.	Do you sometimes have a feeling of inferiority?	no	39%
C +	21.	Are you impulsive?	yes	63%
R +	22.	Do you like games of chance?	yes	59%
D −	23.	Do you have difficulty in asserting yourself during discussions with your peers?	no	71%
D +	24.	Would you like to be always the first?	yes	25%
R −	25.	Do certain things frighten you?	no	24%
R +	26.	Do you go in for dangerous exercise or sports, or would you like to?	yes	52%
D +	27.	Do you find it unpleasant to be given orders?	yes	58%
C −	28.	Do you need time to think before engaging in a bold venture?	no	18%
R +	29.	Do you experience pleasure in undertaking a risky action?	yes	69%
C +	30.	Do you make your decisions rapidly?	yes	61%

[*]C : self-confidence
 D : dominance
 R : risk

[**]The percentages are indicated for the responses corresponding to the positive pole of the factor (C, D, or R).

NOTES

1. This research program was realized at the Laboratoire de Psychologie Sociale, University of Paris 7, with the technical assistance of Danièl Alaphilippe and of Daniele Duda.

2. We wish to express our thanks to the director of ENSEPS, the director of the high school at Châtenay-Malabry and all the professors and teachers at these two schools for having received us with kindness, thus making it possible for us to carry out this study.

3. Recall that in the betting task, subjects have a choice between five values of probability or of stake, while in the perception task, involving estimates of the number of dots or of the length of a line, the number of possible values is very large.

4. Ranks indicate the relative value of the influence of each individual in the group (rank 1 to 6). Scores were defined earlier when task descriptions were given.

REFERENCES

Lambert, R. Risky shift in relation to choice of metric. *Journal of Experimental Social Psychology,* 1972, *8,* 315-318.

———. Extrémisation du risque en groupe. *Journal de la Société de Statistique de Paris,* 1971, *112,* 11-22.

———. Extrémisation du comportement de prise de risque en groupe et modèle majoritaire. *Psychologie Française,* 1969, *14,* 113-125.

———. Autorité et influence sociale. In P. Fraisse and J. Piaget (Eds.), *Traité de psychologie expérimentale.* Vol. IX. *Psychologie sociale.* Paris: Presses Universitaires de France, 1965.

Zaleska, M. Majority influence on group choices among bets. *Journal of Personality and Social Psychology,* 1976, *33,* 8-17.

———. The effects of discussion on group and individual choices among bets. *European Journal of Social Psychology,* 1974, *4,* 229-250.

4

SOME EXPERIMENTAL RESULTS:
MAJORITY INFLUENCE ON GROUP DECISIONS

Maryla Zaleska

Depending on the type of task, several models predicting group decision-making behavior have been proposed in the past. The classic model of convergence on the mean of initial individual choices proves satisfactory when the task consists of estimating physical properties of some stimulus. In this type of task, groups are confronted with a great number of possible responses ordered on a unidimensional continuum.

A majority-rule decision-making model has been used as early as 1938 by Thorndike, and later by other authors, in order to predict group decisions on certain tasks of the problem-solving type, involving a small number of different choice possibilities. Recently, Lambert (1969, 1971) has shown that his model of decision-making by majority-rule accounts, under specific conditions, for the well-known group "polarization phenomenon." It can be demonstrated that if the majority, or the plurality choice, is systematically adopted, the mean group choice necessarily inclines further toward the pole initially predominating on the scale. In other words in order to explain significant changes of risk level in groups, as well as group attitude change following discussion, it would be sufficient to replace the classic model of convergence on the mean by the model of convergence on the mode. It remains to be seen to what extent the experimental results confirm this hypothesis.

To answer this question, I shall refer first to Figure 1 showing the rate of agreement between one or the other of the two models, and actual decisions of small groups. The percentages shown in this figure are based on five experiments bearing on different populations in various situations involving risk. In the first two of these experiments subjects were making choices among bets and were actually winning or losing money. Experiment I involved choices between a sure gain—a 10 out of 10 probability of winning—and probabilities ranging from 9/10 to 1/10 of receiving greater gains (up to $25) of expected value approximately equal to that of the sure gain. This value was different for each of the six items. In Experiment II, subjects were gambling with their own money and for each of the six values of the stake they had to select one of seven probabilities of winning ranging from 1/1 to 1/12. All the bets were of zero expected value. In both experiments, one bet only was actually played for money. Results of these two studies showed significant group risky shifts for the three items with relatively low values of the sure gain or of the stake, while only slight differences were found between group decisions and the mean of initial individual choices on the items involving comparatively large potential losses (Zaleska, 1972, 1975, 1976).

In the other three experiments, subjects responded to questions concerning hypothetical situations. Five choice dilemmas of the well-known Wallach and Kogan Questionnaire (see Kogan & Wallach, 1964, Items 1, 2, 3, 7, and 8) were used in their original form in Experiment III, and in Experiment IV in a slightly modified version (Zaleska, 1972). With the exception of the Item 2, these choice dilemmas have typically yielded a significant group risky shift following discussion. For Experiment V, a different set of five hypothetical situations had to be devised in order to make these situations relevant for the populations used in this study: juvenile delinquents, and boys of the same age attending a trade school of carpentry.

For each of the five experiments briefly described above, the percentage of group decisions in conformity with the model of convergence on the mean or on the mode was calculated in the following way. Initial distributions of choices made by individuals within each group were used as a baseline for predicting group decisions. The model of convergence on the mean predicts that group members would agree on the value of the scale closest to the arithmetic mean of their first choices, while the model of convergence on the mode predicts the adoption of the modal choice within the group. The latter requires, however, additional assumptions in case of deadlocks and of uniform distributions. It was assumed that in the first case, groups would agree in equal proportion on the choice made by the more risky and the more conservative subgroup, and in the second,

Figure 4-1

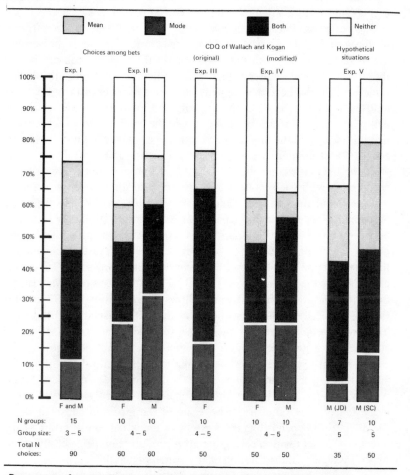

Percentage of group decisions in conformity with the model of convergence on the mean of initial choices of group members (Mean), the model of convergence on their mode (Mode), both models (Both) and neither of them (Neither). Female (F) and male (M) students from various departments of the Paris University participated in Experiments I, II, III and IV; juvenile delinquents (JD) and boys attending a trade school of carpentry (SC) participated in Experiment V

that they would adopt a compromise solution by adopting the choice closest to the mean of initial responses. Thus, when individual preferences within a group are all different at the outset, the predictions of both models are identical. The percentages presented in Figure 4-1 were obtained by calculating the proportion of observed group decisions in conformity with the predictions of one or the other of the two models, of both, or of neither.

These percentages are shown in the following manner: the lower part of each column, horizontally hachured, corresponds to the observed percentage of group decisions in conformity with the model of convergence on the mean, while the vertically hachured section represents the percentage of those agreeing with the predictions of the model of convergence on the mode. It will be seen that the predictions of both models will sometimes be identical; this happens when each member of the group gives a different answer, or when the majority and minority choices within the group are very similar, or again, when the choices are symmetrically distributed around the mode. The percentage of these cases is shown in the center of each column, hachured both horizontally and vertically.

If the figure is examined, it is seen that the proportion of group choices conforming with each model varies according to the type of experiment, and the population studied. There is, for example, a noticeable difference between female groups participating in Experiments III and IV, and also between female and male groups in Experiment II. On the whole, the use of the model of convergence on the mean alone (see the horizontally hachured section plus the section hachured both horizontally and vertically), allows the prediction of 42% to 65% of the decisions, whereas the model of convergence on the mode allows the prediction of 38% to 66% (see the vertically hachured section plus the section hachured both ways). Thus, we can only state that the predictive value of each model is variable and that the superiority of one over the other cannot be unequivocally established over all five experiments. Without going into detail, it may be added that majorities are followed on the average three times out of four, while pluralities, that is, the largest subgroups, are only followed about every fourth time. The predictive value of the model of convergence on the mode thus depends to a large extent on the initial configuration of the individual choices within each group, this configuration being partly determined by the initial distribution of the overall population decisions.

In order to compare now the predictions of Lambert's decision-making model (i.e., mode-convergence as described above) with the actual group choices, I shall refer to the curves corresponding to the predicted results, and those observed in the course of the same five experiments. In each figure (see Figure 4-2: a, b, c, d, e, and f), the abscissa represents the scale of choices proposed, and the initial means of the group are entered on this axis. The groups initially taking the greatest risks, i.e., the lowest probabilities of success, are found to the right of each scale, and the most cautious groups to the left. The average shifts towards risk and towards caution of the same groups are entered on the ordinate, the former being marked with a plus and the latter with a minus. Beside the continuous curve which represents the actually observed results is the broken curve which corresponds to the predictions of the model of convergence on the mode. The predictions of this model were determined in the manner described above, i.e., the choice of the majority or of the largest subgroup was attributed to the group, while in case of deadlocks group decisions were assigned in equal proportion to the more risky and the more conservative subgroups. Finally, when individual choices within the group were all different, their arithmetic mean was computed and group decision was assumed to be the scale value closest to that mean. Group decisions determined in this manner were subtracted from the means of initial individual choices within each group in order to calculate predicted shifts.

Figure 4-2

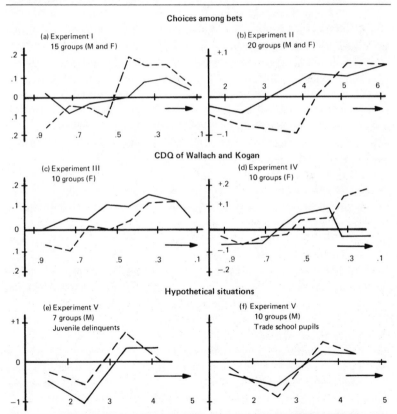

Risky and conservative shifts in relation to initial means of individual choices. The magnitude of the shifts—risky (with a plus sign) and cautious (with a minus sign)—is to be read on the ordinate, and initial means of groups on the abscissa. Observed shifts are represented by a continuous line, shifts predicted by the model of convergence on the mean by a broken line

Thus, the distance between the points on the broken curve and the abscissa represents the average predicted shift for more or less risky, moderate and cautious groups, while the corresponding distance between the points on the continuous curve and this axis represents the average observed shift of the same groups.

Examination of the broken curve shows that the model of convergence on the mode predicts shifts towards risk in the groups initially inclined towards risk, and towards caution in the groups initially cautious. Generally, only very slight shifts are predicted for groups whose initial score of risk is situated about the middle of the scale. In each of the figures, the broken curve, representing predicted shifts, rises above the abscissa towards the risk pole (to the right) and sinks below this axis towards the pole of conservatism (to the left of the scale).

The continuous curves which represent the observed results are similar in appearance to the broken curves insofar as they generally also rise above the abscissa to the right of the choice scale and fall below it to the left. There are, however, differences in relation to the predicted results. In some cases, actual group decisions are closer to the initial mean choice than predicted by the model, in others, on the contrary, observed shift is larger than the predicted shift. In the latter case, it appears that the influence of majorities and pluralities can explain partly, but not entirely, the group polarization phenomenon.

It should be noted that the data reported here refer only to comparisons between initial individual choices and group decisions. The term "polarization" is used when the average group choice following discussion becomes closer to one or other of the poles on the choice scale, as compared to the mean of initial choices made by group members. This does not preclude the use of the same term in reference to comparisons between individual pre- and postdiscussion scores. However, in order to avoid any confusion, it is necessary to specify whether the polarization effect examined is a group or individual effect.

Examination of results presented in Figure 4-2 shows clearly that the model of convergence on the mode cannot be applied to all the decisions taken in the course of group discussion. This would be expected insofar as the model does not at all allow for the influence of minorities. To deny them any role during discussion is obviously not justified. In many cases, minority and majority negotiate a compromise, one of which is an agreement closest to the mean of the initial positions. The minority may also impose its choice but, on the whole, this case is seen relatively seldom and cannot be used alone to explain the polarization of group choices.

In certain experiments, however, the polarization effect is accentuated, or else there is a shift contrary to the prediction of the majority-rule model, due to the uncompromising attitude, or to persuasive arguments provided by the minorities who adopt extreme positions. The degree of risk then becomes greater, or the increase in caution less, than predicted by the model.

An interesting case is Experiment III, which bears on five hypothetical situations of the Wallach and Kogan Questionnaire (Figure 4-2c). It is to be observed that the groups, whatever their initial degree of risk, take more risky decisions than predicted by the model of convergence on the mode. The analysis of the characteristics of the situations proposed reveals that most of them contain imprecise or dissimulated information which provides arguments in favor of risk-taking if used. In the course of one of my experiments, I observed that a great number of individuals do not detect this information, or draw no conclusions from it on a first reading. Thus, the highly significant difference ($p < .001$) observed in Experiment III between the predictions of the model of convergence on the mode and actual group choices, is explained, in my opinion, by the arguments in favor of risk put forward, not only by members of the majorities, but also by members of the minorities. This difference disappears, as Figure 4-2d shows, when the subjects reply, in Experiment IV, to a modified version of the same situations, where the information given has been made more precise, and lends itself less to arguments favorable to risk.

In the experiments reported here, the influence of minorities who opt for extreme caution is generally negligible. With a few exceptions, moderate and relatively conservative minorities are also less influential than those in favor of risk. As far as members of minorities are concerned, their chances of convincing the group do not only depend on the extremeness of their choices but also, and above all, on the position they defend. Thus, final group decisions depend not only on the distribution of initial choices within the group but also on the content of the responses in each specific situation.

The results discussed here seem to be similar in some respects to those observed by Thorndike (1938) and Timmons (1942) in different tasks of the problem-solving type involving value judgments. For both these authors, the criterion for the "correct" answer was that of an informed expert. Their results show that, depending on their size, majorities carry the group more often, but they have more influence when they are "correct" than when they are "wrong" by the criterion adopted. In the situations involving social values and norms, such as risk-taking situations, the responses which are in conformity with dominant values or norms may be considered as being to some extent "socially correct." Generally, these responses have a higher probability of being adopted by the group than others, and may sometimes be accepted even if they are advocated by a single group member against a strong majority.

In conclusion, I would suggest that when groups are confronted with a choice between several competing and unverifiable propositions or responses, those initially most frequent are likely to gain wider acceptance in the groups than others. High initial frequency indicates in general the existence of a systematic factor influencing individual choices, such as for example, a cognitive bias, a dominant social value or norm. Proponents of most frequent responses would thus be more confident in their position and in the arguments supporting it; they would defend it more vigorously and manifest more resistance to persuasion than other group members. If groups are randomly assembled, the most frequent answers have, moreover, majority or plurality support in most groups. Through a combination of these factors, the proportion of the initially most frequent responses would be likely to increase in groups following discussion. This type of group process probably occurs in various situations when groups, homogeneous with respect to status and initial resources, are confronted with choices among a limited number of untestable responses or propositions. The generality of the process described here remains however a matter for further study. The conditions under which it occurs can only be specified by gathering and analyzing more experimental data.

REFERENCES

Kogan, N., and M.A. Wallach. *Risk Taking: A Study in Cognition and Personality.* New York: Holt, Rinehart and Winston, 1964.

Lambert, R. Extrémisation du risque en groupe. *Journal de la Société de Statistique de Paris,* 1971, *112,* 11-12.

–––. Extrémisation du comportement de prise de risque en groupe et modèle majoritaire. *Psychologie Française,* 1969, *14* 113-125.

Thorndike, R.L. The effect of discussion upon the correctness of group decision, when the factor of majority influence is allowed for. *Journal of Social Psychology,* 1938, *9,* 343-362.

Timmons, W.M. Can the product superiority of discussors be attributed to averaging or to majority influence? *Journal of Social Psychology,* 1942, *15,* 23-32.

Zaleska, M. Majority influence on group choices among bets. *Journal of Personality and Social Psychology,* 1976, *33,* 8-17.

–––. The effects of discussion on group and individual choices among bets. *European Journal of Social Psychology,* 1974, *4,* 229-250.

–––. Comparaison des décisions individuelles et collectives dans des situations de choix avec risque. Unpublished doctoral dissertation, University of Paris V, 1972.

5

ACTIONS AND JUDGMENTS:
COLLECTIVE AND INDIVIDUAL STRUCTURING

Willem Doise

Collective polarization is doubtlessly a complex phenomenon resulting from the intervention of a multiplicity of processes. The first part of this paper describes one of these processes at the cognitive level and shows the specific manner in which groups organize or structure material in the course of a discussion that must result in consensus. The second part will deal with cognitive structuring in a more precise and Piagetian sense. In it we shall discuss the structuring activity of collective interaction as a factor in individual cognitive development. We shall expound and expand upon the thesis that intellectual activity—considered as an internalized and reversible coordination of schemes of action after the fashion of Piaget—is first of all a social coordination of actions, at least at certain stages of cognitive development. It will perhaps seem that the link between the two parts of our paper is the inevitable result of a certain ambiguity associated with the notion of structuring. Still, it is a fact that the research described in the second part actually arose from the problems and research described in the first part but transplanted into a "Geneva context."

THE "STRUCTURING" OF COLLECTIVE DECISIONS

In the discussion section of our first study on collective polarization we presented some results which indicated that groups would be more "unidimensional" than individuals:

> Isolated individuals can envisage a problem from different angles and
> give a wide gamut of responses to different items. In a group
> situation this diversity is lost. Individuals tend to have a multidimen-
> sional approach to a problem, while groups tend to use an unidimen-
> sional one ... The increase in polarization in the experimental
> condition can perhaps be explained by the fact that this condition
> furnishes the group with a ready-made judgmental dimension.
> (Doise, 1969, p. 143.)

However, the experimental condition of this experiment implied a comparison between an ingroup and an outgroup, thereby allowing the experimental groups to produce a salient dimension more easily.

This interpretation has subsequently been supported by a number of
experimental results, and has been formulated more explicitly:

> Groups, more than individuals, put stress on certain aspects of the
> material under discussion in order to make interaction between their
> members possible; this allows them to find agreement on sharply
> distinct judgments, and thus end up with collective polarization.
> What does really happen when several individuals, following the
> order of the experimenter, must discuss in order to formulate a
> common decision or judgment? When different aspects of the prob-
> lem are differently striking for different individuals, agreement is
> only possible after the situation has been redefined: One or more
> aspects must become dominant for everybody and prevail over the
> considerations of different kind which may have pushed the answers
> of the individuals in different directions. The group is thus led to
> bring about a veritable work of cognitive organization, whether it is
> in the sense of a new departure—when a new dimension takes first
> place—or in the sense of an organization which is already present in
> several members of the group and comes to impose itself on all of
> them. (Doise, 1976, p. 71.)

But what is the experimental data in support of this thesis? Four
experiments, carried out with varied techniques, have confirmed that
collective judgments, more than individual judgments, organize themselves
around main features of the material on which collective deliberations are
requested.

The first experiment (Doise, 1970) aimed at comparing the judgments
given by individuals with those of groups on social stimuli ordered along
one main dimension. Compared with the individuals, the groups were
hypothesized to position the different stimuli in a neater and more
consistent way along the given dimension. In this experiment, the main
dimension had been made very salient, both in the material to be judged

and in the categories of answers required from the members (something that will not necessarily be the case in the other experiments).

The experimental material was a modified version of eleven narratives from Luchins and Luchins (1961) describing the behavior of a pupil, Jim (in French Jean), who is very introverted in the first narrative but becomes progressively more extroverted in the others. The members of the group, pupils in a technical lycée (high school), had to describe Jim's behavior by circling one and only one of the three adjectives: "introverted," "extroverted," "equiverted" appearing under each description. The stimuli were presented in random order for twelve groups of subjects, in an introverted to extroverted order for six groups and the other way around for another six groups. Every group consisted of four subjects who gave preconsensus, consensus, and postconsensus judgments for each of the eleven narratives.

The results shows that for the first five narratives "introverted" is given more frequently for the "consensus" and "postconsensus" judgments than for the "preconsensus," while "equiverted" is given more frequently for the two middle narratives and "extroverted" for the last four. The results also show that the variability of the answers diminishes significantly at the consensus and postconsensus levels as compared to the variability of the answers at the preconsensus level for the three groups of extreme and intermediary stimuli. The main dimension of the material thus appears to be better perceived by groups than by individuals.

With the help of data provided by Moscovici, Zavalloni, and Weinberger (1972) we have been able to show (Doise, 1973)—again for less structured material—that groups detect a more salient dimension than individuals do. In the Moscovici et al. experiment, members of four-person groups described individually each of five rather uncharacteristic photos of men on twelve seven-point scales (preconsensus). Then, each group reached agreement for each description (consensus). In our reanalysis of the results we have been guided by the following line of argument: if it is true that the groups put more weight on some aspects of the photos than others, then as a consequence the first factor in a factor analysis on which the photos are projected will account for more of the variance in collective answers than the first factor accounting for the individual answers. This, in fact, happened for eight out of ten groups. If we calculate the variance accounted for by the first two factors, groups prevail in nine cases out of ten.

The same kind of analysis allowed us to verify another prediction that the members of the group who exercise the most influence in the consensus process are those who had already shown the strongest organization of the material at the preconsensus stage. This corroboration was accomplished by means of two different calculations, both of which were carried out under the assumption that the individual most influential in establishing the group consensus was the one whose preconsensus answers were most similar to the consensus answers. We first considered as most influential the individual who changed his answers least in passing from preconsensus to consensus. For these individuals, the average saturation of the first factor of individual answers was 49.06%, and for the others 42.85%. But this prediction can also be verified at the level of the organization underlying the answers, with the most influential individual this time being the one whose individual cognitive structure most closely resembles the cognitive structure of the collective answers. For each group we located this individual by calculating the correlations between the projections of the five photos on the first factor of each group member's answers and the projections of these photos on the first factor of consensus. The individual achieving the highest correlation was considered the most influential. The average saturation of the first factor was 47.67% for the most influential individuals, and 43.22% for the others. Thus, the cognitive structure of groups is not only stronger than that of individuals, but it is also the case that those individuals who have already structured the material around one factor exercised more influence during efforts to reach consensus.

The third and fourth experiments relevant to the same hypothesis (Doise, 1973) were carried out in collaboration with Mugny at Geneva. In both cases the subjects were children of ten to twelve years of age, and thus at the higher operative stages of concrete thinking.

In the course of the third study we no longer compared consensus with preconsensus answers, but instead those of individuals and three-member groups who had not given individual answers. The task material was also very different; it consisted of a series of eight boards with geometrical figures glued on them. The figures were arranged according to three criteria which were varied systematically: color (either orange or blue), shape (triangular or square), and size and number (two large and two small). Thus, the main characteristics of the material were controlled. The task was simple: whether individuals or groups of three, subjects had to choose the board which "would be best suited to decorate a classroom." After the first choice, the selected board was returned and put aside. The subjects were then asked to choose another and this continued until all eight boards were classified.

The structuring of choices was measured as follows. We calculated separately the totals of the orders of merit attributed by each subject, or group, to blue boards, boards with small figures, and those with squares. Then, we calculated the differences between each of these sums and a value of eighteen which would correspond to a random choice. The total sum of squares of these differences reflects the structure underlying the choices. Once again, the structuring of collective decisions proved to be stronger than that of individual decisions—and this with younger subjects.

Will the same difference be noticed if the children are faced with social material not actually present but only called to mind? Our fourth experiment carried out in Geneva allows us to give an affirmative answer. Here we again used the traditional paradigm of consensus and preconsensus. Using the method of paired comparisons, children gave their preferences for five professions and, for each case, the reason for their preference. In our analysis, we took into account two indices: (a) the number of different criteria used to justify the ten choices, and (b) the number of cases of intransitivity calculated according to Kendall's (1955) formula. The latter index provided the number of intransitive triads of the type "A is preferred to B, B to C, but C to A." Assuming again that collective decisions result from a more stable, or less variable, approach than decisions by single individuals and, from earlier experimental results, that collective choices operate on more hierarchicalized criteria than individual choices, we predicted that collective choices would present fewer cases of intransitivity than individual choices. This was verified by our results in which only one consensus out of ten showed a case of intransitivity, while there was an average of one case of intransitivity per individual at the preconsensus stage. Collective structuring was thus the stronger as a greater amount of information was dealt with by the groups; the number of different criteria averaged 7.60 for collective answers as opposed to 6.30 for individual responses.

SUMMARY

Different indices show that groups which must reach consensus organize the task material to a greater degree than individuals who make decisions, on the same material, alone. It is a process which takes place when there is collective polarization, which probably accounts for some of this organization. Indeed, once a dimension is made salient or, if the criteria of decisions are well hierarchicalized, judgments and decisions can become very clearcut, as demonstrated in group polarization studies (Moscovici & Doise, 1974).

But, in a quite different field of research, several authors (for instance, Flavell and collaborators, 1968, and Smedslund, 1966) have suggested that the particular aspect of social interaction which leads individuals to organize their different approaches to a problem is also a powerful factor of cognitive development, and especially so for children. They hypothesize, in a very general way, that the structuring effects of social interaction also take place at the level of Piaget's cognitive structures. Therefore, in the following discussion, we shall first describe Piaget's own view on the links between social interaction and cognitive development, and then mention some of our own research on the structuring effects of social interaction in cognitive development. In this way we hope not only to publicize some of Piaget's conceptions, which are often ignored by social psychologists, but also support them with some empirical evidence.

SOCIAL INTERACTION AND COGNITIVE DEVELOPMENT

When Piaget (1965) describes the isomorphism between structures of social interactions and cognitive operations, he gives as an example the exchange between two individuals which results in credit for one and debt for the other. Reaching the equilibrium of an exchange during the course of time would necessarily imply—apart from the use of a common scale of values—a certain conservation and a certain reversibility, viz., the possibility of returning at any particular moment to previously accepted criteria of validity, and the awareness that what is debt for one is credit for the other, and vice versa. He similarly analyzes the exchange of propositions or views, since discussion implies a coordination of points of view, with the conservation of propositions previously accepted, and reversibility, which allows one to come back both to one's own and to the interlocutor's affirmations.

Piaget gives these analyses—summarized here very briefly—in order to illustrate his thesis that social interaction in equilibrium manifests the same characteristics of "conservation" and "reversibility" shown by individual cognitive operations. For Piaget, cognitive and social development go together: "They form the two inseparable aspects of one and the same reality, social and individual at the same time." (Piaget, 1965, p. 63.) Recently, Piaget (1976, p. 226) has reasserted his thesis in the course of his comments on some of our research, upon which we shall presently expound:

> It is still clear that the coordinations of actions and operations are identical, whether the links are intra- or interindividual; the more so, because the individual is himself socialized, and reciprocally collective work would never function if each of the members of the group was not provided with a nervous system and the psychobiological regulations which it carries with itself.

The same author admits, nevertheless, that social interaction exercises a certain influence on cognitive development. This is reflected not only in early writings (e.g., Piaget, 1932, on moral judgment) but also in a recent work (i.e., Piaget, 1967): "Human intelligence develops in the individual in relation to social interactions which are generally only too much neglected" (p. 260), and

> From the psychogenetic point of view these interindividual or social regulations (not hereditary) constitute a new fact as compared with individual thinking which, without them, is exposed to all kinds of egocentric deformations, and a necessary condition of the formation of a decentralized epistemic subject (p. 413).

In an article on comparative studies in genetic psychology, Piaget (1966) enumerated the factors of cognitive development. Social factors of interindividual coordination are mentioned after the biological factors and the factors which equilibrate actions, but before those of educational and cultural transmissions. Therefore, if cognitive development occurs less rapidly in some children, the reason may perhaps be found at the level of social factors of interindividual coordination. Piaget, in fact, suggests this explanation for the differences in cognitive development he observed.

The aim of our recent research has addressed precisely this link between interactions and interindividual regulations on one side and cognitive development on the other. Social interaction, therefore, has here the status of an independent variable, and we examined its effect on the cognitive structuring of individuals. However, the idea that social interaction plays a causal part in cognitive development is not the same as admitting that the intelligence of the individual is passively shaped by regulations which are outside of it. Our conception is similar to Piaget's, interactionistic and constructionistic: the individual, by acting on the external world, elaborates the systems of organization of his own activity; nevertheless, he does not act on reality in isolation. It is precisely by coordinating his own actions with those of others that he can then elaborate the systems of coordination of his own actions—systems which are reproduced in an autonomous way. Thus, interaction leads the individual to master certain coordinations which will allow him to take part in more elaborated social interactions which, in turn, become sources of new developments. This conception, therefore, is somewhat analogous to that defended by Piaget which considers the equilibrium process as progressing spirally as the individual resolves perturbations encountered by his actions on the environment (Piaget, 1974). The work of internal equilibration and coordination is only made possible by the coordination of one's actions with those of others.

It is now possible to summarize some of our earlier results as well as recent findings that have not yet been reported. An initial set of results concerned the structuring influence (in the strict sense of the words) of social interaction. By this we mean that individuals who interact with one another in order to solve a given problem achieve more effective performances—at least at some stages of their development—than individuals acting alone. This result has been verified by the use of different tasks, especially those requiring coordination of movements and spatial transformations.

The material for tasks of coordination of movements may be found described in detail elsewhere (Doise and Mugny, 1975). The subjects, either alone or several together, manipulated via pulleys and strings, a movable object along a given course. With this device we observed that the performances of two individuals coordinating their actions are better than those of one individual as long as their age was less than seven to eight years. For older children (nine to ten years) the differences between individual and collective performances decreases. This result agrees, therefore, with our general thesis that coordinations are first elaborated in social interaction, and only later acquired by the individuals one by one. With the same device it has been possible to "individualize" some social interactions by reducing the communications between members of a group or by imposing a leader upon them. These manipulations had a very disturbing effect on the younger children, but not on the older ones who had already mastered, individually, the coordinations necessary for success in their task.

The spatial transformations task consisted of an adaptation of the "Three Mountains" task developed by Piaget and Inhelder (1948). The material utilized in this case required two identical games of three houses. One of these games is arranged by the experimenter on a support. The subjects must copy this village on an identical support using the three houses of the model. When the copy is turned around in relation to the model, the results of Doise, Mugny, and Perret-Clermont (1975) confirmed that pairs of subjects succeeded better than individuals working alone. A second experiment with the same material, but with a pretest, showed that 50% of the dyads composed of one child who did not make any transformation and one who made an incomplete transformation succeeded in at least one complete transformation, when the two copies are made together (Mugny & Doise, in press). In the conclusion of this paper we shall show that other experimenters have similarly observed this "developmental progress" of children who have interacted, as compared with children who act alone.

A second set of inquiries was conducted to verify that social interaction had some effect on the structuring of subsequent actions by the individual. Perret-Clermont has focused her research primarily on this problem. One study, using the decanting test (Doise, Mugny, and Perret-Clermont,

1975), showed that nonconserving children improved after taking part in a cooperative task with conserving children. This progress is well reflected in the amount of individual structuring. Those children who had taken part in the social interaction subsequently were able to propose arguments in the posttest which had not been advanced previously. These results were later replicated both in a test of conservation of liquids and in a test of number conservation (Perret-Clermont, 1976). In addition, these researches have shown that the kinds of progress elicited experimentally go together with progress in other tests, which is in line with the "natural" progress studied by the Geneva school. On the other hand, a specific interaction does not provoke progress in each and every individual; a certain degree of competence is required in order to facilitate the subject's asserting himself in a sociocognitive interaction. Thus, in the experiment concerning the acquisition of number conservation during a social interaction, only those children capable of carrying out the process of counting or making one to one correspondences can improve. These kinds of competence would have been acquired in the course of previous interactions.

In a more recent version of his model of equilibration, Piaget (1975) has emphasized the role of perturbation when passing from one equilibrium to another at a higher level. We believe these perturbations are mainly of a sociocognitive order and, more specifically, that the new coordinations have their origin in the need for the resolution of conflicts resulting from opposing centrations, in order that a common action can be achieved. Such differences in centrations between individuals were illustrated in the previously mentioned experiment on spatial transformation (Mugny and Doise, in press).

That was the beginning of our research on the role of sociocognitive conflicts in the development of knowledge. A more direct investigation of this problem (Doise, Mugny, and Perret-Clermont, 1976; Mugny, Doise, and Perret-Clermont, 1976) was aimed at comparing the effect of an incorrect opposing centration with the effect of a model who correctly coordinated opposed centrations on a test of the conservation of lengths. The results showed that the sociocognitive conflict was a sufficient condition to make children progress. Significant progress was provoked not only by the model but also by the incorrect opposed centration. This leads us to think that the progress provoked by a model is really the result of a conflict between the coordinations suggested by the model (or certain elements of these coordinations) on one side and by the centrations of the subject on the other side.

We are currently preparing a more comprehensive set of experiments on sociocognitive conflict. Our preliminary results appear to confirm those of the previous experiment. One of the aims of our inquiries is to separate, as much as possible, the social from the purely cognitive aspects of the sociocognitive conflict.

Finally, let us also mention that several other investigators have reached similar conclusions regarding the importance of social interaction for cognitive development. For example, Murray (1972) has shown that, of the children who used a consensus method to solve different problems of conservation, some also made individual progress. Silverman and Stone (1972) have also observed significant advances after an interaction on a test of space conservation. Silverman and Geiringer (1975) have verified that the social interaction necessary to perform on a given test can generalize to progress on other tests. Maitland and Goldman (1974) have observed progress through interaction on problems of moral judgments, while Miller and Brownell (1975) recorded similar results in length and weight conservation. Our first experiments, undertaken without knowledge of these investigations, serve as an independent validation.

Several others (Kuhn, 1972; Rosenthal and Zimmerman, 1972; Murray, 1974; Zimmerman and Lannaro, 1974) have also observed improvement in the field of conservation resulting from the mere observation of models. Does this mean that an explanation of cognitive development based on the notion of sociocognitive conflict is thus insufficient? We do not think so, because the effect of the model can very well arise from the conflict the model itself generates. Kuhn (1972, p. 843) writes,

> Thus, observation of a model performing a task in a manner discrepant from (but not inferior to) the child's own conceptualization of the task may be sufficient to induce in the child an awareness of alternative conceptions and will perhaps lead to disequilibrium and reorganization.

We agree, but only on the condition that she omit the restriction in parentheses. In fact, we shall shortly report an investigation showing that precisely this intervention by an inferior model can lead to improvement.

An area toward which we are directing our subsequent inquiries is that of formal thinking. Laughlin and Jaccard (1975) have shown that at this stage of cognitive development the group also prevails over the individual. With a different task, but one which also requires hypothetic-deductive thinking, Stalder (1975) has showed, on the other hand, that some variables which modify social interaction in the groups also modify the cognitive strategies of group members during this interaction. Whether or not this leads to subsequent other effects following interaction remains to be examined.

In order to fully explain the collective polarization phenomenon it may be useful to take into account the occurrence of collective processes which structure, in a particular way, the different aspects of the problem discussed by a group of individuals. But, whereas research on group polarization and collective decisions focuses mainly on the dynamics of collective processes, another area of research is developing which bears on the effects of social interaction in the individual's mastering of cognitive structures. In a series of experiments we were able to show that children interacting with each other not only better structure their approach to certain cognitive tasks than children do alone, but also that they individually perform more advanced cognitive operations after their participation in such a social interaction. This suggests that social interaction might be an important factor in cognitive growth, at least at certain stages of an individual's development.

REFERENCES

Doise, W. *L'articulation psychosociologique et les relations entre groupes.* Bruxelles: De Boeck, 1976.
– – –. La structuration cognitive des décisions individuelles et collectives d'adultes et d'enfants. *Revue de Psychologie et des Sciences de l'Education,* 1973, *8,* 133-146.
– – –. L'importance d'une dimension principale dans les jugements collectifs. *L'année Psychologique,* 1970, *70,* 151-159.
– – –. Intergroup relations and polarization of individual and collective judgments. *Journal of Personality and Social Psychology,* 1969, *12,* 136-143.
Doise, W., and G. Mugny. Recherches socio-génétiques sur la coordination de'actions interdépendantes. *Revue Suisse de Psychologie Pure et Appliquée,* 1975, *34,* 160-174.
Doise, W., G. Mugny, and A.N. Perret-Clermont. Social interaction and cognitive development: Further evidence. *European Journal of Social Psychology,* 1976, *6,* 245-247.
– – –. Social interaction and the development of cognitive operations. *European Journal of Social Psychology,* 1975, *5,* 367-383.
Flavell, J.H., P.T. Botvin, C.L. Fry, J.W. Wright, and P.E. Jarvis. *The Development of Role-taking and Communication Skills in Children.* New York: John Wiley, 1968.
Kendall, M.G. *Rank Correlation Methods.* London: Griffin, 1955.
Kuhn, D. Mechanisms of change in the development of cognitive structures. *Child Development,* 1972, *43,* 833-844.
Laughlin, P.R., and J.J. Jaccard. Social facilitation and observational learning of individuals and cooperative pairs. *Journal of Personality and Social Psychology,* 1975, *32,* 873-879.
Luchins, A.S., and E.H. Luchins. Social influences on impressions of personality. *Journal of Social Psychology,* 1961, *54,* 111-125.
Maitland, K.A., and J.R. Goldman. Moral judgment as a function of peer group interaction. *Journal of Personality and Social Psychology,* 1974, *30,* 699-704.
Miller, S.A., and C.A. Brownell. Peers, persuasion and Piaget: Dyadic interaction

between conservers and nonconservers. *Child Development*, 1975, *46*, 992-997.

Moscovici, S., and W. Doise. Decision making in groups. In C. Nemeth (Ed.), *Social Psychology: Classis and Contemporary Integrations*. Chicago: Rand McNally, 1974.

Moscovici, S., M. Zavalloni, and M. Weinberger. Studies on polarization of judgements: II person perception, , ego involvement and group interaction. *European Journal of Social Psychology*, 1972, *2*, 92-94.

Mugny, G., and W. Doise. Socio-cognitive conflict and structuration of individual and collective performances. *European Journal of Social Psychology*, in press.

Mugny, G., W. Doise, and A.N. Perret-Clermont. Conflit de centrations et progrès cognitif. *Bulletin de Psychologie*, 1976, *29*, 199-204.

Murray, F.B. Acquisition of conservation through social interaction. *Developmental Psychology*, 1972, *6*, 1-6.

Murray, J.P. Social learning and cognitive development: Modelling effects on children's understanding of conservation. *British Journal of Psychology*, 1974, *65*, 151-160.

Perret-Clermont, A.N. L'interaction sociale comme facteur dans le développement cognitif. Thèse polycopiée, Université de Genève, 1976.

Piaget, J. Postface. *Archives de Psychologie*, 1976, *44*, 223-228.

———. *L'équilibration des Structures Cognitives*. Paris: P.U.F., 1975.

———. *Adaptation Vitale et Psychologie de l'Intelligence*. Paris: Hermann, 1974.

———. *Biologie et Connaissance*. Paris: Gallimard, 1967.

———. Nécessité et signification des recherches comparatives en psychologie génétique. *Journal International de Psychologie*, 1966, *1*, 3-13.

———. *Etudes Sociologiques*. Genève: Droz, 1965.

———. *Le Jugement Moral Chez l'Enfant*. Paris: P.U.F., 1932.

Piaget, J., and B. Inhelder. *La Représentation de l'Espace Chez l'Enfant*. Paris: P.U.F., 1948.

Rosenthal, T.L., and B.J. Zimmerman. Modeling by exemplification and instruction in training conservation. *Developmental Psychology*, 1972, *6*, 392-401.

Silverman, I.W., and E. Geiringer. Dyadic interaction and conservation induction: A test of Piaget's Equilibration Model. *Child Development*, 1973, *44*, 815-820.

Sliverman, I.W., and J.M. Stone. Modifying cognitive functioning through participation in a problem-solving group. *Journal of Educational Psychology*, 1972, *63*, 603-608.

Smedslund, J. Les origines sociales de la décentration. In *Psychologie et Epistémologie Génétique, Thèmes Piagétiens*. Paris: Dunod, 1966.

Stalder, J. *Lernen in kleinen Gruppen*. Inauguraldissertation der Philosophisch-historischen Fakultät Bern. Bern: Kopierservice, 1975.

Zimmerman, B.J., and P. Lanaro. Acquiring and retaining conservation of length through modeling and reversibility cues. *Merrill-Palmer Quarterly of Behavior and Development*, 1974, *20*, 145-161.

PART II

COOPERATIVE INTERACTION:
SOCIAL-EMOTIONAL ASPECTS

Introduction by Hermann Brandstätter

The papers in this section all deal with the impact of emotional relations on persuasion in group discussion. There are three ways in which emotionally tuned social relations can affect the influence people exert on each other when involved in a discussion in order to reach agreement: (a) Learning the other's stand on an issue provides a person with the opportunity to verify his own position. To agree with an attractive other is particularly comforting in matters of value. (b) Learning the other's demand for conformity to his view induces yielding to this demand, especially if the other is liked. (c) Learning the other's arguments provides new information about the issue at stake. If the other is liked, one may pay more attention to what he has to say.

Although the authors do not explicitly differentiate these three types of social influence, one can derive from their discussion or description of experimental designs the manner by which social emotional responses were thought to facilitate, or make more difficult, movement toward conformity. Experiments with friendly versus unfriendly remarks of a disucssion opponent, or with applause versus disapproval of an audience following a discussant's arguments, focus on the demand for yielding. Experiments with partners who like or dislike each other, because of satisfying or annoying prior experience with the partner, make any social comparison with the other's stand on the issue salient, especially if the rating of the decision preferences is private, hence preventing either partner from controlling the other's response.

Brandstätter reviews the theory, methods, and results of an extensive series of experiments performed during the past five years at the University of Augsburg. These experiments, three of which are reported in detail in this chapter, resume the examination of problems that were first studied in the fifties within the context of social comparison theory. They were designed to analyze the very process by which a liked versus disliked and friendly versus unfriendly discussant, and an applauding versus disapproving audience exerted influence on participants and observers of a discussion.

Two kinds of experiments with subjects observing a discussion (observational setting) are reviewed: (a) Observed discussants presented their arguments with either friendly, hostile, or neutral personal remarks; and (b) observed discussants exchanged their arguments without emotionally tuned remarks and were either applauded or disapproved of by an audience or a moderator of the discussion. As expected, applause by an audience, accompanied by the approval of a moderator, promoted influence. The effects of discussion style (friendly versus neutral, hostile versus neutral) on observers are not quite clear yet. On the whole observers seem to be more strongly influenced by a speaker who attacks his opponent than by one who presents his arguments in a friendly way.

That a liked person exerts more influence on his discussion partner than a disliked one is a common-sense notion predicted by various theories. The corroboration of such an unspecified hypothesis is, therefore, not very surprising and does not add much knowledge. But any of the four experiments where subjects exchanged arguments (interaction setting) brings about some interesting interaction effects of liking with other variables (e.g., the time series, the expectation of future interaction, the partner's friendliness).

The review article points only briefly to the as yet inconclusive results of a field study which utilized real decision-making groups in an attempt to generalize the experimental results beyond the laboratory environment.

In the first of the Augsburg group discussion studies to be reported in this chapter, the subjects either observed (i.e., read), listened to, or watched a discussion between two opponents who earned either applause or disapproval from an audience; in the second, subjects discussed a disciplinary court decision while a confederate behaved in either a friendly or unfriendly (but nonverbal) way; in the third study real decision-making groups were used.

To work with randomly selected telephone owners, as von Rosenstiel and Stocker-Kreichgauer did in their observation experiment, was an attempt to gain a broader range of generalizability. They paid a rather high price in that quite a few subjects didn't comprehend the instructions and hence generated unreliable data which led to their exclusion from the analysis. Earlier analyses of these data had shown that an applauded discussant influenced observers more strongly than a discussant before a disapproving audience. This analysis relates the effects of vicarious social reinforcement to the attractiveness of the reinforcing agent, and explores these effects separately for the "final influence" of the whole discussion, the "momentary influence" of the two discussants, and the "differential influence" of the reinforced compared to the not reinforced arguments. Observed applause and disapproval by an audience affected the "final influence" of the discussants on the observers only when the audience was rated positively by the subjects. A closer look at the data shows that this holds only for the adherents of the minority position among the subjects. Whether this has to do with minority position as such or with the specific content of the minority position is an open question. As to the "momentary influence" of a discussant the results are again rather complicated. Whereas the proponent of the minority position gains nothing from the applause of a positively valued audience but loses a great deal by the applause of a negatively valued audience (boomerang effect), the proponent of the majority position, which is at the same time the punitive alternative ("member of radical parties should be excluded from civil service"), gains from the audience applause whether the audience is rated as attractive or unattractive. These and other results of the observation experiment imply a warning against simple generalizations. They also underline the importance of exploratory data analysis in addition to hypothesis-testing.

In the dyadic interaction experiment of Schuler and Peltzer, a subject discussed a disciplinary court case with a confederate in order to decide whether the alleged criminal behavior had really taken place. Half of the participating subjects met with a friendly while the other half met with an unfriendly confederate, who in both conditions opposed the subject's decision preference. Friendliness or unfriendliness was expressed in a nonverbal way. Half of the dyads were joined by an observer-subject who also rated his preferences in the same manner as the interacting partners. Thus, the interaction and observation setting was realized within one design allowing a better comparison of the two situations.

There was a clear-cut persuasive effect of friendliness, which affected the interacting and the observing subjects about the same. More subjects than in any previous experiment changed over to the partner's side, most of them in the condition with a friendly partner. The effect of friendliness could still be observed eight weeks later. That the nonverbal friendliness of a discussant affects the attitude change of an interacting partner in the same way as that of an observer deserves special attention, since verbal friendliness seems to facilitate influence on the discussion partner only, while the observer tends to be more easily convinced by a verbally aggressive speaker (cf., Brandstätter in this volume). Showing friendliness through the polite reception of an opponent's argument does not increase the influence on an observer as much as showing hostility does, through remarks abasing the opponent's arguments.

Rüttinger gives a brief outline of a field study designed to test the hypothesis that friendliness in discussion style among the members of real life decision-making groups intensified the movement toward conformity. The friendliness was defined in terms of Interaction Process Analysis Categories 1 and 12.

A conformity measure (Kendall's W) was derived from the group member's individual preference ratings of all the alternatives that were listed as possible solutions to the decision problem before the discussion started. The preference ratings were repeated after the group had reached a decision. Generally, there was a movement toward conformity following group discussion, but the effect of friendliness proved nonsignificant. Better statistical control over other conformity-affecting variables (e.g., distribution of arguments, differences in expertness and status, kind of decision problem) may help in detecting the impact of friendliness on movement toward conformity. Nevertheless, the result of this field study reminds us that social-emotional relations are just one among many other determinants of agreement. Even if agreement is facilitated by friendliness, one has to question whether a decision reached in such a manner is a good one.

Verhagen is interested in the assumed advantage that accrues to an expert from high participation (i.e., extensive contribution of arguments) in group decision making with a nonexpert, when the subject (nonexpert) is alone with the expert or is supported by a co-oriented peer (also a nonexpert). Since co-orientation means perceived similarity in life situations and values generally leading to interpersonal attraction, this study deals implicitly with social-emotional factors. The subjects were required to render a decision on a town planning problem after exchanging written messages with either a fictitious expert or with a fictitious expert and a real co-oriented peer. As had been expected, the influence of the opposing expert decreased markedly when the subject's position was supported by a co-oriented peer. The degree of the expert's participation (i.e., the relative

number of arguments contributed by him) did not make significant difference. Verhagen recognized that, in this experiment, agreement with
another person might have been the crucial point in resisting the expert's
influence, and not the presence of a co-orientated peer. Using results of a
second experiment aimed at separating the effect of co-orientation from a
majority-minority effect, Verhagen adduces additional evidence for the
importance of co-orientation with a peer in resisting an expert's influence.

One may finally ask whether social-emotional responses are a hindrance
to adequate decision-making that should be overcome by self-control and
group training, or rather an opportunity allowing one to forcefully promote important goals. There is of course no general answer to this
question. To like someone who shares the same values, and hence be more
open to his influence, may often be as helpful as harmful, depending on
the other's expertness, sincerity and specific goals. If the attractive person
is also prominent in knowledge, morality, and benevolence, all would be
fine. Since that is rarely the case, it may be wise to be aware of the
function of social emotions within the persuasion process in order to cope
with them in the proper way. As a means of gaining influence in group
situations, educators, supervisors, politicians, and advertising agencies
attempt to monitor the social-emotional responses of the target persons.
They too may be able to learn from experimental results, such as we have
discussed, a more efficient and, let us hope, more responsible and consid-
erate use of emotional stimuli.

6

SOCIAL EMOTIONS IN DISCUSSION GROUPS

Hermann Brandstätter

Previous research on attitude change through persuasive argumentation has focused on a large number of characteristics of the source, the message, and the receiver (see McGuire, 1969), most of which were either not immediately related to the emotional aspects of the influence process, or were not analyzed in the context of discussion. During the last decade the choice shift phenomenon has almost completely absorbed the research activities in the area of group discussion (see Cartwright, 1971; Pruitt, 1971; Sauer, 1974; Meyers, and Lamm, 1976), with little attention paid to social-emotional factors. A variety of explanations for the rather regularly observed movement of mean group preference away from the indifference point toward one or the other pole of bipolar scales have been proposed, one of which has turned out especially promising. The proportion of pro and con arguments arising in the discussion (Burnstein, 1969; Burnstein et al., 1973; Ebbesen and Bowers, 1974; Bishop and Myers, 1974) seems to determine the choice shift, thus pointing to the importance of informational influence (Deutsch and Gerard, 1955).

There is no doubt the distribution of arguments referring to the probabilities and values of possible consequences of a decision is a very potent determinant of attitude change. But what is to be said about the social-emotional components of the conversation that modify the informational influence of arguments in several ways and possibly to a remarkably degree? It is this component of the influence process on which a research project at the University of Augsburg, Germany, concentrates. Its aim is to explore how preestablished attraction to and actual friendliness of a discussant or an audience affects the participants and observers of a discussion.

To look for the impact of preestablished attraction to and actual friendliness of a discussant on the decision preferences of participants as well as observers of the discussion within the same research project may be justified by functional similarities of attraction and friendliness on the one hand, and participation and observation on the other. (a) Social emotions may be elicited in stable patterns by the mere presence (real or symbolic) of another person (liking or disliking), or by his/her behavior being perceived as friendly or unfriendly. These two kinds of emotional responses are closely related to each other: enduring liking or disliking can best be understood as an effect of prior rewarding (pleasant) or punishing (unpleasant) interaction with a person. Both preestablished liking or disliking and emotional responses to actual behavior also entail expectation of future rewards and punishments, which function as incentives modifying the behavior in a specific way. (b) To participate in a discussion also means to listen to the arguments of the discussion partners and to observe the interaction between others. To observe a discussion as an outsider usually entails partisanship with one speaker or the other and generation of arguments by oneself.

REVIEW OF EXPERIMENTAL LITERATURE

Before describing the method and results of our research the reader may be reminded of studies dealing with the attraction-persuasion problem that have been published during the last twenty-five years.

The various experiments were based on Festinger's (1950, 1954) theoretical concepts of social comparison (Back, 1951; Festinger and Thibaut, 1951; Gerard, 1954; Argyle, 1957; Jackson and Saltzstein, 1958; Berscheid, 1966); theories of cognitive consistency, particularly Newcomb's (1968) ABX model (Burdick and Burnes, 1958; Brewer, 1968; Sussmann and Davis, 1975); Festinger's (1957) theory of cognitive dissonance (Kiesler and Corbin, 1965; Jones and Brehm, 1967, Himmelfarb and Arazi, 1974); attribution theory (Kelley, 1967; Goethals, 1972; Goethals and Nelson, 1973; Eagly and Chaiken, 1975); classifactory concepts of Kelman (1961) or French and Raven (1959; Mills and Harvey, 1972; Horai et al., 1974); or no specific theory at all (Kiesler, 1963; Mills and Aronson, 1965; Snyder and Rothbarth, 1971).

There is one theoretical paper comparing the persuasive communication with the forced compliance situation, trying to explain by an extension of Heider's (1946) cognitive balance model why in persuasive communication experiments interpersonal influence usually increases with interpersonal attraction, whereas the opposite seems to be true in the forced compliance situation.

The following brief review of the experimental literature on the function of attraction in the persuasion process comprises only the few discussion experiments, almost exclusively performed in the fifties (Back, 1951; Festinger and Thibaut, 1951; Gerard, 1953; Gerard, 1954; Argyle, 1957; Brewer, 1968).

Most later studies used one-way communication in order to show how source attractiveness relates to persuasiveness. Within the perspective of this review, they are less relevant than the early studies. Nevertheless some of them offer useful additional information on conditions modifying the relation between attractiveness and influence which might be effective in one way or another in the group discussion situation too. Because of space limitations they are only mentioned here without further details of the experimental design and results.

ATTRACTION AND INFLUENCE IN GROUP DISCUSSION

Probably the first experiment on the relation between attraction and opinion change following group discussion was performed by Back (1951), an associate of Leon Festinger at the Research Center for Group Dynamics at the Massachussets Institute of Technology. The experimental task for each member of a dyad demanded looking individually at a set of three pictures, writing a story about it, discussing their stories, and writing individually a final version of the story. A content analysis of the initial and final stories provided the scales for measuring change. Cohesiveness was varied in three ways: (a) you will like each other; (b) the best group performance will win a prize; (c) you and your partner are more able than any other pair to solve this kind of problems. Although the subjects rated their liking for the partner, no results on differences in liking between the three conditions of cohesiveness are reported. All three kinds of cohesiveness were effective in inducing agreement. Cohesiveness also increased the number of influence attempts.

Festinger and Thibaut (1951) studied groups with six to fourteen members, seated at a round table, each with a letter card for identification and a card showing the scale value of his opinion. The two design factors were pressure for agreement and perceived homogeneity of interests and abilities. Because of contamination of interests and abilities, the results are not clear with respect to attraction, as Jones and Gerard (1967) point out for this experiment and for a similar one performed by Gerard (1953). Nevertheless this study is noteworthy for its application of continuous measurement of attitude, although the report does not refer to the time series data.

Gerard (1954) obtained less ambiguous results with a face to face discussion of three-person groups who had been informed they were to be or not to be composed of congenial people. High attraction produced more influence attempts, more influence, and more resistance to a later attempt of counterpersuasion.

Argyle (1957) wanted to test the hypothesis that a person, having privately rated the esthetic value of a painting after having exchanged written notes with his partner, would agree more in a final rating when the rating was public and when the partner's messages were unfriendly. Standardized messages, e.g. "What you say is so trivial, for this picture is so meaningless as a whole," or "I respect your opinion, but the picture. . . . ," were forwarded to the subjects, either by the experimenter interrupting the exchange of messages or by a confederate. Unfriendly remarks were expected to be more persuasive, based on the assumption that subjects would have a stronger need for acceptance in this situation and therefore yield more in order to be accepted. The hypothesis was not confirmed. There was a tendency in the opposite direction.

Brewer (1968), testing Newcombs ABX model, found that liking in dyads discussing the pros and cons of capital punishment fostered agreement and induced initial perception of high attitude similarity. The relation between initial similarity and postdiscussion attraction and the patterns of communication did not turn out as predicted. In this case, changing one's own attitude seemed to have been the dominant reaction to the perception of imbalance.

ATTRACTION AND INFLUENCE IN
ONE-WAY PERSUASIVE COMMUNICATION

Most of these studies are aimed at specifying conditions which modify the impact of attractiveness on influence: stated desire to influence (Mills and Aronson, 1965), relevant and irrelevant similarity with attraction held constant (Berscheid, 1966), informing the subjects on the source attractiveness before or after the communication (Mills and Harvey, 1972), expertness of the communication combined with attractiveness (Horai et al., 1974), need for affiliation (Burdick and Burnes, 1958), expected future interaction with the group (Kiesler et al., 1966; Kiesler and Corbin, 1965), source with same or different data basis for judgment (Goethals, 1972), discussion of belief or value issues (Goethals and Nelson, 1973), desirability of advocated position (Eagly and Chaiken, 1975) agreement and disagreement between two partners, one liked, the other disliked (Sussmann and Davis, 1975) attractive versus unattractive audience applauding or disapproving some of the speaker's arguments (Kelley and Woodruff, 1956; Landy, 1972).

As a résumé of the various studies, it may be stated that a source of communication exerts more influence on the recipients of the communication the better the source is liked for one reason or another only (a) if the subjects have no choice whether to expose themselves to the communication or not, and (b) if the subjects do not expect further interaction with the source.

In the case of free exposure, an unattractive source tends to be more influential than an attractive one (cf. Kaplan and Baron, 1974). The expectation of further interaction with the source results in roughly a U-shaped relation between attraction and influence with high attraction connected with high influence, medium attraction with low influence, and low attraction with medium influence. There is also some evidence that liking is more important in matters of values than in matters of facts, and that need for social approval makes especially sensitive a variation in friendliness of the speaker. Finally, one may partial out or hold constant the perceived expertness of the source and the remembering of arguments without attenuating the genuine effect of liking.

THEORETICAL CONSIDERATIONS

The theoretical position taken here is described in the following (see Brandstätter, 1976): (a) A person responds to any perceived or imagined situation giving or denying need satisfaction with emotions. These provide him with an immediate, spontaneous feedback of whether something is good or bad for him, whether to approach or to avoid it, to continue an activity or to stop it. There is an intimate tie between motives and emotions, the kind and intensity of motives determining the kind and intensity of emotions that are elicited by characteristics of the situation relevant to the activated motive (cf. Lersch, 1954; for a similar view, cf. Arnold, 1960). (b) Emotions originally elicited only by cognitions of situational characteristics relevant to motives can be conditioned to irrelevant characteristics of the situation (classical conditioning of emotions). (c) The involuntary action tendency of emotions can be monitored (released, suppressed, diverted) by considering the possible consequences of action and by problem-solving in order to arrive over the long run at a gratifying result.

To predict a person's reaction to someone's behavior in a debate, one must know or make several assumptions: (a) whether the behavior elicits positive or negative feelings; (b) to which of the situational elements are these feelings mainly conditioned; (c) how the person intellectually copes with the situation.

Each point may be elaborated in more detail. First, whether another's specific discussion behavior elicits positive or negative emotions depends on personal traits and on the situational context. A person who is rather in need of social approval will be affected more by supportive or discouraging behavior of another person than someone who is self-reliant. To be blamed by a liked person is more startling than by someone who is not attractive.

Second, the emotional response to a rewarding or punishing person tends to be conditioned to other elements of the situation, which are not only simultaneously present but cognitively related to the primary emotional stimulus. The speaker and what he says are perceived as a unit, and therefore emotions elicited by the speaker become conditioned to his arguments and to his position, for which his arguments plead.

Since there are always several situational elements which are cognitively linked to the primary emotional stimulus, the emotional conditioning usually affects more than one element. The intensity of conditioning depends on the strength of the cognitive bond. So if my opponent in a discussion acknowledges the originality of my arguments, which would please me, this emotion will be conditioned not only to the complimenting person, but also to my way of arguing. Two conflicting forces impinge on my attitude toward the topic of discussion. The increased emotional value of my argument strengthens my position, and the increased emotional value of my opponent entices me to yield. The outcome depends on the relative strength of the two cognitive bonds or, the equivalent, on the selection of elements to which I attribute the origin of emotion.

Third, besides the impact of emotional conditioning which is, although cognitively induced, functioning automatically, there usually is also a problem-solving process going on. For example, if I want my opponent to like me, and if I am convinced he wouldn't like me strongly opposing him, I would perceive yielding as a means to acquire or to maintain his benevolence. Whether I actually give in to achieve that goal depends on the whole set of expected consequences, e.g. loss of self-esteem, loss of support by friends, and so on. Theories of cognitive consistency (Abelson et al., 1968), to which many of the experiments on attraction and persuasion refer can be seen as special theories of problem-solving.

Hitherto only the effects of positive emotions have been discussed. What about the effects of negative feelings provoked, for example, by the partner's deprecatory remarks or by his expressed doubts about my competence or sincerity? Again the negative emotions are going to be conditioned to several elements of the situation, the intensity of conditioning depending on the kind and strength of cognitive bonds between the primary emotional stimulus and the remaining situational characteristics. And there is also problem solving involved, which might interfere with unconditioned and conditioned emotions.

So if my opponent attacks me for my position or my arguments, negative feelings are conditioned both to the opponent and to my position, prompting me on the one side to abandon it, and on the other side calling forth my disliking of the opponent and my resistance to his arguments. Which of the two forces is stronger depends again on the strength of the cognitive bond. If I perceive myself as weak compared with my opponent, attributing the cause of attack to my questionable attitude and viewing the attack as more or less legitimate, the negative emotions will be conditioned to my position, otherwise mainly to my opponent.

Besides being affected by this inescapable emotional conditioning, I am coping with this disturbing situation by intellectual activity, trying to find an acceptable solution or interpretation. So, I might be aware of my emotional reactions, disapprove of them as unacceptable by my standard of objectivity, and agree with somebody else's opinion even if it is imbedded in aggressive remarks.

The results of an experiment will be clear only if it is designed unambiguously, so that most subjects (a) perceive the experimentally manipulated behavior of their opponent in the same way (as emotionally positive or as emotionally negative), (b) are exposed to the same conditioning process, and (c) cope intellectually with a similar strategy.

GENERAL DESCRIPTION OF THE METHOD

Since all experiments of the Augsburg research project were designed according to the same basic structure, a general description of the method will be presented prior to a discussion of individual experiments.

The subjects of our experiments participated in or observed a discussion among two or three people about various issues. One question was whether members of radical parties should be employed in the civil service. Another question dealt with whether or not acquisition and possession of drugs should lead to more severe punishment. A third was whether or not a job applicant whose record threw some doubt on his abilities should be hired. The fourth question was whether or not to plead guilty in a case before a disciplinary court. As an experimental (independent) variable, the perceived similarity of important values between the subject and his partner was manipulated in some studies. The manipulation in other studies was the perceived similarity and competence, or perceived similarity and courtesy of discussion style; in still others, the approving or disapproving behavior of an audience. In addition to these experimentally constructed variables, we included as independent variables, in some of our analyses, the discrepancy between the listener's position and the position of the speaker, the order of pro-con arguments, and some personality characteristics. (For further information on the basic structure of the experiments see Brandstätter, 1972.)

There was altogether a wide variation in: (a) the amount of experimental control and restriction of interaction (the subject communicating with a simulated partner on a computer terminal, the subject interacting with a confederate, or a group discussing some problem in a natural way); (b) the medium through which the discussion was presented to the observers (audiovisual, audio, or written form); (c) the population of subjects (students, bank executives, officer cadets, or randomly selected male citizens of the city of Augsburg, varying in age, education, and occupation).

The most important dependent variable in our experiments was a subjective ratio formed by the person through an overall weighing of the pro and con arguments known to him at the moment. Since these ratios were assessed after each argument, we obtained a time series of preference measures for each subject, a procedure which distinguishes our experiments from nearly all other experiments on group discussion, in which subjects' preferences usually were measured just twice, before and after the discussion. Besides the continuous scaling of preferences, the subjects rated the discussants on several dimensions (liking, dominance, competence, and conscientiousness) before and after the discussion. They were also questioned about their interpretations of the experimental situation.

In the early experiments, analyses of variance have been performed on the sum of individual preference changes immediately following the presentation of the argument. In some experiments, a trend analysis of the whole series of single preference changes was performed, when the variance-covariance matrix of the repeatedly measured dependent variable met the prerequisites of the model.

At the present time, we usually perform an analysis of covariance with the initial preference score as a covariate and either the final preference or the correlation between the time series and the series of preference scores as dependent measure of influence. A different option would be to perform a principal component analysis on the whole set of dependent variables (usually ten to twenty), to compute factor scores, and to apply univariate analysis of variance on each factor score variable or a multivariate analysis of variance on the whole set of factor scores.

In order to find a suitable theoretically based formal representation of the change process, some reanalysis of experimental data was performed. Thereby, the proportional change model (Anderson and Hovland, 1957) has been modified through the inclusion of the distance to the initial position and different weights for the various experimental conditions. The weights can be estimated by polynominal multiple regression analysis on individuals or groups.

To avoid some problems connected with the questionable scale properties of the preference measures we are now testing discrete models of changing probabilities (Bishop et al., 1975; Wiggins, 1973; Coleman, 1964) thereby hoping to overcome the difficulties related to interindividual variance in proneness to change, to inequality of scale units, and to the specific variance-covariance matrix of repeated measures, which often precludes the use of a trend analysis. Simple counting of the number of moves in the direction of the argument or away from it and performing nonparametric significance tests has already proved useful (see von Rosenstiel & Stocker-Kreichgauer, this volume).

To get a clearer understanding of the process of change we are planning to experiment with the method of thinking aloud as well as the measurement of GSR in order to improve the identification of critical, emotion-arousing events.

A REVIEW OF THE AUGSBURG EXPERIMENTS

The main purpose of the Augsburg research project on group discussion is to explore the very process by which the attraction to the speaker, the friendliness of the speaker, and the applause supporting the speaker affects his influence on participants and observers of a discussion. Up to now the outcome of group discussion but not the process itself had been studied.

OBSERVATIONAL SETTING

In a series of three experiments, the subjects ($N_1 = 28$, $N_2 = 82$, $N_3 = 29$) had to read an alleged transcript of a discussion about liberalizing drug use, featuring pro and con arguments. Whereas in the control condition all three discussants (one arguing for liberalization, one against, and the third for the status quo) avoided attacks, one of the speakers in the experimental condition, who held an extreme position, was verbally aggressive against his opponent.

The results of these experiments were inconclusive. In the first experiment (Brandstätter and Rüttinger, 1974), there was a statistically nonsignificant tendency for an increased influence of the aggressive speaker (especially on people who held the same position). In the second and third experiments (Rüttinger, 1974), verbal aggressiveness tended to diminish the influence on subjects who held the same position, and also on subjects who held the opposite position. The functioning of verbal aggressiveness seems to be more complex than we had assumed.

Further investigation should consider the possibility of individual differences in perceiving and reacting to verbal aggressiveness, which might have blurred the results of our experiments. It is quite possible that some subjects are intimidated by the attacks and yield, whereas others reject an aggressive speaker and move away from his position. Still others may be pleased to see that their "representative" attacks his opponent who is also their adversary. So far our efforts to find a personality measure correlated with differences in reactions to verbal aggressiveness have not been very successful. However, there is some evidence in our data that verbal aggressiveness is perceived less negatively by subjects who hold a position which implies aggression, and that these subjects yield relatively more to the aggressive speaker than to the nonaggressive speaker.

In a second series of experiments, the subjects were exposed to a discussion between two alleged representatives of two different teacher unions about whether members of radical parties should be employed by the civil service.

In the first experiment of this series (von Rosenstiel and Rüttinger, 1976), forty-nine students in the School of Education watched the discussion on a TV screen. Half of them saw an audience applaud one of the speakers while behaving neutrally towards the other speaker. The other half saw an audience behave neutrally towards both speakers. The data analysis demonstrated that applause increased the influence of the applauded speaker to an astonishingly high degree.

In the second experiment in this series (von Rosenstiel and Stocker-Kreichgauer, 1975), the participants were 257 male citizens of Augsburg, randomly selected from the telephone directory. There were seven different applause conditions combined with three different media conditions (TV screen, tape recorder, and a written form) for a total of twenty-one experimental combinations. The subjects were influenced more strongly by the applauded speaker, especially if the other speaker was treated neutrally by the audience and if the audience was liked.

Stocker-Kreichgauer and von Rosenstiel (1976) performed an experiment with 176 subjects in a 3×9 design (audiovisual, acoustic, and written media presentation and nine social reinforcement conditions: friendly, unfriendly, and neutral behavior of the two discussants in various combinations), using again the civil service problem. The hostile speaker was more influential than the friendly one.

In an experiment carried out by Stocker-Kreichgauer (1976), 136 students watched a videotaped discussion of supervisors about a personnel decision problem. A third participant served as moderator, but he seemed to be biased, as evidenced in various ways by his remarks. Simple agreement or disagreement with the arguments of one side, advanced by the moderator without contributing his own arguments, increased the influence of that speaker who had been favored by the moderator.

INTERACTION SETTING

All experiments described above were conducted with subjects who were observers of a discussion presented in various media. Now we proceed to experiments in which subjects interacted with each other.

In an experiment performed by Schuler (1975) the subjects, after reading a case study which contained a mixture of positive and negative judgments about a job applicant's skills, had to decide on whether to accept or reject the applicant for the position of a bank teller. A list of eight arguments were then given to each subject, justifying the decision he had made about hiring or not hiring the applicant. Each subject was told to select those five arguments from among the eight which, in his opinion, were most persuasive and which he would use to try to convince someone else. In sessions consisting of approximately fifteen participants, all of whom were acquainted with each other, each participant judged five members of the group with respect to dominance, liking, and conscientiousness. After these preparations designed to manipulate the variable of liking, the subject got a larger set of fifteen arguments which included the five arguments he himself had selected. The instructor told the subject that two other anonymous participants had each selected five arguments, and that one of his two partners had judged the subject as very likeable, whereas the other had made no judgment of him. The arguments were arranged in such a way that five proposed to accept the applicant, five proposed to reject him, and five pleaded for not deciding without further information, and were presented regularly in alternating order. The subject's task was, as in all other experiments, to rate his decision preference after each argument.

The main results are that the arguments stemming from a liked partner are more influential, and the difference in influence between the liked and the neutral partner diminishes during the series of arguments. The influence measure used as the dependent variable was the sum of changes of preferences towards the position of the speaker immediately following the arguments of the specific partner.

The effect of the partner's similarity, the partner's competence, and the expectation of a personal encounter in the near future has been tested by Schuler and Peltzer (1975) with the same personnel decision problem. About eighty students, in groups of fifteen to twenty people, interacted on computer terminals with a simulated partner in one of the eight conditions of the $2 \times 2 \times 2$ design. The main results are that similar partners are liked more, especially when the subject does not expect a personal encounter, similar partners are more persuasive, and the correlation between initial and final rating of liking is higher with dissimilar partners than with similar partners.

The combined effect of preestablished liking and friendliness of behavior has been studied by Peltzer and Schuler (1976) again with the personnel decision problem, and with about eighty subjects interacting on computer terminals. The $2 \times 2 \times 2$ design combined two levels each of partner similarity (which induced liking), partner's friendliness (in using acknowledging or disapproving remarks before presenting the argument), and the order of arguments (with subject or partner starting the discussion). These are the results: (a) similar partners are liked more than dissimilar ones, to a lesser degree even after a controversial discussion; (b) the difference between similar and dissimilar partners in influencing subjects was greater at the beginning of the discussion than at the end; (c) partners using unfriendly remarks more often elicited unfriendly responses than partners using friendly remarks; (d) yielding to an argument is followed more often by a friendly remark, while withdrawing in the opposite direction is more likely to be followed by an unfriendly remark; (e) the correlation between initial and final rating of liking was higher with dissimilar partners than with similar ones.

In contrast to the preceding experiments, where the participants interacted via computer terminals or by exchanging notes, the fourth experiment (Schuler and Peltzer, this volume) was contrived to test the effect of friendliness on real two-person discussion groups, with a confederate, opposing the subject's view and behaving in a friendly or unfriendly way using nonverbal cues. Participants had to decide on a case from a disciplinary court. Half of the discussions were watched by an observer. Both the observer and the discussants continuously rated their preferences after an acoustic signal every minute. Before and after the discussion, which lasted about twenty minutes, the discussants mutually rated their impressions of each other. The observer rated both discussants.

The results suggested that the friendly confederate was rated by the interacting and by the observing subject as more attractive, and the friendly confederate exerted more influence on both the interacting and the observing subject. The observer's presence had no significant effect on the discussant's behavior. An inquiry by mail six to eight weeks later showed about the same difference in personality ratings, but a diminished difference in influence, though still a significant one.

THE FIELD SETTING

To ascertain the generalizability of the experimental results beyond the laboratory situation, videotapes were made of twenty real-life decisions of four-person groups within business organizations, civil service, and university departments. The discussion was unrestricted, but before and after the discussion each participant rated his preference for possible solutions of the problem, the supposed preferences of the other three participants, and perceptions of own and others' competence, friendliness, and dominance. Interaction analysis of the videotapes has been completed and computation is underway. The main topic of this analysis is again of the modifying effect of liking and friendly behavior on persuasiveness. The correlation between friendliness of interaction and movement toward conformity is not significant in the field setting although it is in the predicted direction (Molt et al. 1975, Rüttinger, this volume).

Summing up the results of the various experiments and integrating some of their most interesting features we may state:

(a) Whereas observers of a discussion were more strongly influenced by an unfriendly speaker, participants yielded more to a friendly partner.

Since in the observational setting the discussions stressed the value aspects of the problem and in the interaction setting the discussion focused on facts, the generalization just stated is only tentative. If further experiments systematically varying the content of discussion corroborate the difference between the observed and the experienced friendliness in discussion style, it may be explained in the following way.

Verbal aggressiveness in an observational setting is perceived as less disturbing than in the interactional setting, not only by subjects holding the same position as the aggressor but also by his opponents among the observers. To feel directly attacked by the discussion partner leads to devaluation of the aggressor, thus neutralizing the reinforcement effect of punishment.

(b) Observers of a discussion who stick to the implicitly aggressive alternative were more strongly influenced by the aggressive speaker, whether he adhered to the aggressive or the nonaggressive alternative, than the observers favoring the opposite alternative. There seems to be an affinity between the implicit aggressiveness of the preferred alternative and the reaction to aggressiveness of discussion style. Whether this is related to stable characteristics of persons who favor punitive actions is not yet clear. It may be that the specific reaction to verbal aggressiveness is related more to a state than to a trait of aggressiveness.

(c) Observers of a discussion are influenced more strongly by that speaker who is supported by an audience (applauding him and/or disapproving of his opponent). This relation is more prominent if the observers like the audience than if they dislike it. This rather plausible result may be explained in terms of vicarious reinforcement.

(d) Whereas the perceived attractiveness of a dissimilar opponent in a discussion does not change much from the beginning to the end of the discussion, this is not true with a similar opponent. In this case, the correlation between initial and final liking is low, and the attractiveness decreases on the average. This result may be explained by cognitive consistency concepts. A dissimilar opponent does not stimulate any change in personal attractiveness rating or decision preference. Being dissimilar and being an opponent in a discussion fit together. The situation is different with a similar and therefore, at least initially, liked opponent. Experiencing this kind of inconsistency leads some persons to change their decision preference, some to devalue the opponent, and some to both reactions. The present data base does not allow any prediction about which of these reactions takes place.

(e) In the field studies the impact of social-emotional behavior on movement toward conformity is not significant. We may assume that uncontrolled variables like quality of arguments, talkativeness, status differences, and kind of decision problems have blurred the effects of friendliness. There are also some doubts about the validity of the measures of conformity and friendliness. So the generalizability of the experimental results has to be tested in more field studies.

CONCLUSIONS

People involved in a discussion in order to reach a decision try to influence each other and are influenced by each other mainly in three ways: (a) they communicate their preferences and learn the other's stand; (b) they communicate promises and threats, rewards and punishments for yielding or resisting the attempted influence (i.e., they learn the other's demands); (c) they communicate the reasons for these preferences and learn the other's arguments.

The first facet has been studied mainly within the tradition of conformity (Sherif, 1936; Asch, 1951) and social comparison theory (Festinger, 1954).

The second vein of the influence process is related to effect dependence, and as Jones and Gerard (1967) have remarked, has so far been neglected. Except for a series of experiments stimulated by Festinger's theory of informal communication in the early fifties, only a few studies have been performed on that topic during the last twenty years. To be sure, the literature on experimental bargaining and negotiation (Rubin and Brown, 1975) comprises many studies focusing on these variables. But the structure of experimental games is so different from the structure of group discussion on rather poorly defined problems that generalization would be hazardous.

The third area is the domain of integration theory (Anderson, 1971; Anderson and Graeser, 1976). Burnstein et al. (1973) and Ebbesen and Bowers (1974), although not explicitly referring to integration theory, also stress the importance of the relative number of pro and con arguments in explaining the choice shift following group discussion. Jones and Gerard (1967) denote the basis of this kind of influence as information dependence.

Liking of the other person based on past experience, or like of his present behavior can affect each of these three types of influence.

(a) A person in need of social validation of his beliefs and values, and perceiving a discrepancy between his and the other's position, is prone to conform in order to feel secure. To agree with a liked person provides more security than to agree with a disliked one, especially on issues of value.

Most experiments do not differentiate the perception of another's position (stand) from the perception of another's desire to influence (demand). One exception is a study by Mills and Aronson (1965) which suggests that to know someone's position does not itself cause conformity, if the subject assumes that the other does not want to exert influence. The perception of demand is also less effective if there is no way by which the other could check whether his influence attempt results in yielding or not. So one can assume that (in those experimental conditions where the subjects give only a private rating of their preferences and/or overhear a discussion as outsiders) any effect of liking is tied to the perception of the other's stand rather than to the perception of the other's demand, especially if there is no demand stated explicitly, as in those studies where the subjects know only the group consensus.

(b) The demand of a liked person is less objectionable than the demand of a disliked one for two reasons. If liking is based on rewards received in the past, yielding is an act of restoring equity (Adams and Freedman, 1976). It is also a means of preserving friendship and obtaining rewards or avoiding punishment in the future (Jones, 1964).

Although the subjects of our experiments perceive only weak, if any, effect dependence (Jones and Gerard, 1967), the desire to influence, i.e., to demand, is communicated quite frankly. It is therefore likely that in our experiments both the perception of a stand and the perception of a demand are affected by social-emotional responses.

(c) Whether liking affects not only the influence of stand and demand perception, but also the influence of persuasive argumentation, possibly by enhancing attention and remembering, is hard to say. There seems to be no difference in remembering the arguments of a liked and a disliked person.

Even if the arguments of a liked person were perceived as more convincing than the arguments of a disliked one, this may be due to some kind of post hoc explanation of the subject, e.g., "I have been influenced; therefore, the arguments must have been convincing, since I am a reasonable person who would not be seduced by personal attraction in finding the right answer to a problem."

It will be the admittedly difficult task of further theoretical work and of more sophisticated experimentation to separate the various ways in which social-emotional responses affect the influence process.

REFERENCES

Abelson, R.P., E. Aronson, W.J. McGuire, T.M. Newcomb, M.J. Rosenberg, and P.H. Tannenbaum (Eds.). *Theories of Cognitive Consistency: A Source Book*. Chicago: Rand McNally, 1968.

Adams, J.S., and S. Freedman. Equity theory revisited: Comments and annotated bibliography. In L. Berkowitz and E. Walster (Eds.), *Advances in Experimental Social Psychology, Vol. 9*, New York: Academic Press 1976, 43-90.

Anderson, N.H. Integration theory and attitude change. *Psychological Review*, 1971, *78*, 171-206.

Anderson, N.H., and C.C. Graeser. An information integration analysis of attitude change in group discussion. *Journal of Personality and Social Psychology*, 1976, *34*, 210-222.

Anderson, N.H., and C.H. Hovland. The representation of order effects in communication research. In C.H. Hovland (Ed.), *The Order of Presentation in Persuasion*. New Haven: Yale University Press, 1957.

Argyle, M. Social pressure in public and private situations. *Journal of Abnormal and Social Psychology*, 1957, *54*, 172-175.

Arnold, M.B. *Emotion and Personality*. New York: Columbia University Press, 1960.

Asch, S.E. Effects of group pressure on the modification and distortion of judgment.

In H. Guetzkow (Ed.), *Groups, Leadership, and Men*. Pittsburgh: Carnegie, 1951.

Back, K.W. Influence through social communication. *Journal of Abnormal and Social Psychology*, 1951, *46*, 9-23.

Berscheid, E. Opinion change and communicator-communicatee similarity and dissimilarity. *Journal of Personality and Social Psychology*, 1966, *4*, 670-680.

Bishop, D.G., and D.G. Myers. Information influence in group discussion. *Organizational Behavior and Human Performance*, 1974, *12*, 92-104.

Bishop, Y.N.N., S.E. Fienberg, and P.W. Holland. *Discrete Multivariate Analysis: Theory and Practice*. Cambridge: MIT Press, 1975.

Brandstätter, H. Soziale Verstärkung in Diskussionsgruppen. In H. Brandstätter and H. Schuler (Eds.), *Entscheidungsprozesse in Gruppen*. Bern: Huber, 1976.

Brandstätter, H. Grundplan für Experimente zur Gruppenentscheidung. *Problem und Entscheidung*, 1972, *8*, 33-45.

Brandstätter, H., and E. Rüttinger. Verbale Aggression als Mittel der Beeinflussung in Gruppendiskussionen. *Zeitschrift für Sozialpsychologie*, 1974, *5*, 48-54.

Brewer, R.E. Attitude change, interpersonal attraction and communication in dyadic situations. *The Journal of Social Psychology*, 1968, *75*, 127-134.

Burdick, H.A., and A.J. Burnes. A test of "strain toward symmetry" theories. *Journal of Abnormal and Social Psychology*, 1958, *57*, 367-370.

Burnstein, E. An analysis of group decisions involving risk. *Human Relations*, 1969, *22*, 381-395.

Burnstein, E., A. Vinokur, and Y. Trope. Interpersonal comparisons versus persuasive argumentation: A more direct test of alternative explanations for group induced shifts in individual choice. *Journal of Experimental Social Psychology*, 1973, *9*, 236-245.

Cartwright, D. Risk taking by individuals and groups: An assessment of research employing choice dilemmas. *Journal of Personality and Social Psychology*, 1971, *20*, 361-378.

Coleman, J.S. *Models of Change and Response Uncertainty*. Englewood Cliffs, N.J.: Prentice-Hall, 1964.

Deutsch, M., and H.G. Gerard. A Study of normative and informational social influence upon individual judgment. *Journal of Abnormal and Social Psychology*, 1955, *51*, 629-636.

Eagly, A.H., and S. Chaiken. An attribution analysis of the effect of communicator characteristics on opinion change: The case of communicator attractiveness. *Journal of Personality and Social Psychology*, 1975, *32*, 136-144.

Ebbesen, E.B., and R.J. Bowers. Proportion of risky to conservative arguments in a group discussion and choice shift. *Journal of Personality and Social Psychology*, 1974, *29*, 316-327.

Festinger, L. *A Theory of Cognitive Dissonance*. Evanston: Row, Peterson, 1957.

―――. A theory of social comparison processes. *Human Relations*, 1954, *7*, 117-140.

―――. Informal social communication. *Psychological Review*, 1950, *57*, 271-282.

Festinger, L., and J. Thibaut. Interpersonal communication in small groups. *Journal of Abnormal and Social Psychology*, 1951, *46*, 92-99.

French, J.R.P., Jr., and B.H. Raven. The bases of social power. In D. Cartwright (Ed.), *Studies in Social Power*. Ann Arbor: Institute for Social Research, Univ. of Michigan, 1959, 150-167.

Gerard, H.B. The anchorage of opinions in face to face groups. *Human Relations*, 1954, *7*, 313-326.

―――. The effect of different dimensions of disagreement of the communication process in small groups. *Human Relations,* 1953, *6,* 249-271.

Goethals, G.R. Consensus and modality in the attribution process: The role of similarity and information. *Journal of Personality and Social Psychology,* 1972, *21,* 84-92.

Goethals, G.R., and E. Nelson. Similarity in the influence process: The belief-value distinction. *Journal of Personality and Social Psychology,* 1973, *25,* 117-122.

Heider, F. Attitudes and cognitive organisation. *Journal of Psychology,* 1964, *21,* 107-112.

Himmelfarb, S., and D. Arazi. Choice and source attractiveness in exposure to discrepant messages. *Journal of Experimental Social Psychology,* 1974, *10,* 516-527.

Horai, J., N. Naccari, and E. Fatoullah. The effects of expertise and physical attractiveness upon opinion agreement and liking. *Sociometry,* 1974, *37,* 601-606.

Jackson, J.R., and H.D. Saltzstein. The effects of person-group relationships on conformity processes. *Journal of Abnormal and Social Psychology,* 1958, *57,* 17-24.

Jones, E.E. *Ingratiation: A Social Psychological Analysis.* New York: Appleton, 1964.

Jones, E.E., and H.B. Gerard. *Foundations of Social Psychology.* New York: Wiley, 1967.

Jones, R.A., and J.W. Brehm. Attitudinal effects of communicator attractiveness when one chooses to listen. *Journal of Personality and Social Psychology,* 1967, *6,* 64-70.

Kaplan, K.J., and R.M. Baron. An integrative balance notion for the attractiveness-persuasiveness relationship in persuasive communication versus forced compliance. *Human Relations,* 1974, *27,* 287-301.

Kelley, H.H. Attribution theory in social psychology. In D. Levine (Ed.), *Nebraska Symposium on Motivation,* Vol. 15, Lincoln: Univ. of Nebraska Press, 1967, 192-240.

Kelley, H.H., and C.L. Woodruff. Members reaction to apparent group approval of a counternorm communication. *Journal of Abnormal and Social Psychology,* 1956, *52,* 67-74.

Kelman, H.C. Processes of opinion change. *Public opinion quarterly,* 1961, *25,* 57-78.

Kiesler, C.A. Attraction to the group and conformity to group norms. *Journal of Personality,* 1963, *31,* 559-569.

Kiesler, C.A., and L.H. Corbin. Commitment, attraction, and conformity. *Journal of Personality and Social Psychology,* 1965, *2,* 890-895.

Kiesler, C.A., M. Zanna, and J. DeSalvo. Deviation and conformity: Opinion change as a function of commitment, attractions, and presence of a deviate. *Journal of Personality and Social Psychology,* 1966, *3,* 458-467.

Landy, D. The effects of an overheard audience's reaction and attractiveness on opinion change. *Journal of Experimental Social Psychology,* 1972, *8,* 276-288.

Lersch, P. *Aufbau der Person.* 5. Aufl. München: Barth, 1954.

McGuire, W.J. The nature of attitudes and attitude change. In G. Lindzey and E. Aronson (Eds.), *The Handbook of Social Psychology,* 2nd ed., Vol. III. Reading, Mass.: Addison-Wesley, 1969.

Mills, J., and E. Aronson. Opinion change as a function of the communicator's attractiveness and desire to influence. *Journal of Personality and Social Psychology,* 1965, *1,* 173-177.

Mills, J., and J. Harvey. Opinion change as a function of when information about the communicator is received and whether he is attractive or expert. *Journal of Personality and Social Psychology*, 1972, *21*, 52-55.

Molt, W., B. Rüttinger, and R. Brand. Entscheidungsverläufe in realen Entscheidungssituationen. *Problem und Entscheidung*, 1975, *14*, 109-126.

Myers, D.G., and H. Lamm. The group polarization phenomenon. *Psychology Bulletin*, 1976, *83*, 602-627.

Newcomb, T.M. Interpersonal balance. In R.P. Abelson et al. (Eds.), *Theories of Cognitive Consistency: A Source Book*. Chicago: Rand McNally, 1968, 28-51.

Peltzer, U., and H. Schuler. Personwahrnehmung, Diskussionsverhalten und Präferenzänderung in Dyaden. In H. Brandstätter and H. Schuler (Eds.), *Entscheidungsprozesse in Gruppen*. Bern: Huber, 1976.

Pruitt, D.G. Conclusions: Toward an understanding of choice shifts in group discussions. *Journal of Personality and Social Psychology*, 1971, *20*, 495-510.

Rosenstiel, von, L., and B. Rüttinger. Die Wirkung von Applaus für Beiträge in Fernsehdiskussionen auf die Einstellungsänderung der Zuschauer. In H. Brandstätter and H. Schuler (eds.), *Entscheidungsprozesse in Gruppen*. Bern: Huber, 1976.

Rosenstiel, von, L., and G. Stocker-Kreichgauer. Der Einfluss stellvertretender Verstärkung auf den Entscheidungsverlauf der Beobachter von Gruppendiskussionen. *Problem und Entscheidung*, 1975, *14*, 17-77.

Rubin, J.Z., and B.R. Brown. *The Social Psychology of Bargaining and Negotiation*. New York: Academic Press, 1975.

Rüttinger, B. Die Wirkung verbaler Aggression auf den Sprechereinfluss und den Sprechereindruck in Entscheidungsgruppen. Dissertation, Universität Augsburg, 1974.

Sauer, C. Zur Erforschung der Gruppenextremisierung nach Diskussion. *Zeitschrift für Sozialpsychologie*, 1974, *5*, 255-273.

Schuler, H. *Sympathie und Einfluss in Entscheidungsgruppen*. Bern: Huber, 1975.

Schuler, H., and U. Peltzer. Ahnlichkeit, Kompetenz und die Erwartung künftiger Interaktion als Determinanten von Diskussionsverhalten und Partnerbeurteilung. *Problem und Entscheidung*, 1975. *14*.

Sherif, M. *The Psychology of Social Norms*. New York: Harper, 1936.

Snyder, M., and M. Rothbart. Communicator attractiveness and opinion change. *Canadian Journal of Behavioral Science*, 1971, *3*, 377-387.

Stocker-Kreichgauer, G. Stellvertretende Verstärkung in Gruppendiskussionen. Dissertation, Universität Augsburg, 1976.

Stocker-Kreichgauer, G., and L. von Rosenstiel. Der Einfluss der Sprecherfreundlichkeit auf den Entscheidungsverlauf der Beobachter von Gruppendiskussionen. *Problem und Entscheidung*, 1976, *18*, 23-77.

Sussmann, M., and J.H. Davis. Balance theory and the negative interpersonal relationship: Attraction and agreement in dyads and triads. *Journal of Personality*, 1975, *43*, 560-581.

Wiggins, L.M. *Panel Analysis: Latent Probability Models for Attitude and Behavior Processes*. San Francisco: Jossey-Bass, 1973.

7

FRIENDLY VERSUS UNFRIENDLY NONVERBAL BEHAVIOR: THE EFFECTS ON PARTNER'S DECISION-MAKING PREFERENCES

Heinz Schuler and Ulf Peltzer

In a discussion that is aimed to lead to a joint decision of two or more persons, the discussion partners utter arguments which are in favor of one or the other of the alternatives, which support the speaker's opinion (or, in the case of ambiguity, reflect his contradictory ideas) and, if there is an internal or external pressure to come to an agreement, should convince the partner of the speaker's opinion.

How much each of the interacting persons is busy convincing the others of his opinion depends, first, on all the factors that are known from the field of attitudes and attitude change, e.g., interconnectedness with other beliefs, the importance of self-image, expected reinforcing consequences of maintenance from others, and so on. In addition, there may be an endeavour to dominate others, to bring influence to bear, and to make one's own opinion the group's opinion, explainable in dispositional terms of the person, by reinforcing properties of the situation, by the role-taking of the participants, and so on. With growing motivation to influence discussion partners, a participant will choose those arguments, out of the total he is able to produce, which he expects a priori or concludes from his partner's reactions to be most influential.

Besides the content and quality of the arguments chosen and uttered in the discussion, there are various other signals, e.g., the amount of time speaking, the number of presented arguments, or reinforcements for the partner's behavior (especially for something like yielding on the part of the partner). We are interested most of all in this second dimension of influence, in the variables of influence which lie beyond the quality of argumentation. For the moment, we are focusing on the question: if and how much rewarding behavior enhances influence on the other participants of discussion.

As Brandstätter (this volume) explained, mutual positive reinforcement during discussion may work in opposite directions, that is, changing the partner's mind *or* stabilizing him in his position, depending on whether it is seen as an expression of positive evaluation of the partner's whole person or as a reinforcement of single arguments. In the first case, interpreted as a sign of positive evaluation or liking, we should expect it to evoke reciprocal liking and in this way enhance the partner's willingness to join in the speaker's opinion or to find a more acceptable compromise. This effect should be expected especially when there are no, or only restricted, possibilities of reducing inconsistency or, in terms of exchange theory, finding other rewarding elements which may serve as exchangeable goods.

But reinforcement could work otherwise, such that the partner does not feel positively evaluated as a person, although his opinion is reinforced. This may produce the contrary effect, namely, that he persists in his opinion more than before and shows less willingness to compromise. His impression of the other should be positive in this case also, because the reinforcing person will gain a positive quality via conditioning of emotions (for example by contributing to the positive self-esteem of the recipient) to the extent that the reinforced statement are seen as an aspect of one's own person.

So while the impression rating of a discussion partner should be positive in both cases, changes of preference should be significantly affected by whether the other's behavior is seen as distinct reinforcement of one's opinion or as positive evaluation of the person. This distinction, however, remains still more plausible than empirically confirmed. Although there was some support for this theoretical statement within the frame of the Augsburg project on group decision-making, most of the studies concerned with positive evaluation more or less resulted in influence-increasing effects, independent of reinforcement being interpretable as more related either to the partner's person or to his single arguments, thus confirming the predictions derived from diverse social psychological theories (Schuler, 1975).

The different realizations of the central variable were direct expression of liking (Brandstätter et al., 1971), information about similarity (Schuler, 1975), and discussion remarks either appreciating or disapproving the partner's arguments (Schuler and Peltzer, 1975; Peltzer and Schuler, 1976). To improve generalizability, some other conditions were varied, like discussion topic, medium of communication, and group size. The primary common result was that rewarding behavior in all its forms showed a weak (in terms of ratios of variance) but reliable and significant influence on the decision-making preferences of the discussion partners. This effect, although diminished, still appeared after eight weeks. Time by treatment interactions also showed that the influence-enhancing effect of arguments stemming from a liked partner already decreased over the course of the discussion. Largely consistent with the above were results concerning other dependent variables of "discussion style" and "impression ratings of the discussion partners." However, there were several promising results which could not be verified in later studies, for example, a theoretically plausible interaction between extroversion and style of performance, indicating that introverts reciprocated their partner's behavior, while extroverts dominated a verbally friendly partner and yielded to an aggressive one (Schuler, 1974).

The present experiment is designed to examine if rewarding friendly behavior can also be shown on the *nonverbal* dimension to produce the aforementioned effects. Nonverbal effects seem to be separable quite well from other aspects of discussion behavior, especially from the content and the quality of the arguments, although there is a certain empirical correlation (Mehrabian, 1972). That friendliness or liking may be expressed by nonverbal behavioral cues has often been shown (e.g., Argyle et al., 1972). Argyle[1] takes nonverbal signals in many cases as even more important than verbal ones (especially, of course, in situations and contexts where verbal behavior is subject to rather restricting social norms). Those dimensions of nonverbal responses assumed best able to express liking are gaze and eye-contact, or mutual gaze (Argyle and Cook, 1976), as well as posture of body and arms (Mehrabian, 1968), facial expressions, and body orientation (Argyle, 1969; Ekman and Friesen, 1968). To investigate the effects of only one or another of these dimensions did not seem to be adequate, as we show and perceive all of them together as *behavioral patterns* (Mehrabian, 1972). Concerning the dimension of interpersonal distance, we had to allow our subjects a certain amount of freedom because people differ in what they consider the most comfortable distance from one another (at least within the range of approximately 1-1.5 m in dyadic talking situations). This amount of freedom was also allowed in order not to disturb the "equilibrium," i.e., we did not want to produce a degree of intimacy uncomfortable to some persons which could lead them to counterresponses. "If one of the components of intimacy is changed, one or more of the others will shift in the reverse direction in order to maintain the equilibrium" (Argyle and Cook, 1976, p. 64). According to Argyle, one need not expect that within this range of distance the partner's likability is influenced.

Behavioral signals which express different dimensions of interpersonal behavior or attitudes have to be avoided in our context. So, for example, body erectness, head raising, and loudness of voice are perceived more on the dimension of dominance or superiority (Argyle, 1969). Mehrabian distinguishes besides "positive evaluation" (liking) and "potency" (status, dominance), "responsiveness" (activity) as a third dimension, which is expressed among other means as frequency and speed of talking. Our behavioral pattern had to exclude this sort of signal. Also to be avoided were those nonverbal cues which could have worked as reinforcements to specific arguments, e.g., head nods, as we intended to produce a sort of global social approval. Also, the design of the experiment had to assure that the expressed friendliness was not perceived as a general interpersonal behavioral style, but as especially directed to the person of the discussion partner.

As one has to consider large interpersonal differences in the ability to decode nonverbal signals (Argyle, 1969), our nonverbal cues had to be clear enough to exceed most of these differences, while at the same time being realistic and credible. Performances of friendly and unfriendly patterns of behavior do not need to have the same intensity as one can take into account that by means of cultural norms there will already be perceived a slighter degree of unfriendliness than of friendliness by the target person: "There are considerable restraints on the expression of negative attitudes or emotions, so that spontaneous expressions are often concealed" (Argyle, 1972, p. 249).

In addition to the responses of those subjects who themselves participate in the discussions (hereafter, "participants"), it might be investigated further if an observer of the discussions perceives the behavior in the same way, if he too is influenced more by a friendly acting participant of the discussion, and if he rates the discussion persons in the same manner. We are also interested in whether the observer's presence has a notable influence on the discussant's behavior. We look at this question in order to render possible comparisons with parallel investigations that are run in the same research project (von Rosenstiel & Stocker-Kreichgauer in this volume).

In addition to the measures taken in the course of the experiment, we took follow-up measures of decision preferences and impression rating several weeks after the experiment in order to have a look at long-term effects.

To summarize our hypotheses, we expect participants of discussion treated with nonverbal friendliness to change their decision preferences more in their partner's direction than unfriendly treated ones. This effect should diminish with time, but still be observable eight weeks later. In addition, we expect friendly behaving participants to be rated more positively on the "social-emotional factor," but not on the "dominance factor." As to the variables of experimental condition (participants/observers and presence/absence of an observer), we cannot yet formulate direct hypotheses.

METHOD

Sixty-nine male students from the Teacher's College at the University of Augsburg participated in the experiment. Diverging from most of our experiments in which an interaction between the participants was possible only in written form or via computer terminals, respondents interacted face-to-face in dyadic discussions.

The case to be decided dealt with a teacher accused of an indecent assault on a pupil (modified from Peters, 1970). The subjects had to imagine they were members of a disciplinary court deciding this case. To avoid the social-desirability components of a decision *in dubio pro reo,* the accusing girl, who meanwhile was of full age, was said to be in danger of being condemned for having committed perjury. In this way, a decision had to be made between a negative consequence for the teacher or a negative consequence for the pupil. After a pretest with a random sample of thirty students from the Department of Economics and Social Sciences at the University of Augsburg, the information about the case was modified to the extent that a balance was nearly obtained regarding the alternative decisions.

Independent variables were (1) the experimental situation and (2) the nonverbal friendliness or unfriendliness of the discussion participants. The *experimental situation* was varied in three ways: (a) one subject was an active discussion participant while a second participated as a passive observer; (b) one subject was an active discussion participant without a second subject as observer; (c) one subject was a passive observer of the discussion. Each of the four male confederates was trained to show both nonverbal friendliness and unfriendliness. *Nonverbal friendly behavioral cues* were frequent eye contact, friendly countenance (e.g., smiling if suitable), bodily orientation towards the partner sitting at the corner seat, and emotionally warm voice. *Unfriendly cues* were avoidance of eye contact, neutral or hostile countenance, bodily orientation rather away from partner or a reserved poise, and indifferent or aggressive voice. Furthermore, every confederate had to be able to argue *for* as well as *against* the facts of the case. For both decision alternatives binding lists of arguments were prepared. The aim of the training was that every confederate should appear convincing in his various roles and that the number and quality of arguments were not confounded with the roles to be played. This was pretested with uninformed observers.

Three subjects and two confederates were invited to every experimental session. At the beginning of every session the subjects had the opportunity of talking to each other for some minutes in order to form "first impressions" of one another. During this initial period the instructed subjects (confederates) had orders to behave as neutrally as possible so that the naive subjects did not interpret the friendliness or unfriendliness expressed later in the discussion as a typical behavioral style of his partner but perceived it as specifically directed to their own person.

The case was presented to the subjects in written form. After fifteen minutes they had to decide what percent of the facts specified argued for or against the case. As it had to be expected that some of the subjects would not come to a conclusion, they had additionally to make an alternative decision ("rather pro" or "rather con"). This was necessary to determine the direction of the confederate's argumentation in the following discussion.

According to their individual decisions, the naive subjects were assigned to the experimental conditions. In order to control individual and scaling effects and to make sure that the subjects' initial opinions were distributed homogeneously among the experimental conditions, each one of the instructed subjects had to play every role at approximately the same frequency.

With three naive and two instructed subjects it was possible to set up two discussion groups simultaneously: (a) one group with an observer who had made the same alternative decision as the naive discussion participant,

TABLE 7-1
Experimental design with cell frequencies

	Participants in a discussion *with* observer	Participants in a discussion *without* observer	Observer
Nonverbal friendliness	12	12	9
Nonverbal unfriendliness	12	13	11

and (b) one group without the corresponding observer. The same decision by participant and observer in the first group allows a direct comparison of the influence of nonverbal friendliness on the active versus passive participants in a discussion.

Before discussion started the two discussion participants had to rate each other on a nine-item semantic differential, taken from Cohen (1969). The observers had to rate both discussion participants. After the mutual rating, the subjects received a booklet in which, on each of the approximately thirty pages, the figure of an eleven-point quasi-ratio scale was shown (100:0, 90:10, . . . 0:100) (cf. Peltzer and Schuler, 1976). The extreme points 100:0 and 0:100 were marked verbally as for or against the facts of the case.

The confederate—informed only at the very beginning of the discussion of which role he was to play—had to open the discussion with a contribution making his opinion clear, e.g., "Well, I mean that . . ." During the discussion, the participants stated their decision preferences on the quasi-ratio scale every minute. The moment was announced by an acoustic signal. After having made their statements, the subjects had to turn over the leaf to the next page. Thus, they could not see the last marking they had made. The opinion change described by the average of the last three scores was analyzed as a dependent variable in the experiment. After twenty-two minutes the discussion was ended. Then the discussion participants rated each other once more on the semantic differential items used before the discussion. The judgment of the partner after the discussion in relation to the rating before the discussion was analyzed as the second dependent variable.

Since a previous investigation (Schuler and Peltzer, 1975), in which almost the same items of Cohen (1969) were used, found a high correlation between the items, it seems possible at least partly to summarize the items as *rating factors* or *clusters*. This reduction of the nine items to possibly a few homogeneous rating aspects was based on the intercorrelations of the items as rated before the discussion by means of the hierarchical cluster analysis of Johnson (1967). The sum scores of clustered items were used as the dependent variable.

At the end of the experiment, the subjects were interviewed alone in order to control possible sources of error and to get information about the individual course of the decision. As immediate debriefing was not possible, the interviews had to make sure that no lasting disturbance was caused by the partner's unfriendly behavior. In two cases assurances were offered and accepted. Eight weeks later a questionnaire was sent to all of the subjects whose addresses were known to examine the long-lasting

Figure 7-1

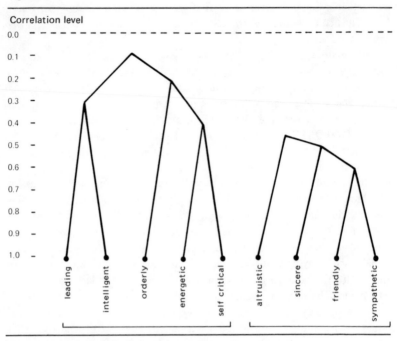

Hierarchical clustering of the semantic differential

effects of the discussions on the development of preferences and on the impression ratings.

RESULTS

DEFINITION OF THE PARTNER RATING DEPENDENT VARIABLE

The intercorrelation matrix of the nine semantic differential items of all sixty-nine subjects was submitted to an hierarchical cluster analysis. As shown in Figure 7-1, the nine items can be divided into two clusters: one factor of *social-emotional evaluation* and one factor of *activity-potency*. For further analysis, we summed the respective items into two scores. The correlation of the two dimensions was $r = .157$ among all subjects; thus, they can be considered independent.

INITIAL DECISION AND EXTREMITY OF INITIAL RATING

Of the sixty-nine subjects, twenty-four decided for and forty-five against the facts of the case. This distribution deviated significantly from the equal distribution expected from the pretest ($\chi^2 = 6.35$, $p < .05$).

Presumably, the student teachers identified themselves more with the accused teacher than did the "neutral" students of economics in the pretest. This may possibly cause the student teachers to regard the assault as less probable, or to associate the alternative "not to condemn the teacher" with a greater social value, although we had tried to procure a counterbalance in the prospect of eventual perjury by the girl. However, possible assault by the teacher was discussed, not perjury by the pupil. The principle of *in dubio pro reo* was probably applied to the teacher rather than to the girl.

The case as such may be taken as realistic and reliable, since doubts about authenticity were uttered neither in the experiment nor in the postexperimental interview.

In accord with our expectation, the extremity of the initial rating, with respect to the indifference point of 50:50, correlated positively with the extremity of scaling at the end of the discussion. In addition, pro-subjects yielded more than con-subjects. The extremity of the initial attitude and the decision shall therefore be used as additional predictors in the regression analysis of the *opinion change* dependent variable to improve total prediction.

DIFFERENCES BEFORE THE DISCUSSION AND CONTROL OF POSSIBLE ERROR INFLUENCES

Table 7-1 shows the allocation of the sixty-nine subjects within the experimental design. Because the initial ratings were counterbalanced, there are no significant differences between the experimental conditions, neither for the initial decision nor for the extremity of the first opinion expressed. Also, there are no differences concerning the share of speech time of the confederates in the total discussion time (average 60.84%). This result is important in so far as possible differences in the experimental conditions, especially in the friendliness condition, are not explainable by different speech rates. By means of a random sample of record discussion protocols it was determined that the number and quality of arguments used by the confederates were constant among the experimental conditions. No notable difference could be found here.

No significant difference in the experimental conditions for either index of partner rating before discussion can be stated. There was, however, a trend showing discussion observers as rating confederates less positively than active debaters with respect to the social-emotional as well as the activity-potency aspect. Perhaps the expectation of directly confronting another person leads, at least in tendency, to a more positive judgment of this person.

TABLE 7-2

Regression analysis for the criterion of preference after discussion

Variable	Corr.	Regr. coeff.	Std. error of regr. coeff.	t	Sign.
Friendliness	0.34	1.12	0.32	3.46	**
Type of participation	0.12	0.80	0.41	1.93	
Type of discussion	0.03	0.12	0.39	0.31	
Decision	0.45	0.76	0.17	4.45	***
Extremity	0.37	0.64	0.19	3.41	**

Multiple correlation = 0.67
Std. error of estimate = 1.34

Analysis of variance for the regression

Source	SS	DF	MS	F	Sign.
Attrib. to regression	92.6	5	18.5	10.33	***
Dev. from regression	112.9	63	1.8		
Total	205.6	68			

EFFECTS OF THE EXPERIMENTAL CONDITIONS IN THE DISCUSSION

Altogether twelve subjects changed their minds fundamentally in the course of the discussion, i.e., from pro to con or vice versa. Nine of these were participants in a friendly discussion and three in an unfriendly one (Fisher's Exact Test, $p = .039$). Six of these yielding subjects were debaters in a discussion with an observer, four without an observer present, and two were observers. For more detailed analysis of the effects of experimental conditions on the dependent variable of *opinion change,* a regression analysis was computed with five predictors: friendliness/unfriendliness; type of participation, i.e., debater or observer; type of discussion, i.e., with or without an observer; decision at the beginning of discussion; extremity of opinion at the beginning of discussion, i.e., distance from the indifference point of 50:50.

The results of the regression analysis are shown in Table 7-2. The aforementioned effects of initial decision and extremity proved significant. Also, as mentioned above, the choice supporting the teacher and thus against the pupil seemed to have more social desirability. Since we worked with a quasi-control group design and took care to strictly counterbalance the initial scores between experimental conditions, the effect of extremity cannot bias the effect of the friendliness variable.

The effect of the *friendliness* condition proved to be significant in the expected direction. Friendly discussion participants had more influence on their partners than unfriendly ones. For the *situation* variable no significant differences could be found. However, a clear trend appears, scarcely missing the .05 level of significance, which would have shown that subjects actively participating in discussion changed more in the direction of their partners than observers did. Here it is striking that debaters also moved to agree with an unfriendly partner somewhat, while observers withdrew farther from the unfriendly debater's point of view (Figure 7-2).

Figure 7-2

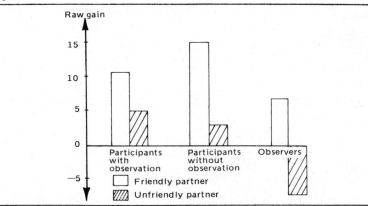

Effects of experimental conditions on preference (represented by raw gain differences)

Figure 7-3

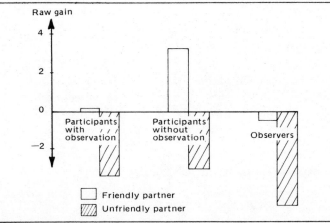

Effects of experimental conditions on "social emotionality" (represented by raw gain differences)

TABLE 7-3

Regression analysis for the criterion of "social emotionality"
after discussion

Variable	Corr.	Regr. coeff.	Std. error of regr. coeff.	t	Sign.
Friendliness	0.38	4.05	0.89	4.53	***
Type of participation	0.36	1.84	1.13	1.63	
Type of discussion	0.29	1.63	1.04	1.56	
"First impression"	0.35	0.53	0.14	3.71	***

Multiple correlation = 0.64
Std. error of estimate = 3.64

Analysis of variance for the regression

Source	SS	DF	MS	F	Sign.
Attrib. to regression	600.6	4	150.2	11.35	***
Dev. from regression	846.7	64	13.2		
Total	1,447.3	68			

For the social-emotional aspects of *partner rating* after discussion, a regression analysis was computed with predictors of friendliness/unfriendliness, type of participation, type of discussion, and judgment before discussion (Table 7-3). A friendly discussion participant is judged more positively than an unfriendly one (Figure 7-3). The *first impression* also maintains its effect if more information about the partner is available during the discussion. This is even more true for an unfriendly ($r = .75$) than for a friendly debater ($r = .36$).

The experimental situation as a variable shows no significant effects; observers tend to be more critical (less positive) than active participants, and unobserved debaters judge their opponent more positively than observed ones do. The corresponding calculation referring to the activity-potency aspects of partner impression after discussion showed no significant effects.

LONG-LASTING EFFECTS OF THE DISCUSSION

The postexperimental questionnaire, sent to subjects eight weeks later, was returned by 83.6%. Observers returned their questionnaires sooner than active debaters; after the first week already 70.6% of the observers, but only 38.6% of the debaters ($\chi^2 = 5.02$, p $<$ .05), had answered. The corresponding trend for the friendliness condition was not significant.

A regression analysis for the significant predictors in the main experiment, (a) friendliness/unfriendliness, (b) decision before the discussion, and (c) extremity of the first decision, showed expected significant effects for the first two predictors (Table 7-4). The influence of extremity in the beginning did not reach significance.

A two-factorial least-squares analysis of variance with repeated measures (Winer, 1971) for the friendliness variable at three points of time (before discussion, immediately after discussion, eight weeks later) showed

TABLE 7-4
Regression analysis for the criterion of preference after some weeks

Variable	Corr.	Regr. coeff.	Std. error of regr. coeff.	t	Sign.
Friendliness	0.32	0.47	0.19	2.52	*
Decision	0.39	0.59	0.19	3.10	**
Extremity	0.16	0.26	0.21	1.23	

Multiple correlation = 0.53
Std. error of estimate = 1.32

Analysis of variance for the regression

Source	SS	DF	MS	F	Sign.
Attrib. to regression	31.0	3	10.3	5.92	***
Dev. from regression	80.3	46	1.7		
Total	111.3	49			

TABLE 7-5
Analysis of variance for the preference

Source of variation	SS	dF	MS	F	Sign.
Friendliness	33.6	1	33.6	10.00	***
Subj. w. Gr.	161.2	48	3.4		
Time	13.8	2	6.9	6.38	***
Friendl. X time	14.9	2	7.5	6.90	***
Time X subj. w. Gr.	104.0	96	1.1		

both the main effects and the interaction to be significant (Table 7-5). While unfriendly-treated subjects showed only small preference changes over time, friendly-treated ones yielded remarkably as a consequence of the discussion. Their responses to the postexperimental questionnaire eight weeks later, however, again approached somewhat their initial position (Figure 7-4).

A corresponding analysis of variance for the dependent variable of partner rating (social-emotional aspect) showed effects of time and the time-friendliness interaction to be significant (Table 7-6). The main effect of friendliness scarcely missed the .05 significance level, which may be explained by a slight initial difference in favor of the later unfriendly-act-

TABLE 7-6
Analysis of variance for the "social emotionality"

Source of variation	SS	dF	MS	F	Sign.
Friendliness	117.5	1	117.5	3.92	
Subj. w. Gr.	1,259.3	42 +	30.0		
Time	174.7	2	87.3	15.30	***
Friendl. * time	167.4	2	83.7	14.66	***
Time * subj. w. Gr.	479.9	84	5.7		

+ As six Ss did not completely fill in the postexperimental inquiry, degrees of freedom for the analysis of variance were reduced.

Figure 7-4

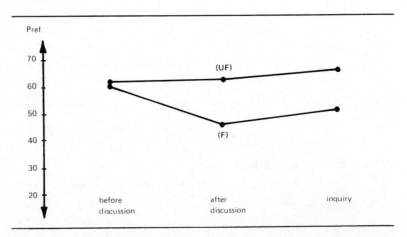

Changes over time for preference for friendly (F) and unfriendly (UF) partner

Figure 7-5

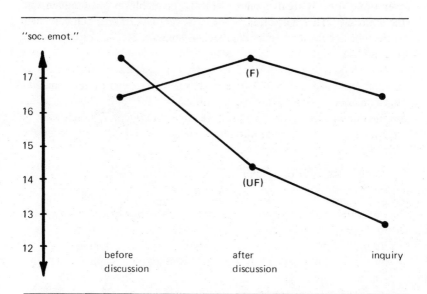

Changes over time for "social emotionality" for friendly (F) and unfriendly (UF) partner

ing debaters. The significant decrease of positive judgments over time is almost exclusively explained by the behavior of unfriendly partners, as shown in the significant interaction.

While friendly discussion partners are rated rather constantly over time, the evaluation of unfriendly discussion partners deteriorates (Figure 7-5).

DISCUSSION

BEHAVIORAL STYLE AND INFLUENCE

The twelve observed fundamental changes of decisional preference are, relative to the sixty-nine total subjects, more than what had occurred in all our previous experiments of this series. We cannot decide at the moment if this large tally is due to the special form of interaction, namely face-to-face interaction, or if it has to be attributed to the case decided by the participants. According to our experience in the postexperimental interview, we prefer the interpretation that this experimental situation—direct confrontation with another person—caused much higher involvement than did our previous forms of interaction (via written statements or computer terminals). But the case under discussion—a teacher accused of an indecent assault on a pupil—in its mixture of realism (the subjects were student teachers) and ambiguity (more than twenty discriminable arguments were used for each side) might also have promoted opinion changes more than other discussion topics, although comparisons within and between our previous studies had never shown any remarkable effects of the topics.

Nine of these twelve fundamental changes were observed under the "friendly style of nonverbal interaction" condition. The results of statistical analyses also show an influence-enhancing effect of friendly behavior on development of the preferences of discussion partners. Given that Brandstätter's argumentation is correct that reinforcement of single arguments should rather lead to a stabilization of a partner's position, we can assume that we succeeded in creating a sort of "global social reinforcement."

Compared with previous results, it seems now to be rather unimportant in which way this social approval concretely appears. The phenomenologically different appearances of our central independent variable had about the same influence-enhancing effect, one of modest size but statistically reliable. Direct manipulation of liking, information about similarity, use of friendly and courteous remarks, and, in the present case, friendly, socially-accepting nonverbal behavior, all enhanced—in comparison to the control groups—influence on the discussion partner and at the same time resulted in a more favorable partner rating by the latter.

Herein we see a confirmation of our suspicion that the reactions of discussion partners, and thus the interactional process, do not depend so much on the specific actually-appearing behavioral dimension nor even on special elements of behavior. The characteristic which appears in all this information is distinctive; it is perceived by the partner as an expression of benevolence directed to him and interpreted as positive evaluation of his person, which he in turn answers with symmetrically positive evaluation, with heightened readiness to listen and to accept the other's arguments, and with increased approach tendencies.

Eight weeks after the discussion took place, the difference in influence between friendly- and unfriendly-acting debaters was somewhat reduced, but still remained significant. In a similar experiment (Schuler and Peltzer, 1975), the difference had diminished more obviously, which led us to compare this result with the sleeper effect described by Hovland and Weiss (1951). The minor loss of influence over time in the present case could well be a result of higher involvement, caused by real face-to-face interaction and probably by the more interesting topic of decision as well. One might be tempted to see herein support of Nuttin's provocative *response contagion theory of persuasion* (1975), postulating changes of *attitude responses* through activation, and, instead of enduring attitude changes, *stability of changed attitude responses,* if measured with the same instrument, caused by resistance to altering a once-emitted attitude response. However, Nuttin's hypothesis gives no explanation for the influence-enhancing effects of friendly, rewarding behavior as measured at two different points of time, unless one expects—contrary to all experience—that friendly behavior of a sort which is usual in a discussion induces more activation or confusion than unfriendly behavior does.

RATING OF THE DISCUSSION PARTNER

The rating data reflect the intended behavior of the confederates: At both points of postdecisional measurement friendly-acting discussants were rated higher by far on the items clustered around the *social-emotional* or *liking factor* than unfriendly-acting persons. We consider it remarkable that there were no differences at all for the second factor, the *achievement* or *dominance factor.* This supports Argyle's assumption (1969) of two orthogonal factors of nonverbal behavior, *like-dislike* and *dominance* or superiority. Obviously it was possible to manipulate, as intended, only the first of these two dimensions and at the same time have the second remain constant. There was no indication of a third *activity factor,* independent of *dominance,* as postulated by Mehrabian (1972). The reason may be that frequency and speed of talking, which should be important behavioral elements of such a factor, were held constant.

The difference in the correlation coefficients of ratings before and after discussion in the present as well as in our former experiments, being higher for unfriendly than for friendly discussants, may find different explanations. Possibly, all four confederates succeeded equally in performing the friendly role, while their performance of the unfriendly role was somewhat dependent on their expression and behavior in the initial neutral situation. Another possible explanation is that negative first impressions might have a higher impact or more consistent effects on later person perception processes.

Brandstätter[2] suggests a cognitive consistency explanation, assuming that a friendly-acting partner (or a similar liked partner) who represents a position in discussion contrary to one's own position creates cognitive inconsistency, and thus provokes different and in some cases irritated responses, while an unfriendly (or dissimilar) partner's position is quite consistent with his behavioral style and is responded to in a similar manner by all the subjects.

The development of the partner rating concerning the liking-factor from the first to the second postdiscussional inquiry seems remarkable to us. While the positive rating of the friendly discussants slightly diminished over the course of eight weeks, the unfriendly partners' scores did not, as probably expected, subsequently rise, but rather became even worse. Unfriendly behavior, which fails to correspond to social norms of politeness and kindness and is eventually more unusual, shows a longer-lasting and even increasing effect on person perception processes, instead of diminishing and fading as is the case with positive impressions.

As to the rating of the friendly discussants, the gain in liking from predecisional to the first postdecisional response may even be underestimated because of a ceiling effect. More than for competing theories, these results are assumed to speak for conditioning of social emotions as formulated by Brandstätter (1976 and this volume).

COMPARISON BETWEEN PARTICIPANTS AND OBSERVERS

Comparison between active participants of discussions and observers did not show any weighty differences between these two groups. The only significant difference was in the return of postexperimental inquiries. This corresponds to the impression we had after the postexperimental interviews, that observers of discussions were highly interested in participating actively in such a discussion in the future. Eventually, this observation could be of some use in the recruitment of volunteer subjects.

However, with respect to the main points of decision and impression formation processes, i.e., development of decision preferences and the responses to independent variables in the forms of yielding and partner rating, there was no really important difference. Summarizing the differences which did occur as trends, observers seemed to be somewhat more critical than participants, that is, they rated the confederates somewhat less positively and showed less yielding. Additionally, they seemed to react somewhat more sensitively to the confederates' behavioral styles.

This result—only a statistical trend—also coincides with our observations in the interviews. The observers' distance and lower ego involvement may facilitate a critical attitude and frank expression of their opinions. That unobserved discussants rated their partners somewhat more positively than observed ones may be interpreted as the observers' presence having induced some distance in the role of an active participant.

This was only the first systematic comparison between the two modes of participation in a decision process—active participation versus observation—within the Augsburg research project on discussion. It has shown shades rather than differences and may allow further attempts at theoretical unification of the different approaches which have developed, using partly different methods, within this project.

NOTES

1. M. Argyle, Non-verbal communication. Paper presented at the 2nd Summer-School of the European Association of Experimental Social Psychology. Oxford, 1976.
2. H. Brandstätter, Social Emotions in persuasive argumentation. A review of the Augsburg research project on discussion. Paper presented at the 31st International Congress of Psychology (Symposium on social influence). Paris, 1976.

REFERENCES

Argyle, M. Non-verbal communication in human social interaction. In R.A. Hinde (Ed.), *Nonverbal Communication.* Cambridge: Cambridge University Press, 1972.
– – –. *Social Interaction.* London: Methuen, 1969.
Argyle, M., F. Alkema, and R. Gilmour. The communication of friendly and hostile attitudes by verbal and non-verbal signals. *European Journal of Social Psychology,* 1972, *1*, 385-402.
Argyle, M., and M. Cook. *Gaze and Mutual Gaze.* Cambridge: Cambridge University Press, 1976.
Brandstätter, H. Soziale Verstärkung in Diskussionsgruppen. In H. Brandstätter and H. Schuler (Eds.), Entscheidungsprozesse in Gruppen. *Zeitschrift für Sozialpsychologie,* Beiheft 2. Bern: Humber, 1976, 65-82.
Brandstätter, H., W. Molt, L. von Rosenstiel, B. Rüttinger, H. Schuler, and G. Stocker-Kreichgauer. Der Einfluss in Entscheidungsgruppen als Funktion der Sympathie und des Unterschieds in den Handlungspräferenzen. *Problem und Entscheidung,* 1971, *6*, 2-71.
Cohen, R. *Systematische Tendenzen bei Persönlichkeitsbeurteilungen.* Bern: Huber, 1969.
Ekman, P., and W.V. Friesen. Non-verbal behavior in psychotherapy research. In J. Shlien (Ed.), *Research in Psychotherapy.* Vol. 3, Washington, D.C., 1968.
Hovland, C.I., and W. Weiss. The influence of source credibility on communication effectiveness. *Public Opinion Quarterly,* 1951, *15*, 635-650.
Johnson, S.C. Hierarchical clustering schemes. *Psychometrika,* 1967, *32*, 241-254.
Mehrabian, A. *Nonverbal Communication.* New York: Aldine-Atherton, 1972.
– – –. The inference of attitudes from the posture, orientation, and distance of a communicator. *Journal of Consulting Psychology,* 1968, *32*, 296-308.
Nuttin, J.M., Jr. *The Illusion of Attitude Channge.* London: Academic Press, 1975.
Peltzer, U., and H. Schuler. Personwahrnehmung, Diskussionsverhalten und Präferenzänderung in Dyaden (LIDIA II). In H. Brandstätter and H. Schuler (Eds.),

Entscheidungsprozesse in Gruppen. *Zeitschrift für Sozialpsychologie*, Beiheft 2. Bern: Huber, 1976, 105-117.

Peters, K. *Fehlerquellen im Strafprozess*, Bd. 1, Karlsruhe: C.F. Müller, 1970.

Schuler, H. Sympathie und Einfluss in Entscheidungsgruppen. *Zeitschrift für Sozialpsychologie*, Beiheft 1. Bern: Huber, 1975.

―――. Soziale Verstärkung und Diskussionsverhalten bei simulierter Interaktion (LIDIA I). *Problem und Entscheidung*, 1974, *12*, 26-37.

Schuler, H., and U. Peltzer. Ahnlichkeit, Kompetenz und die Erwartung künftiger Interaktion als Determinanten von Diskussionsverhalten und Partnerbeurteilung (LIDIA III). *Problem und Entscheidung*, 1975, *14*, 78-107.

Winer, B.J. *Statistical Principles in Experimental Design*. New York: McGraw Hill, 1971

8

VICARIOUS SOCIAL REINFORCEMENT

Lutz von Rosenstiel and Gisela Stocker-Kreichgauer[1]

ON THE ACTUALITY OF THE PROBLEM

People often form their opinions and decisions about social or political problems while they listen to controversial arguments about these questions and simultaneously observe the reactions of other people confronted with the same arguments. A paradigm for this situation is the "pro and con" program in German television. This program presents two parties discussing controversial conceptions about actual problems; at the same time the reactions of a representatively chosen audience are presented. This paradigm corresponds to many other social situations in real life, e.g., to public election speeches, shareholder meetings, tenant associations, all kinds of decision committees, and also to party and family conversations. In all these cases observers do not participate in the controversial discussion themselves, but form their opinions and decisions after having heard the information and observed its evaluation. It is obvious, and theoretically explicable in many ways, that a person more easily accepts opinions positively valued by others. It is, however, also plausible, and again in many ways explicable, that evaluations of persons positively valued by oneself are more effective. We shall discuss here the question of how vicarious social reinforcement of arguments influences observers' attitude change and how essential the evaluation of the reinforcing agent is in that attitude change.

EXPERIMENTS CONCERNING
OUR RESEARCH PROBLEM

Experiments on our question were conducted by Kelley and Woodruff (1956) and by Landy (1972); another study, with an experimental design which is similar to the experiment discussed here, was performed by von Rosenstiel and Rüttinger (1976). Kelley and Woodruff (1956) confronted their subjects, who were students of a progressively oriented teachers college, with a lecture in which the speaker argued against training behavior usually approved by the subjects. The lecture was presented via an audio recording in which central passages of the lecture were applauded by an audience. Subjects were divided into two groups receiving different information about the applauding audience. The first group was informed that they were members or prior members of the college; the second group was instructed that they were academically educated people of a nearby town. The results corresponded to the hypothesis: there were more opinion changes in the direction of the applauded position of the speaker when applause came from a "membership-audience" than when it came from an "outsider-audience."

In the study of Kelley and Woodruff, only the source of applause was varied, not the kind of audience reaction; furthermore, they did not include a lecture presentation with no audience reaction at all (i.e., a control group), nor with an audience showing dislike.

Landy (1972) paid attention to this point in his study. He systematically varied two independent variables, the kind of audience reaction—applause, no reaction, dislike—and the evaluation of the audience—subjects were informed that the audience consisted of former students of the same college (positive evaluation) or of members of the American Nazi party (negative evaluation).

Landy stated that applause regardless of the source was more efficient in changing the preferences of listening subjects in the intended direction than no response at all; the latter condition, however, was more effective than dislike shown by the audience. The predicted "boomerang effect" when applause or dislike was expressed by the "wrong side" could not be proved.

Regarding the results obtained by Landy (1972), von Rosenstiel and Rüttinger (1976) attempted to take into account the evaluation of the audience in their experimental study. They were concerned with the question of how a controversial discussion about the "Radikalenerlass der Ministerpräsidenten" (members of extreme political parties should not be taken into public employment) affected the preferences of subjects in two different applause situations. In the experimental group, one of the speakers was applauded by the audience, while in the control group there were no reactions by the audience. It was shown that the reinforced speaker was more effective in influencing the subjects' preferences than the "no reaction" speaker in the control group.

Corresponding to the study of von Rosenstiel and Rüttinger (1976), von Rosenstiel et al. (1975) developed a more comprehensive experimental design in which two speakers discussing the "Radikalenerlass" in a controversial form were exposed to seven different conditions combining different reactions by an audience: applause, no reaction, and disapproval. The design of this experiment is shown in Figure 8-1.

In this study the results of von Rosenstiel and Rüttinger (1976) were replicated to some extent. Subjects were significantly more influenced by speakers applauded by the audience than by speakers disliked by the audience. Yet there was no significant difference between these two conditions and the control condition (no reaction of the audience).

In the study of von Rosenstiel et al. (1975), evaluation of the applauding audience was not varied systematically, but was measured in the six experimental conditions by a semantic differential after presentation of the entire discussion. The question we are asking here is whether the results reported by von Rosenstiel et al. (1975) must be differentiated with respect to evaluation of the audience.

Figure 8-1

| | Reinforcement condition | | | | | | |
	1	2	3	4	5	6	7
Reaction to B (arguing con or 0:100)	+	+	0	0	−	−	0
Reaction to M (arguing pro or 100:0)	0	−	−	0	0	+	+

+ = reward (applause)
0 = no reaction
− = punishment (disapproval)

Experimental design

THEORETICAL CONSIDERATIONS

The experiment described here was designed within the theoretical framework of vicarious social reinforcement. Observers are not reinforced directly, but vicariously, by the two speakers whose discussion is presented through one of three media. The social reinforcers employed here are of presumably positive and negative valence: approval and disapproval by an audience listening to the speakers' discussion. It is assumed that vicarious positive reinforcement, like direct positive reinforcement, will raise the intensity or frequency of the behavior contingently reinforced (Bandura, 1969, p. 217 ff., p. 253 ff.; 1971, p. 4 ff.; Mowrer, 1960a, p. 70 ff.; 1960b, p. 63 ff.).

Vicarious reinforcement can be defined according to Flanders (1968, p. 312) as the operation of exposing O (the observer) to a procedure of presenting a reinforcing stimulus, i.e., a presumed or confirmed reinforcing stimulus for O, to M (the model) after and contingent on a certain response by M.

We shall discuss the effects of vicarious reinforcement on the observers within a cognitive-emotional framework. We already know from empirical studies that the efficiency of such a reinforcer can be modified by different qualities of the model. A positively evaluated model will be more effective in modifying the observers' behavior than a negatively evaluated model (Bandura, 1969, p. 136; Kanfer and Phillips, 1970, p. 108 ff.; Miller and Dollard, 1941, p. 165 ff.). The evaluation of the model can take place on different dimensions: competence (Baron, 1970; Longstreth, 1971), interpersonal attractiveness (Landy and Aronson, 1968; Lepper, 1970), social power (Argyle, 1972, p. 281; Baron and Kepner, 1970), and credibility (McGarry and Hendrick, 1974, p. 86; McGuire, 1969, p. 179 ff.).

Additionally, we suppose that the effectiveness of a reinforcer on observers' behavior will be modified by the evaluation of the reinforcing agent. We hypothesize that a positively evaluated reinforcing agent will modify the observers' behavior corresponding to the quality of the reinforcer he is transmitting, while a negatively evaluated agent will cause boomerang effects in reinforcing. Stocker-Kreichgauer (1976, p. 362 ff.) studied this question with a group discussion moderator in the role of a reinforcing agent; she could not confirm the hypothesis. Bandura (1969) showed that, in direct social reinforcement, a friendly reinforcing agent was more effective than an unkind one. Lepper (1970), however, reported that anxiety of the observer (here, children) can affect this relation as a moderator variable: "Under high anxiety the negative experimenter (showing negative interaction) was more effective than the positive one, while under low anxiety the positive experimenter was more effective in modifying the children's behavior by social reinforcement." (Lepper, 1970, p. 704) Since we are not aware of an analogous study for adults, it is not clear whether this result is limited to children.

In our study, we predict an interaction between the kind of vicarious social reinforcement and the observers' evaluation of the reinforcing agent (the audience) on the attitude change of observers. The failure of Landy (1972) to prove such an interaction in his experiment does not discourage us because it is possible that his subjects "forgot" the experimentally induced valence of the audience during the discussion and therefore only reacted to the reinforcer itself.

In our case, we shall have some difficulty determining causality in the relation between reinforcement, evaluation, and opinion change. Since we did not manipulate the evaluation of the reinforcing audience experimentally, but only measured it at the end of the discussion, evaluation of the audience cannot be interpreted as an independent variable. This difficulty also arises in the case of awareness measurements after an operant conditioning experiment (Spielberger and DeNike, 1966). Among others, the following relations are possible: (a) the reinforcement condition affects evaluation of the audience; the latter is affecting attitude change; (b) the reinforcement condition affects attitude change; the latter is affecting evaluation of the audience; and (c) the reinforcement condition is affecting both evaluation and attitude change at the same time.

It is obvious that a demonstrated relation between evaluation of the audience and attitude change cannot be interpreted in a causal way. Another experimental design with evaluation induction by the experimenter (see Kelley and Woodruff, 1956; Landy, 1972) or evaluation measurements in advance would help to clarify these relations. There still remains the problem of evaluation modification during the discussion. A positive or negative evaluation of the audience at the beginning of the experiment may change during the discussion if the observer is judging audience reaction in a different way, i.e., fair, unfair, in the course of the discussion. This latter case is taken into account in the present study.

EXPERIMENTAL DESIGN AND SUBJECTS

Subjects were male citizens of Augsburg selected by chance from the telephone directory. Originally 257 persons (average age of 48 years, SD = 14 years) had participated in the experiment; 128 subjects remained after having met the elimination criteria (see von Rosenstiel et al., 1975, p.

36 ff.): incomplete data; data which were not suitable for the statistical design, i.e., subjects holding an extreme position at the beginning on the attitude scale (100:0 or 0:100, see Figure 8-2); data which indicated that subjects presumably did not understand instructions. In the analysis presented here, the 18 subjects of Condition 4 (no applause or disapproval) were also eliminated because they could not evaluate the audience, as well as 13 other subjects who did not evaluate the audience in spite of instruction. Therefore, only 97 subjects remained for the present analysis. That is a great amount of disqualification, yet not too surprising since many subjects had little experience with complicated paper and pencil tasks.

We will briefly describe the experimental procedure. (a) Subjects were welcomed and thanked. (b) Subjects were instructed as to the "quasi-ratio scale" to continuously record their own preferences about the decision. (c) Subjects were assigned to the twenty-one different experimental conditions by chance. There were twenty-one conditions in that three different media (television, tape recorder, and written reports) were combined with the seven different reinforcement conditions (see Figure 8-1). (d) Subjects marked their initial preference for the proposition, "In the future every candidate for public employment should be refused if he is a member of an extreme political party." (e) Subjects described on a six-point bipolar

Figure 8-2

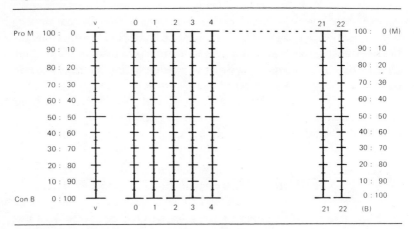

The attitude scale

scale how sure they were of their initial preference. (f) Subjects observed the presentation of the controversial discussion by one of three media; they scaled their actual preference continuously after each argument of the two speakers. (g) Subjects described how sure they were of their terminal preference. (h) Subjects described their impressions of the audience by means of a semantic differential. (i) Subjects answered some questions about their contingency awareness. (j) Subjects made a self-classification concerning their social status by a method created by Kleining and More (1968); inquiry was made of the age of the subjects. (k) Subjects answered the personality inquiry by Fahrenberg and Selg (1970), "Freiburger Persönlichkeitsinventar" (FPI). (l) Subjects were thanked and payment of ten deutsche marks made to every subject.

We used a partial reinforcement schedule where only arguments 1, 2, 5, 7, and 10 of each speaker were reinforced. We defined three kinds of influence as dependent variables. (1) *Final* influence is represented as a frequency distribution of subjects on three categories. We scored "+1" when subjects preferred the issue at the end of the discussion more than they had at the beginning, "0" when there was no difference between the initial and terminal position on the scale, and "−1" when subjects preferred the issue less at the end of the discussion. This measure drops the metric differences, regarding only the direction of change. This seems adequate since unsystematically performed interviews showed that subjects understood well the direction of the scale but had difficulties in interpreting the intervals. (2) *Momentary* influence is the number of moves towards a speaker minus the number of moves away from the speaker immediately following his arguments. (3) *Differential* influence of reinforcement is the net number of moves towards the position of the reinforced arguments minus the net number of moves towards the position of the nonreinforced arguments. Net number means moves towards minus moves away from the position of the argument.

HYPOTHESES

On the basis of the theoretical considerations above, we have stated some hypotheses postulating interactions between intensity of vicarious social reinforcement and evaluation of the audience as reinforcing agent.

Hypothesis 1. If the audience is evaluated positively, the *final* influence of a speaker is congruent with the positive reinforcement or punishment by the audience. In case of negative evaluation, influence is opposite to the kind of reinforcement. Operational definition of Hypothesis 1: There is a significant positive correlation between final influence and the product of the reinforcement condition and evaluation of the audience.

Hypothesis 2(B). If the audience is evaluated positively, the *momentary* influence of a speaker, B, is congruent with the positive reinforcement or punishment by the audience. In case of negative evaluation, influence is opposite to the kind of reinforcement. Operational definition of Hypothesis 2(B): There is a significant positive correlation between momentary influence and the product of the reinforcement condition and evaluation of the audience.

Hypothesis 2(M): Ditto for speaker M.

Hypothesis 3(B): Reinforced arguments of speaker B are more influential than nonreinforced arguments (differential influence or reinforcement), especially if the audience is positively evaluated. Operational definition of Hypothesis 3(B): There is a positive correlation between differential influence and the product of the reinforcement condition and evaluation of the audience.

Hypothesis 3(M): Ditto for speaker M.

Evaluation of the audience was measured by the factor score of a semantic differential.

RESULTS

Testing Hypothesis 1, we computed the product of the "evaluation" factor score and the reinforcement condition of the observer without considering the medium. The subjects in the control condition (no reinforcement by the audience) were eliminated because it was not possible to evaluate the audience in this condition. The remaining six experimental conditions were weighted in the following way:

−3: applause/no reaction (+/0);
−2: applause/disapproval (+/−);
−1: no reaction/disapproval (0/−);
+1: disapproval/no reaction (−/0);
+2: disapproval/applause (−/+);
+3: no reaction/applause (0/+);
+/0 was weighted higher than +/− because Wissner and von Rosenstiel (1974) found by means of paired comparisons that condition +/0 was classified as more pleasant than condition +/−.

The correlation of the product of the reinforcement condition and evaluation of the audience with final influence is significant ($r = .29$; $p < .01$), confirming Hypothesis 1.

This correlation is higher, but not significantly higher, than the correlation between the reinforcement condition and final influence ($r = .22$; $p < .05$). There is no correlation between evaluation of the audience and final influence ($r = -.01$). The bias caused by a correlation between the initial position of the observer and reinforcement for the speaker expressing the same attitude as the observer is small. The correlation between audience evaluation and degree of reinforcement of the speaker whose position the subject shares is $r = .19$. The distribution of data showed no signs of nonlinear correlation between the two variables, neither for persons sharing the position of Speaker B nor for persons sharing the position of Speaker M.

Testing Hypotheses 2(B) and 2(M), we found that the product of the six reinforcement conditions and evaluation of the audience is not significantly correlated with momentary influence (Speaker B, $r = -.11$; Speaker M, $r = .05$). The correlation of momentary influence with reinforcement condition alone is not significantly greater (Speaker B, $r = .10$; Speaker M, $r = .16$). There is no significant correlation between momentary influence and evaluation of the audience (Speaker B, $r = .06$; Speaker M, $r = .11$) either. Thus, Hypotheses 2(B) and 2(M) could not be confirmed.

Testing Hypotheses 3(B) and 3(M), we found that the correlation between differential influence and the product of the newly defined reinforcement conditions (see Figure 8-3) and evaluation of the audience was $r = -.04$ for Speaker B (n.s.). The correlation of differential influence and reinforcement condition alone was $r = .19$, and between differential

Figure 8-3

	Reinforcement condition						
	1	2	3	(4)	5	6	7
For B	+	+	0	0	−	−	0
For M	0	−	−	0	0	+	+

Weights for B: +1 in cond. 1, 2 (reward)
   0 in cond. 3, 7 (no reaction)
   −1 in cond. 5, 6 (punishment)

Weights for M: +1 in cond. 6, 7 (reward)
   0 in cond. 1, 5 (no reaction)
   −1 in cond. 2, 3 (punishment)

Classification of reinforcement conditions used in the analysis of differential influence

influence and evaluation, $r = -.04$, as well. The corresponding data for M were $r = -.16$, $r = .07$, and $r = -.11$. Thus Hypotheses 3(B) and 3(M) could not be confirmed. The results even tend in the opposite direction.

SUMMARY AND DISCUSSION

By means of three measures of influence—final, momentary and differential—we studied the effects of vicarious social reinforcement in group discussions as a function of the evaluation of the reinforcing audience. We tested our hypotheses by correlational analyses. Since we did not regard metric differences on the attitude scale but counted all attitude changes only with respect to their direction, one could argue that a correlational analysis is not suited to our data. Yet, we think that this method is adequate since the number of changes is compatible even with a ratio scale.

The main results are that the correlation between the product of audience evaluation and reinforcement condition with final influence is significant, thus demonstrating the interactional effects of evaluation on attitude change within vicarious reinforcement in group discussions. There are no analogous significant effects of evaluation on the two other influence measures, momentary and differential influence. The interaction between evaluation of the audience and reinforcement condition seems to

TABLE 8-1

Distribution of subjects evaluating the audience *positively* with regard to the final influence of Speakers B and M

	Number of Ss moving to speaker B	Number of Ss moving to speaker M	
B is rewarded M is punished reinforcement condition 1, 2, 3	12	4	16
M is rewarded B is punished reinforcement condition 5, 6, 7	7	16	23
Total	19	20	39

chi^2 = 5.8 (p $<$ 0.05)

affect final influence only, and not the special momentary influence of each speaker nor the single reinforced arguments.

There remain some questions with respect to our significant result. (a) Does the correlation depend to equal extents on a strengthening effect on reinforcement of positive evaluation of the audience on one hand, and on a boomerang effect of reinforcement in case of negative evaluation on the other? To answer this question we computed χ^2 for a 2 × 2 table, defined by reinforcement condition (reward and punishment) and final influence (subjects moving to Speaker B or Speaker M), for positive and for negative evaluations of the audience. Subjects showing no final attitude change were not considered in this analysis. The results are shown in Tables 8-1 and 8-2.

As shown in Table 8-1, the rewarded speaker compared to the punished one has a significantly greater final influence if the audience is evaluated positively. On the contrary, as shown in Table 8-2, the punished speaker is not more influential if the audience is evaluated negatively; there is no boomerang effect. There is no reversal of the effects of reinforcement condition in case of negative evaluation of the audience, but nearly complete reduction of these effects.

(b) Are these effects caused to the same degree by observers holding the position of Speaker M (M′) and of Speaker B (B′)? We tested this question by separate chi-squared tables for M′ and B′. It could be shown that the strengthening effect of positive evaluation of the audience is mainly caused by B's ($\chi^2 = 5.06$) and not by M's ($\chi^2 = .37$). We do not know why, but

TABLE 8-2
Distribution of subjects evaluating the audience *negatively* with regard to the final influence of Speakers B and M

	Number of Ss moving to speaker B	Number of Ss moving to speaker M	
B is rewarded M is punished reinforcement conditions 1, 2, 3	9	11	20
M is rewarded B is punished reinforcement conditions 5, 6, 7	6	10	16
Total	15	21	36

$\text{chi}^2 = 0.06$ (n. s.)

TABLE 8-3

The distribution of subjects with *positive* evaluation of the audience
influenced above or below average by Speaker B
with regard to reinforcement condition

| | Momentary influence by speaker B | | |
	Above average	Below average	
B is rewarded M is punished (reinf. cond. 1, 2, 3)	13	8	21
B is punished M is rewarded (reinf. cond. 5, 6, 7)	13	13	26
Total	26	21	47

chi^2 = 0.27 (n. s.)

perhaps the reason lies in the liberal or conservative attitude position of B$'$
versus M$'$, or in the knowledge that B$'$ is in a minority and that M$'$ is in a
majority. There was no difference between B$'$ and M$'$ in the case of
negative evaluation of the audience; neither B$'$ ($\chi^2 = .00$) nor M$'$ ($\chi^2 =
.20$) reacted in the sense of a boomerang effect.

TABLE 8-4

The distribution of subjects with *negative* evaluation of the audience
influenced above or below average by Speaker B
with regard to reinforcement condition

| | Momentary influence by speaker B | | |
	Above average	Below average	
B is rewarded M is punished (reinf. cond. 1, 2, 3)	10	17	27
B is punished M is rewarded (reinf. cond. 5, 6, 7)	16	7	23
Total	26	24	50

chi^2 = 4.04 (p $<$ 0.05)

As already pointed out, we do not know if attitude change is the cause or effect of evaluation of the audience. We only know that the evaluation of the audience was surprisingly weakly affected by whether the audience applauded or showed disapproval of the speaker expressing an attitude near or opposite to that of the observer. As already mentioned, the correlation is only $r = .19$.

Hypotheses 2(B) and 2(M) could not be proved. However, the correlation concerning Speaker B ($r = -.11$) was analyzed in greater detail by χ^2 tests on 2 × 2 tables for positive and for negative evaluation of the audience (see Tables 8-3 and 8-4). It is obvious that the correlation referring to Speaker B is based on a boomerang effect in case of negative evaluation of the audience ($\chi^2 = 4.04$). When the audience is evaluated positively, reward and punishment of Speaker B do not affect the observers' preferences in the hypothesized way ($\chi^2 = .27$). This is not true for Speaker M. His influence on observers' preferences is affected by audience reactions regardless of how the audience is evaluated (see Table 8-5).

One possible interpretation of these results is that an audience reacting to the majority-speaker (here, M) is affecting attitude change regardless of its evaluation. Observers disregard the evaluation of the reinforcing agent when they know him to be in congruence with the majority. In case of reinforcement given to the minority position (here, B), evaluation of the reinforcing agent becomes more important. If he is evaluated positively the effects of reinforcement are equal to the tendency to yield to the majority

TABLE 8-5

The distribution of subjects with positive *and* negative evaluation of the audience influenced above or below average by speaker M with regard to reinforcement condition

| | Momentary influence by speaker M | | |
	Above average	Below average	
M is rewarded B is punished (reinf. cond. 5, 6, 7)	32	17	49
M is punished B is rewarded (reinf. cond. 1, 2, 3)	21	27	48
Total	53	44	97

$\text{chi}^2 = 4.55$ ($p < 0.05$)

position. If he is negatively evaluated a boomerang occurs; reinforcement works in the opposite attitudinal direction. Yet, it must be noted that in the long run applause and disapproval show the effects intended by the audience (see final influence). It is also possible that it is not a majority-minority explanation which is adequate but another interpretation referring to the liberal versus conservative position of the two speakers.

There is another interesting result relating to differential influence, and, although the correlation concerning differential influence (see Hypotheses 3(B) and 3(M)) is not significant, it is worth further analysis (see Table 8-6). As Table 8-6 shows, the specific influence of reinforced arguments compared with nonreinforced ones brings about some paradoxical effects. The rewarded arguments are more effective than the punished ones, but this effect is, to our surprise, most distinct in the case of negative evaluation of the audience.

This paradoxical differential influence is hard to explain. We believe that, since it is only observed in the case of negative evaluation of the audience, it is possible that the subjects change their preferences spontaneously upon having heard the reinforced argument, according to the kind of reinforcement. After having responded, they realize they were influenced by a negatively evaluated reinforcing agent and withdraw their concession after the next, usually not reinforced, argument of the same speaker. Computing the differences of preference changes following reinforced and not reinforced arguments (by the definition of differential influence), the paradoxical results appear.

A related, but more general, explanation might be that the intention of an attractive reinforcing agent is distinctly perceived and considered, even if he does not state his preferences explicitly. However, an unattractive reinforcing agent loses his influence as soon as he fails to react on the basis of his preferences.

TABLE 8-6

The distribution of subjects with positive or negative evaluation of the audience for specific reward/punishment condition with differential influence combined for Speakers B and M

| | | Differential influence | |
		Above average	Below average
Positive evaluation	B/M is rewarded	19	16
	B/M is punished	10	11
Negative evaluation	B/M is rewarded	20	9
	B/M is punished	10	29

It should be noted that our results can hardly be interpreted as an artifact of the distribution of subjects with respect to initial preferences nor their distribution over experimental conditions (specific reinforcement condition and medium). Comparing the combined conditions of reward and punishment, there is nearly an identical distribution of preferences at the beginning.

A more serious problem is posed by evaluation of the audience. The evaluation was not varied systematically by experimental manipulation nor measured at the beginning of the discussion. Thus, the question remains open whether it must be regarded as cause or effect, or both, of the preference changes. Little is known about the formation of the evaluation. Further research including interviews of the subjects is necessary to make clear the phenomenological representation of the results reported here.

NOTE

1. The authors are grateful to Mrs. G. Albers for her kind assistance with statistical analyses.

REFERENCES

Argyle, M. *Soziale Interaktion.* Koln: Kiepenheuer und Witsch, 1972.

Bandura, A. *Social Learning Theory.* New York: General Learning Press, 1971.

———. *Principles of Behavior Modification.* London: Holt, Rinehart and Winston, 1969.

Baron, R.A. Attraction toward the model and model's competence as determinants of adult aggressive behavior. *Journal of Personality and Social Psychology,* 1970, *14,* 345-351.

Baron, R.A., and C.R. Kepner. Model's behavior and attraction toward the model as determinants of adult aggressive behavior. *Journal of Personality and Social Psychology,* 1970, *14,* 335-344.

Flanders, J.P. A review of research on imitation behavior. *Psychological Bulletin,* 1968, *69,* 316-337.

Kanfer, F.H., and J.S. Phillips. *Learning Foundations of Behavior Therapy.* New York: Wiley, 1970.

Kelley, H.H., and C.L. Woodruff. Members' reactions to apparent group approval of a counternorm communication. *Journal of Abnormal and Social Psychology,* 1956, *52,* 67-74.

Landy, D. The effects of an overheard audience's reaction and attractiveness on opinion change. *Journal of Experimental Social Psychology*, 1972, *8*, 276-288.

Landy, D., and E. Aronson. Liking for an evaluator as a function of his discernment. *Journal of Personality and Social Psychology*, 1968, *9*, 133-141.

Lepper, M.R. Anxiety and experimenter valence as determinants of social reinforcer effectiveness. *Journal of Personality and Social Psychology*, 1970, *16*, 704-709.

Longstreth, L.E. A cognitive interpretation of secondary reinforcement. *Nebraska Symposium on Motivation*, 1971, 33-80.

McGarry, J., and C. Hendrick. Communicator credibility and persuasion. *Memory and Cognition*, 1974, *2*, 82 ff.

McGuire, W.J. The nature of attitudes and attitude change. In G. Lindzey and E. Aronson (Eds.), *The Handbook of Social Psychology* Vol. 3. Reading, Mass.: Addison-Wesley, 1969, 136-314.

Miller, N.E., and J. Dollard. *Social Learning and Imitation*. New Haven: Yale University Press, 1941.

Mowrer, O.H. *Learning Theory and Symbolic Processes*. New York: Wiley, 1960a.

———. *Learning Theory and Behavior*. New York: Wiley, 1960b.

Rosenstiel, von, L., and B. Ruttinger. Die Wirkung von Applaus fur Beitrage in Fernsehdiskussionen auf die Einstellungsanderung der Diskussionsbeobachter. In H. Brandstatter, and H. Schuler, Entscheidungsprozesse in Gruppen. *Zeitschrift fur Sozialpsychologie*, 1976, Beiheft 2, 83-95 (first printing 1974).

Rosenstiel, von, L., G. Stocker-Kreichgauer, and G. Albers. Der Einfluss stellvertretender sozialer Verstarkung auf den Entscheidungsverlauf der Beobachter von Gruppendiskussioner. *Problem und Entscheidung*, 1975, *14*, 17-77.

Ruttinger, B. Die Wirkung verbaler Aggression auf den Sprechereinfluss und den Sprechereindruck in Entscheidungsgruppen. Dissertation, Augsburg, 1974.

Spielberger, C.D., and L.D. DeNike. Descriptive behaviorism versus cognitive theory in verbal operant conditioning. *Psychological Review*, 1966, *73*, 306-326.

Stocker-Kreichgauer, G. Stellvertretende Soziale Verstarkung und Einfluss in Entscheidungsgruppen. Dissertation, Augsburg, 1976.

Wissner, B., and L. von Rosenstiel. Zur Distanz bestimmter Formen sozialer Verstarkung. *Problem und Entscheidung*, 1974, *12*, 68-82.

9

FRIENDLINESS AND GROUP CONSENSUS: FIELD STUDY

Bruno Rüttinger

THE PROBLEM

One of the aspects which has been varied in the investigations of the Augsburg research program, "The impact of social reward and punishment on the preferences of members of decision groups" (cf. Brandstätter, 1972), is the degree of control of conditions in the experimental setting. We conducted strongly controlled experiments (see Ruttinger, 1974; von Rosenstiel, Stocker-Kreichgauer, and Albers, 1975; von Rosenstiel and Ruttinger, 1976; Stocker-Kreichgauer, 1976), less strongly controlled experiments, and finally a field study. A first report of this field experiment dealt with the question of the extent to which group decisions can be predicted by the initial decision preferences of the group members (Molt, Ruttinger, and Brand, 1975).

The results to be outlined in this paper document the connection between the friendliness of the group members during the course of discussions and their movement toward conformity. This question can be studied at two levels. First, one may ask, at the group level, to what extent the friendly climate during the discussion will influence mutual compromise. On the other hand, it is possible to ask, at the individual level, how the friendliness of an individual group member will influence his impact on other group members.

In the following discussion, we will be concerned with the first question. It is expected that the members of a decision group will move further toward conformity the friendlier the discussion between them. We were led to this hypothesis by theories of cognitive consistency (see Abelson et al., 1968) and previous experimental results of the Augsburg research project (see Schuler, 1975; Schuler and Peltzer, 1975).

METHOD

Eighteen decision sessions, each lasting about thirty minutes, were studied. Fifteen of the discussions had four participants, while three discussions contained three persons. Generally, they were members having equal status. The groups were real decision groups in administration (1), industry (5), student body committees (10), and recreation (2). The topics of the discussions were chosen by the groups themselves, and concerned problems just coming into question, e.g., the management of a large supermarket deciding whether or not shoplifting should be denounced.

The experimental data were collected in the following way. (a) Before the discussion took place all members wrote down all desirable and all possible decisions they could conceive concerning the actual topic. (b) These propositions were collected from each member, pooled, and returned to the participants by the experimenter. Each member specified for each proposition the degree of his agreement or disagreement (initial preferences). (c) The ensuing discussion was recorded on videotape and later analyzed by means of the Interaction Process Analysis of Bales. (d) After discussion and decision-making, the members once again rated their agreement or disagreement with the propositions evaluated before the discussion (final preferences). Furthermore, they evaluated the propositions which had been brought up during the discussion and collected by the experimenter. (e) Finally, the members rated each other concerning their friendliness, status, and competence and indicated the degree of their satisfaction with the chosen decision and with the course of discussion. The judgments were made for all of the questionnaires on a nine-point scale.

RESULTS

Friendliness and conformity were operationalized in the following way:

In order to determine the friendliness of a group, Bales' IPA-Categories 1 (friendliness) and 12 (unfriendliness) were put together in the following index:

$$(\Sigma a) / (\Sigma a + \Sigma b).$$

That is, for each group the items of the Category 1 of all members were added and divided by the total number of items of Categories 1 and 12.

Movement toward conformity was found by comparing initial and final conformity. Initial conformity was derived from the preference scale values of the three or four group members for the approximately ten propositions formulated before the discussion. The degree of the initial conformity was measured by Kendall's coefficient of concordance, W.

The final conformity measure for groups was determined in an analogous way, and reflects preferences for the same propositions at the end of the discussion. Conformity increases on the average as a consequence of the discussion. (See Table 9-1.)

Fourteen groups increased in conformity and three decreased. (One group had to be eliminated from the calculations because a member showed no variance in the preferences for the final propositions.) It may be expected that the initial conformity causes variation in both final conformity and friendliness. We therefore partialed out the variance of initial conformity from final conformity as well as from friendliness in order to assess the net impact of friendliness on final conformity. For this purpose the partial correlation between friendliness and final conformity was calculated, $r = .24$, and this value is not significant.

The standard partial regression coefficient is often calculated instead of the partial correlation. It shows in this case the average increase in final

TABLE 9-1

**Intercorrelations among final conformity (X_1),
friendliness (X_2), and initial conformity (X_3)**

Variable	Final conformity	Friendliness	Initial conformity
Final conformity		.05	.58
Friendliness			−.24
Mean	.52	.40	.38
Standard deviation	.16	.24	.16

TABLE 9-2

Regression with final conformity as a function of
both friendliness and initial conformity

	β	b	s_b
Friendliness	.20	.14	.15
Initial conformity	.63	.63	.22
R = .61			

conformity for each increase of a unit of friendliness, with initial conformity held constant. The standard partial regression coefficient $\beta 12.3$ is not significant.

DISCUSSION

The results show that friendliness does not contribute significantly to the prediction of the group members' movement to conformity, when the group is the unit of analysis. It may be asked to what extent this result depends on the experimental setting and the research methods.

Friendliness was determined by means of the Categories 1 and 12 of the Bales' Interaction Process Analysis. These items are relatively rare events which determine only to an extent the impression the discussion participants have of the friendliness in the group. It seemed obvious to include in the analysis at least the items of Categories 3 (agreement) and 10 (disagreement). But we had to leave them out because those actions will also to some extent immediately express the movement to conformity or divergence.

Furthermore, it may be assumed that the friendly or unfriendly actions, in the sense of the Categories 1 and 12 of the IPA, are evaluated by group members in different ways. A friendly action towards a group member is likely to be experienced by other group members inclined to an opposite preference as an unfriendly action. It may be asked, therefore, whether it is possible to construct a friendliness index, at the group level, from Categories 1 and 12.

It is more plausible to pick out only such friendly or unfriendly events which are directed to the total group or uttered in the case of defending one's own point of view, but not such actions which follow the contributions of the other group members. But under such restrictions, it is possible to count only a very small number of actions.

Finally, the result is influenced by the topics which were discussed as well as by the groups themselves. In large part, the topics were relatively trivial and did not evoke a strong emotional engagement. Furthermore, it seems characteristic of the behavioral pattern in organizational decision sessions to suppress emotional reactions as much as possible or to show them in such a differentiated way that an outside observer cannot perceive them.

Finally, the video recording situation may have been obtrusive in that discussants perhaps did not behave with their usual spontaneity.

The low emotional engagement is confirmed by the subjective impression of the discussion participants who gave their ratings at the end of the discussion.

REFERENCES

Abelson, R.P., E. Aronson, W.J. McGuire, T.M. Newcomb, M.J. Rosenberg, and P.H. Tannenbaum (Eds.). *Theories of Cognitive Consistency: A Sourcebook.* Chicago: Rand McNally, 1968.

Bales, R.F. *Personality and Interpersonal Behavior.* New York: Holt, Rinehart and Winston, 1970.

Brandstätter, H. Grundplan für Experimente zur Gruppenentscheidung. *Problem und Entscheidung,* 1972, *8,* 33-45.

Molt, W., B. Rüttinger, and R. Brand. Entscheidungsverläufe in realen Entscheidungssituationen. *Problem und Entscheidung,* 1975, *14,* 108-127.

Rosenstiel, von, 'L., and B. Rüttinger. Die Wirkung von Applaus für Beiträge in Fernsehdiskussionen auf die Einstellungsänderung der Diskussionsbeobachter. In H. Brandstätter and H. Schuler, Entscheidungsprozesse in Gruppen. *Zeitschrift für Sozialpsychologie,* Beiheft 2, 1976, 83-95.

Rosenstiel, von, L., G. Stocker-Kreichgauer, and G. Albers. Der Einfluss stellvertretender sozialer Verstärkung auf den Entscheidungsverlauf der Beobachter von Gruppendiskussionen. *Problem und Entscheidung,* 1975, *14,* 17-77.

Rüttinger, B. Die Wirkung verbaler Aggressionen auf den Sprechereinfluss und den Sprechereindruck in Entscheidungsgruppen. Dissertation, University of Augsburg, 1974.

Schuler, H. Sympathie und Einfluss in Entscheidungsgruppen. *Zeitschrift für Sozialpsychologie*, Beiheft 1, 1975.

Schuler, H., and U. Peltzer, Ahnlichkeit, Kompetenz und die Erwartung künftiger Interakiton als Determinanten von Diskussionsverhalten und Partner-beurteilung (LIDIA III). *Problem and Entscheidung,* 1975, *14,* 78-107.

Stocker-Kreichgauer, G. Stellvertretende Verstärkung and Einfluss in Entscheidungsgruppen. Dissertation, University of Augsburg, 1976.

10

EXPERTNESS, PARTICIPATION, CO-ORIENTATION, AND SOCIAL INFLUENCE

Jan Verhagen

Interaction is the process through which several types of power can be transferred into effective social influence. For instance, expert power is such a resource—the expert becomes influential as soon as he involves himself in communication with others who take an interest in solving a certain problem and who experience some uncertainty with respect to the best solution. This point of view was adopted by the Dutch social psychologist Mulder (Mulder and Wilke, 1970, p. 433) when he tried to interpret certain problems and difficulties that appear in the reviews of field studies and field experiments on participation and democratization.

One purpose of this paper is to stress the point of view that co-orientation, in addition to expert power, is an alternative source of influence: persons tend to be influenced by others who are their equals with respect to personal characteristics, fate, aspirations and value orientations. The second purpose of this paper is to present some thoughts and research concerning the manner in which co-orientation can be effective as a force that weakens, to a certain extent, the transfer of expert power into social influence.

First, the inefficiency of participation as a means to power equalization will be presented. Here Mulder's analysis of discrepancies in expertness between group members will be discussed. Secondly, doubts about the completeness of the analysis will be expressed. Co-orientation theory will be presented as a complementary approach. Thirdly, some ideas will be formulated concerning the manner in which persons react in two types of situations: (a) where the subject as a problem solver receives messages simultaneously from both an expert and a co-oriented peer; and (b) where he only receives messages from the expert.

THE PARADOX

Twenty-eight years ago Coch and French (1948) published their first field experiment on participation. It was presented as a means to overcome resistance to change. Since then many studies on participation have been published and in quite a few of them the data do not fit the theory. For instance, the Norwegian workers studied by French (1960) did not accept the influence that was offered to them. Other studies like Kolaja's (1965) show that in certain participation settings in industry, most proposals are made by managers and academical staff members. In still other studies workers complain about their lack of influence. Mulder, mentioning these and several other examples, remarked that a solid theory about participation is lacking. It is clear that these facts will constitute a serious problem, especially if the achievement of a certain degree of equality and power equalization is considered to be one of the aims of participation.

Mulder's explanation for the failure of participation as an instrument for reaching the goal of power equalization refers to the inequality existent among the participants. Apart from the fact that members of committees, projects and councils often differ tremendously in formal position, a clear difference in expertness also exists. Even where the expert participates with the most democratic intentions, he discovers rather early that his ideas and arguments carry more weight. In fact, such participation appears to become the platform from which expert power convinces (as opposed to commands) the members of the committees about the correctness of proposals.

In this way participation, instead of bringing about power equalization, leads to an even larger discrepancy in power. Moreover one nasty side effect appears: the less expert person, realizing the differences in skill and knowledge that set him apart from the high expert persons, loses his hope of ever gaining any degree of influence. Within the context of the above analyses participation will be effective only when the differences in expertness are very small, thus allowing the less expert person to catch up quickly which subsequently raises his aspirations to exert influence. On the basis of these considerations Mulder and Wilke designed a laboratory experiment in which the following hypotheses were tested:

Hypothesis 1: Higher expert power of person A will result in more effective influence on subject B than lower expert power.

Hypothesis 2: The more expert power person A has and the greater the extent of participation of subject B with A in the decision making, the greater A's effective influence on B.

With respect to the last hypothesis Mulder remarks "that not higher participation in itself (that is, more communication between the persons with restricted expert power and the ones with more expert power) results in power equalization, but that, on the contrary, higher participation enables the ones with more expert power to increase their effective influence over the 'participators.' "

THE TEST OF THE PARADOX

The following 2 × 2 design utilized two levels of expertness and two levels of participation resulting in four experimental conditions:

low expert power — low participation
low expert power — high participation
high expert power — low participation
high expert power — high participation

The subjects in this study each played the role of a townplanner, who was to advise some municipal board about the best site to build a new hospital. Two sites were offered as alternatives. The experimenter handed the subject a booklet filled with cards on which bits of information were placed, that could be used as arguments pro or con a certain site. After he made a provisional decision the subject was invited to communicate with his fictitious partner (the expert). The subject had no idea of his partner's degree of expertness. The subject wrote a message to his partner in which he made known his provisional decision. Then for some time cards were exchanged with the help of a messenger, the experimenter. When the period of exchange was ended, the subject was asked to formulate his definite decision and to make his decision known to the experimenter.

The flow of communication between subject and expert was controlled by a prearranged scheme. The messages that the subject and the expert exchanged were cards, monitored by the experimenter. The subject could choose his messages from arguments that only partly supported his choice, whereas all the arguments of the expert opposed the subject's view. In the low expert power condition, the subject could make use of six arguments

TABLE 10-1

Percentages of subjects changing their decision in accordance
with A's (expert) advocated point of view

	Low participation		High participation	
Low expertness	27.6%	(58)	27.6%	(58)
High expertness	44.8%	(58)	86.3%	(58)

while the expert had five arguments available. In the high expert power condition the subject again had six arguments, while the expert could make use of ten arguments. Participation was operationally defined as the time available for communication about the decision problem. In high participation, the subject and his fictitious partner had twice as much time as in low participation. (The amount of available time was not made known to the subject.)

The most important dependent variable in this experiment was the total number of subjects who changed their final decision in accordance with the position advocated by their fictitious partner (see Table 10-1). It is evident that Mulder's two hypotheses are supported by the data. Other observations, with respect to the subject's attitudes toward A, show the same tendency. For instance, in three of the four conditions the subjects tended to overvalue the quality of their "own" arguments; but as expected they considered their partner's arguments as superior to their own in the high expertness-high participation condition.

Mulder believes that the paradox predicts what is going on in the participation settings in our institutions. The paradox assumes: (a) a considerable difference in expertness between more and less expert persons; (b) high expert persons will not be inclined to explain the key concepts and procedures that will enable the less expert persons to think for themselves; (c) less expert persons, experiencing the large differences in skill and knowledge will see no possibility to reduce the differences to a degree that real participation becomes possible; and (d) less expert persons will attribute an honest and disinterested attitude to the expert person.

Although Mulder's results are quite impressive, they cannot be generalized over all group situations in which an expert is present. For example, if there is a co-oriented peer besides the expert, and both function as referent persons, then the scene can change completely.

In their chapter on social comparison processes referring to Festinger's (1954) theory, Jones and Gerard (1967) proposed that the individual, as a problem solver, generally seeks answers to two types of questions. One type deals with the procedures and steps necessary to reach a certain goal.

Here the expert with his superior knowledge and skills is the appropriate person to consult. In this type of situation the relationship between the two participants tends to be asymmetrical, because the expert's interaction with the nonexpert is from a perspective that is superior to that of the nonexpert. If the question deals with the attractiveness of some considered goal or concerns the moral acceptability of actions or outcomes of actions, then the person should experience a need to communicate with someone with a similar frame of reference, with respect to value orientation, fate, and life perspective. In such a situation the person and his co-oriented peer interact from similar perspectives. Jones and Gerard state that communication with both types of persons will give the subject certainty. It is the purpose of this paper to show that the presence of a co-oriented peer diminishes the expert's influence during high participation more than during low participation.

THE HYPOTHESES

Assuming that the problem-solving person will take an interest in information from both expert and co-oriented peer and, assuming that both types of information will carry a certain weight in his decision-making, one can infer the following hypotheses.

Hypothesis 1: When disagreement exists between expert and nonexpert and where a difference in value orientation appears, the influence of the expert on the decision-making of the nonexpert will be smaller when the nonexpert has a chance to co-orient himself with a peer than when co-orientation is precluded.

Hypothesis 2: During participative decision-making between a low co-oriented expert and a highly co-oriented nonexpert, the effective influence of the expert will increase as a function of the duration of the interaction.

Hypothesis 3: The increase of expert power influence due to increasing participation of expert and nonexpert will be less evident in conditions where the subject can co-orient with a peer than when this type of co-orientation is precluded.

Hypothesis 4: A nonexpert will experience a stronger sense of competence in situations where he achieves a consensus on values (and consistency over modalities) during the process of co-orientating with peers, as compared to situations where such co-orientation is precluded.

To test these hypotheses we must use a group decision problem with alternatives which differ not only in acceptability with respect to rational reasons (means and ends relations) but also with respect to values. Mulder's town planning problem meets these conditions insofar as more weight is given to social values in one solution while the other gives more recognition to the technical and economic aspects of the problem.

Consider the condition where a person, interacting with someone else who appears to be more competent than himself (i.e., an expert) discovers that the solution advocated by the expert differs from his own with respect to value priorities. It stands to reason that the subject will be less influenced in his judgment by such a person than by one who is not only more competent than the subject but at the same time more similar with respect to value priorities. However, in the case where such a person is not present in the situation the subject will be more susceptible to influence by the more competent person. This appears to be a condition of low co-orientation.

The situation, however, will change once the person discovers the presence of a third person, B, who appears to be equal in competence and who apparently shares the same value orientation and preference for one of the solutions. In this case we may expect that the person will be more inclined to continue consideration of his own solution as best. Now disagreements with A will tend to be interpreted as a matter of difference in value orientation. This second situation can be considered as a condition of high co-orientation. Within the low co-orientation condition, high participation will tend to favor A's influence because of his competence. However, while the same tendency might be active within the high co-orientation condition, the value agreement between the subject and his peer will tend to slow down the process.

METHOD

SUBJECTS

Subjects were first-year male students who were invited to volunteer at the end of the introductory class lectures. They were drawn from five disciplines: geography, anthropology, sociology, education, and psychology.

Testing the four hypotheses requires, at a minimum, two co-orientation conditions (high and low), two participation conditions (high and low), and one level of expertness (high). We acknowledge, with respect to the last requirement, that two levels of expertness would have been more desirable for testing the hypothesis of the paradox. Nonetheless, if the paradox is a valid hypothesis, the high expertness-high participation condition should show a greater number of people accepting A's standpoint than the high expertness-low participation condition (by Hypothesis 2).

EXPERIMENTAL PROCEDURE AND CONDITION INDUCTIONS

The subjects were randomly assigned to the conditions, all of which were run in a random sequence. At the start of each session the subjects met the experimenter in groups of two or three persons. One person was in fact the role player who later would act as the expert person. They were invited to consider themselves as a team of town planners whose task it was to give advice to the boards of various institutions. First they completed a test (Raven's progressive matrices) which was allegedly predictive of one's success for the kind of task at hand. The subjects were then requested to study, individually and in separate rooms, a certain planning problem (the choice of a site for a hospital), and then propose a provisional solution, accompanied by five supporting arguments. The experimenter then asked them to begin an exchange of ideas followed by a final decision. This exchange took place by means of written messages taken to and from each subject by a messenger. After the last message had been exchanged the subject wrote down his final decision.

THE MANIPULATION OF EXPERTNESS

As a result of inducing only one level of difference in expertness between the subject and person A, the effectiveness of the paradox could be tested only through the comparison of the high expertness-low participation condition with the high expertness-high participation condition. Expertness was realized in three ways. During the introductory period, the subject saw one of his partners excel on the test that the experimenter had indicated was predictive of success on the experimental task (impression of expertness). Secondly, having arrived in his separate room, the subject was requested by the experimenter to formulate arguments which could support his choice. Therefore, while the arguments were supportive, their quality was generally poor. In contrast with those were the expert's arguments, which were all constructed as syllogisms. In addition, they all referred explicitly to other arguments. Hence, a large difference in the quality of the expert's and subject's arguments was created. Thirdly, in the high participation condition, a subject could produce only half the number of arguments that he would receive from the expert (quantity).

CO-ORIENTATION

This factor was operationalized during the exchange of the messages phase. In the high co-orientation condition the subject communicated simultaneously with both A (expert) and B (peer). B, an equally competent naive subject, could function as such because he had chosen the same alternative as the subject. We deviated from what might be thought ideal, from an experimental point of view, in that B was not a role player—the procedure of the role player was not adopted for the co-orientation factor because the experimenter was not sufficiently acquainted with what one might call the "cues" in the communication that can be considered as typical for co-orientation. As far as the means of communication are concerned, all parties worked exclusively by means of written messages. In the low co-orientation condition the subject could communicate with A only.

PARTICIPATION

Participation was manipulated by varying the number of messages that the subject exchanged with his partners. The high participator wrote ten messages to a partner, whereas the low participator's correspondence was stopped after five messages.

THE DEPENDENT VARIABLES

The main dependent variable was the decision of the subject to leave his earlier choice and to adopt A's point of view. The second dependent variable was the degree of expertness which a subject attributed to both the expert (to a peer) and to himself. This last variable was tapped by means of a questionnaire consisting of seven-point Likert-type questions completed by the subject at the end of the communication period.

ANALYSIS OF THE DATA

It should be mentioned that in the high co-orientation conditions twice as many subjects were run than in the low co-orientation condition. This occurred because in the high co-orientation condition the decision of a subject to adopt or not to adopt A's standpoint was statistically not independent of the partner's decision. Thus, from each pair of subjects in the high co-orientation condition only one of them was randomly selected to have their scores on the dependent variables considered in the analysis. The actual number of "statistical subjects" per cell was thirteen.

The choice data were analyzed by means of chi-square tests, while analyses of variance were used for examining the subject's perceptions of expertness, as measured by the Likert scales.

RESULTS

CHANGE IN THE STANDPOINT OF A SUBJECT

Each subject indicated both at the beginning and end of the task what he believed to be the best solution to the planning problem by answering the following question:

"Looking at my own arguments and at the information I have received from my partner(s), I think that the best site to build the hospital is:
1) the park in the center of the city,
2) the meadow at the border of the city.
Place a circle around the site you want to recommend."

From the results shown in Table 10-2 it is evident that there is only one main effect. That is, subjects in the high co-orientation condition adopted A's point of view less often. It is clear that only Hypothesis 1 is supported by the data. The chi-square for co-orientation was 8.04, $p < .01$. The main effects for participation, expected from Hypothesis 2, and the interaction effect, expected from Hypothesis 3, did not appear.

TABLE 10-2
Number of subjects adopting A's point of view

	Low participation	High participation	Total
Low co-orientation	8	9	17
High co-orientation	2	2	4
Total	10	11	21

TABLE 10-3
Change in relative preference for a certain site

	Low participation		High participation	
	Initial choice	Final choice	Initial choice	Final choice
Low co-orientation	2.24	4.33	2.57	4.18
High co-orientation	2.23	2.67	2.41	2.82

Note: A high score indicates a strong preference for A's choice.

The subject also indicated his relative preference for one of the sites by checking a point on a response scale where the two sites functioned as poles.

Analysis of variance revealed a co-orientation effect: $F(1,48) = 16.50$, $p < .01$. This is apparently due to the stronger adherence by subjects in the high co-orientation condition to their earlier preferences. Furthermore, there also appears a significant shift to A's point of view: $F(1,48) = 66.02$, $p < .001$. However, this shift occurs primarily in the low co-orientation condition: $F(1,48) = 26.36$, $p < .001$.[1] Nonetheless the t test for changes is significant in both co-orientation conditions: t(low co.) $p < .01$, t(high co.) $p < .05$. Thus, the preference data provide some evidence for Hypothesis 1 but not for Hypotheses 2 or 3.

PERCEIVED EXPERTNESS

From Hypothesis 2 we expected that subjects would explicitly recognize A's higher skill and knowledge with the type of problem at hand. In Hypothesis 4 we proposed that those in the high co-orientation condition would perceive smaller differences in expertness between themselves and A. With respect to such perceptions each subject answered the following question: "Did you have the impression that the arguments of other(s) were weaker or stronger than your own arguments?" The responses to this question can be found in Table 10-4.

The answers were given on seven-point Likert scales. Hence, the scale average of 3.5 would indicate that A's arguments and one's own were judged to be of equal strength. From the averages in Table 10-4 one can conclude that A's expertness was explicitly recognized. Analysis of variance indicated that the difference between himself and A was smaller in the high co-orientation condition ($F(1,48) = 5.14$; $P < .05$). When we analyzed the separate judgments for one's own expertness and that of the partner(s), the same tendencies show up. Here, using a repeated measures analysis of variance, A is found once again to be perceived as superior (for the difference between self-other, $F(1,48) = 12.80$; $p < .01$). These differ-

TABLE 10-4
Judgment of A's relative to one's own arguments

	Low participation	High participation
Low co-orientation	4.97	4.76
High co-orientation	4.08	4.35

Note: A high score indicates a favorable view of A's expertness.

ences also appear to be smaller in the high co-orientation condition than in low co-orientation)for co-orientation X difference/self-other, $F(1,49) = 5.57$; $p < .05$). This result is in accordance with hypothesis 4. Answers to other additional questions made it clear that A is also perceived as more logical, systematic and clear in the presentation of his argument (t's are respectively 4.50; 2.50, $p < .05$). We should, however, stress the point that in this last set of data the co-orientation effect was not observed. Hence hypothesis 4 is not supported consistently by all the data.

VALUE ORIENTATIONS

In the method section it was inferred that the subject and A differed in value orientations. An examination of the arguments written by the subjects revealed a predominant concern for social considerations. The messages written for A, however, weighed the social criteria against technical and economic criteria. Therefore we expected that the subjects would attribute a different value orientation to A. To see whether this difference would be significant, and whether it would be stronger in high co-orientation conditions than in low, we inserted a few questions concerning this topic into the final questionnaire. The results for these items appear in Tables 5 and 6.

The tables reveal that the subjects did indeed think that A was more economical and less social in his style of thinking. Both differences were

TABLE 10-5
Degree to which subjects infer social goals from own and A's arguments

	Low participation		High participation	
	Subject	Person A	Subject	Person A
Low co-orientation	4.94	4.25	5.33	3.44
High co-orientation	5.75	3.59	5.28	3.38

Note: A higher score indicates a stronger social orientation.

TABLE 10-6
Degree to which subjects infer economic goals in own and A's arguments

	Low participation		High participation	
	Subject	Person A	Subject	Person A
Low co-orientation	3.57	4.87	3.34	5.35
High co-orientation	3.07	4.85	3.63	5.66

Note: A higher score indicates a stronger social orientation.

significant: $F(1,48) = 65$ and $F(1,48) = 40$, respectively, $p < .001$. As one might expect, when the subject is in the high co-orientation condition, he sees no difference between his own and his partner's (B) value orientation. Therefore, we may conclude that in those conditions the subject experienced low co-orientation between himself and A.

DISCUSSION

The data supported the hypothesis that, when disagreement exists between expert and nonexpert and where a difference in value orientation appears, the influence of the expert on the decision-making of the nonexpert will be smaller when the nonexpert has a chance to co-orient himself with a peer than when co-orientation is precluded. In accordance with this hypothesis subjects did think more favorably about the quality of their arguments when co-orientation with a partner was high. This more favorable judgment about their arguments appears not to generalize, however, to judgment about one's own competence. For instance, subjects in the high co-orientation conditions did not think more favorably of their style and logic of writing than did subjects in the low co-orientation condition.

It becomes evident that the subjects in this experiment did attribute to their more competent partner, A, a different, more economical, value orientation. Surprisingly enough no participation effects showed up. This means that either the paradox is not true or that the difference in expertness employed was not large enough. Since more than 70% of the subjects in the no co-orientation condition changed their standpoints, this last assumption appears not to be valid. Perhaps more definitive conclusions could have been drawn if the design had provided for a low expertness condition.

From Table 10-2 we see that the expert's influence in the low participation-low co-orientation condition is already very considerable—61% of the subjects appear to have changed their point of view. A second interpretation is that the subjects were impressed by A's earlier achievements on the test (ascribed expertness) which, subsequently, made A's arguments more favorable. This second interpretation implies that the other criteria for expertness (number of valid consistent arguments, number of consistently applied modalities) made a weaker impression on the subject. Perhaps the number of arguments and the consistency over modalities do play a less important role for the person who has to decide on a problem where his value orientations are at stake. It may also be that the principle of consistency over persons is more relevant here. These considerations trigger another question: do we have any evidence that our results signify something more than a simple majority effect? Some support for the co-orientation interpretation resides, of course, in the earlier mentioned consensus on social and economic values which the subject perceives with Partner B in the high co-orientation condition.

The answer is inconclusive, on the other hand, if we look at our design, which indeed does not separate the effect of co-orientation from a possible majority-minority effect (i.e., research from Moscovici and Faucheux, 1972, gives evidence supporting manifest majority effects and latent minority influences).

In order to bring some clarity to this problem we conducted a second experiment in which the design allowed us to distinguish between majority effects and co-orientation effects. This was accomplished by utilizing three levels for the co-orientation factor and two levels each for both the expertness factor and the participation factor.

Considerations of space prevent us from presenting a detailed discussion of the procedure and results of this experiment. In comparison with our first experiment, however, the major improvement consisted of the introduction of a co-orientation condition where the subject was confronted with the letters of a peer who shared his values but nonetheless preferred a third solution, a standpoint that did not coincide with either the subject's or the expert's point of view (co-orientation pure). If our co-orientation arguments are valid, a subject should maintain his point of view in this condition as often as he does in the condition where he shares both values as well as standpoint with a peer. The data of this experiment showed exactly this result. That is, under conditions of co-orientation, similarity in value orientations, rather than consensus about specific solutions, is the more decisive variable in explaining the co-orientation effect.

On the other hand, the results of this study do support some of the hypotheses proposed by Mulder. For example, it was found that the influence of expert power on the thinking and decision-making of the nonexperts increased as a function of the difference in expertise between expert and nonexpert. In addition, we also found support for the idea that expertness becomes more effective under conditions of high participation.

NOTE

1. In all cases F was calculated by means of the largest error term available.

REFERENCES

Festinger, L. A theory of social comparison processes. *Human Relations*, 1954, *7*, 117-140.

French, J.R.P., J. Israël, and P. As. An experiment on participation in a Norwegian factory. *Human Relations*, 1960, *19*, 3-20.

Heider, T. *The Psychology of Interpersonal Relations*. New York: Wiley, 1958.

Jones, E.E., and H. Gerard. *Foundations of Social Psychology*. New York: Wiley, 1967.

Kelley, H.H. Attribution theory in social psychology. In D. Levine (Ed.), *Nebraska Symposium on Motivation*. Lincoln: University Nebraska Press, 1967.

Kelley, H.H., and J.W. Thibaut. Problem solving. In G. Lindzey and E. Aronson (Eds.), *The Handbook of Social Psychology*. Reading, Mass.: Addison-Wesley, 1969.

Kolaja, I. *Worker's Councils. The Yugoslav experience*. Tavistrek Publications, 1965.

Moscovici, S. and D. Faucheux. Social Influence, conformity bias, and the study of active minorities. In L. Berkowitz (Ed.), *Advances in Experimental Social Psychology*, Vol. 6. New York: Academic Press, 1972.

Mulder, M., and H. Wilke. Participation and power equalization. *Organizational Behavior and Human Performances*, 1970, *5*, 430-448.

Verhagen, E.J. Koörientatie in machtsverhoudingen. Stichting Studentenpers, Nijmegen, 1976.

PART III

MIXED-MOTIVE INTERACTION

Introduction by Heinz Schuler

"One thousand studies do not a theory make," Fitch (1976) has concluded following his review of Rubin and Borwn's (1975) ambitious collection of studies in bargaining and negotiation. Indeed, this seems to be an accurate assessment, at the moment, of the theory-deficient field of mixed-motive interaction. The following section contains two empirical studies, both of which investigate issues likely to be essential for further fruitful theorizing, and for narrowing the gap between experimental bargaining situations and real-life interaction processes. One of the two other papers to follow is a proposal for categorizing mixed-motive studies, which could easily be interpreted as in competition with Rubin and Brown's taxonomy if it were not for different emphases—especially reflections concerning generalizability. The other theoretical contribution makes a connection between this section and the preceding one by stressing emotional relations in reward allocation processes.

The following section begins with Ian Morley's paper on "The Character of Experimental Studies of Bargaining and Negotiation." Going beyond the sheer enumeration of such studies, he attempts to classify the paradigms now in use in order to outline their specific functions and to discuss some problems of generalizing laboratory results to actual cases. Although Morley gives particular attention to experimental studies, he recognizes the urgency of theoretically framing and integrating the stream of empirical results. For this task, he proposes a solution that differs conceptually from that presented by Rubin and Brown (1975), who tried to set up a complete list of structural and social psychological characteristics of bargaining relationships that would include all relevant studies.

Morley's starting point is that experimental studies are laboratory simulations of real negotiations. By showing the formation process for structural analogies, he tries to reduce the complexity of deciding which sort of bargaining situation is simulated by which laboratory paradigm. In simulating real bargaining, Morley states that the investigator must first define the behavior he is trying to simulate; secondly, he must identify certain key components of that behavior; and, finally, he must translate those components into components of a laboratory task. Thus, differences in tasks are to be recognized as a *mixtum compositum* of different characteristics from real-life situations to be simulated and different problem solutions chosen by the investigator.

Reflecting the state of the art, Morley's paper shows that empirical research has yet to overcome the criticisms of Nemeth (1970) and others. Their central target was the Prisoner's Dilemma, but the accompanying arguments were nonetheless sufficiently general to include most other paradigms as well: these games lack an adequate social context; communication is restricted to an extent that the partner may be forgotten; negotiation lacks multidimensionality; there is a lack of clarity as to which are the exchangeable resources; and so on. These may be the reasons why behavior in experimental games has proven to be extremely instruction dependent and has included less reciprocity in interaction than behavior in naturalistic settings.

Considering these problems, one may conclude that Morley has wisely stressed the concept-paradigm relationship and the problem of external validity. If further experimentation is to result in major advances, its planning must surely proceed from this sort of theorizing rather than from attempts to study some combination of variables that has not been tried heretofore.

The contribution by Geoffrey Stephenson focuses on one of the most neglected determinants of negotiation behavior—the relationship between the negotiators and their respective groups. Loyal members and delegates from competing groups will, as Stephenson sees it, adopt incompatible positions, reflecting or even further sharpening the conflict of interest between the groups. How do negotiators succeed in faithfully advocating their group's interests, yet reach a compromise acceptable to both sides? While the vast majority of empirical bargaining studies abstracts elements from this social milieu, and represents the negotiators as being responsible only to themselves and their own goals, Stephenson pleads for emphasizing the negotiators' *interparty orientation*.

He presents data from actual industrial decisions. The exchanged arguments arising during discussion were submitted to an analysis of *role identifiability,* where subjects attributed the statements from labeled transcripts of discussion to speakers of the respective sides. From the differential accuracy or identifiability he postulates three phases of the decision or negotiation process. The first phase ("interparty exchange") is characterized as a tough demonstration of one's own standpoint and ends in an implicit agreement concerning the relative claims. The second phase ("interpersonal exchange") is interpreted as problem solving behavior, in the course of which the agreement of the first part is formulated in terms of available decision alternatives. Finally, in the third phase ("group decision-making"), the negotiation process is concluded by mutual consent in the form of an explicit agreement.

To what extent the three postulated phases might be heavily dependent upon experimental conditions (the groups negotiated in three sessions at different times) was considered in discussion following the presentation. Other procedural sequences, of course, might well have led to different outcomes. Furthermore, the key theoretical concept of role identifiability could perhaps be operationalized in various ways, and the low percentages of arguments identified suggest other, more reliable categorizations are possible. In any case, Stephenson demonstrated that situational constraints in bargaining experiments may be responsible for many of the problems with external validity often alleged to exist in experimental bargaining and negotiation studies.

The paper by Mikula and Schwinger deals with reward allocations. Mikula and Schwinger consider it a misconception, widely shared among equity theorists, to assume that only one norm of justice exists in a given relationship. In fact, they argue, there are several different justice principles which can be applied (e.g., the contribution principle, the need principle, and the equality principle). Therefore, decisions about the allocation of group rewards can be seen as choices among these different principles. Which allocation rule is chosen should depend, among other things, on the quality of the relationship among the interacting persons. The authors put forward several plausible notions, and also some supporting data, that groups with predominantly positive relations share their goods (by following the equality principle) in a way different from those with neutral or negative relations; persons expecting future interaction will behave differently (e.g., tend more to an allocation which can be expected to produce a favorable image) from those without expectations of future contact.

Mikula and Schwinger discuss in detail the function of what they call the *politeness ritual.* The ritual refers to the generous gesture to pass, as a winner, a higher part of the common reward to the partner than appropriate in light of the contribution principle, or, as a loser, to claim for oneself a smaller share than commensurate with the equality principle. One of the functions of politeness is to fulfill the *norm of responsibility;* further, one may gain social approval and status from a partner and from the experimenter for showing modesty and generosity. Finally, the polite person can one day expect his partner to reciprocate his rewarding behavior.

The observation that this "polite" behavior is rather common in experimental reward allocation leads, of course, to the suspicion that some of the described behavioral regularities might be specific to a situation which is insignificant in view of the minimal resources to be distributed. If one calls to mind, say, wage negotiations as a real-life instance of reward allocation, it seems that at least two essential parameters—importance of resources to be allocated and social attachment to the represented group (see Stephenson)—change the picture so radically from the experimental situation created by Mikula and Schwinger that the empirical results are hardly applicable. In a different sense, however, the reward allocation paradigm is of relatively high external validity, if compared with most of the negotiation games described by Morley or especially those described by Rubin and Brown. While experimental games, especially Prisoner's Dilemma games, are reduced to a type of problem-solving situation that raises many doubts whether subjects even comprehend the situation as a social one, the reward allocation paradigm is doubtlessly understood as a social situation. This consideration should remind us not to focus our attention too narrowly on the tiny financial gains that are divided among subjects in the experiment. The fundamental dogma in equity theory, "Individuals will try to maximize their outcomes" (Austin, Walster, and Utne, 1976, p. 164), surely cannot mean that they are trying to derive only or predominantly financial profit from a bargaining situation. Rather, they may seek other returns that have some sort of reward characteristic, be it only the warm feeling of having acted altruistically. An excellent example of this is provided by one of Mikula's male subjects who waited as long as two hours at the door of the institute for a girl upon whom he generously bestowed a larger part of the common reward than would have been "just" in view of her performance.

Finally, with the sort of bargaining procedure Morley would probably classify as a "distribution game," but which differs from the most popular games by allowing participants to make offers for compromise without restricting the total number of their interactions, Müller and Crott continue a research program, first initiated by Crott and his coworkers (Crott, Lumpp, and Wildermuth, 1976) a few years ago. The central point of this project is the motivational orientation of the negotiators and the relation to rewards and punishments in the bargaining situation.

Müller and Crott investigate how the three motivational components, (a) individualistic motivation, (b) social motivation, and (c) competitive motivation, are influenced by the magnitude of possible gains and by participants' bargaining experience. Neglecting bargaining experience may be another illustration of the reasons that many studies in this field suffer from a lack of external validity. Thus, Müller and Crott's investigation of negotiation experience was particularly valuable. They found that experienced subjects differed in motivational orientation from inexperienced subjects as well as in actual punitive behavior, at least at the beginning of the bargaining process. Another important result was a motivational change in all groups: A decreasing individualistic and competitive orientation, accompanied by an increasing social orientation. At the same time, and seemingly in contrast to the result just reported, a "seesaw effect" was frequently observed in the use of cost-raising penalties.

One problem to be considered was the degree of correspondence between the motivational dimensions and overt behavior. That is to say, is the use of penalties really a behavioral expression of competitive orientation? As the authors themselves recognize, punishment seems to be rather an unsuccessful attempt to induce the partner to comply, and in turn leads to the seesaw effect. Indeed, available reviews on this topic present few studies showing evidence that competitiveness increases during bargaining. The relation between motivational and behavioral variables becomes even more complicated by considering that, during bargaining, the *meaning* of what is called, for example, "individualistic motivation" may be changed. Such conceptual difficulties may lead one to question in principle the usefulness of postulating a "motivational moderator" variable between situational characteristics and observed behavior. On the other hand, everyone seems to agree that theories applicable to mixed-motive situations are at least as urgently needed as further empirical work.

One possible stimulus to further theory not considered in the chapters of this section is a consideration of *power*. What has come to be called *legitimate power* seems a good candidate for conceptual integration into various theories of reward allocation or negotiation. Power, then, might serve the function of a norm-determining factor; the more powerful one of the interaction partners, the more he has the option or the "right" (which could be conceptualized as a preallocation norm) to choose between different allocation norms. As Deutsch (1973) has shown, *legitimate* power can be effective in preventing "autistic" conflicts, while confidence usually is higher when *reward* or *coercive power* is low. And, such a result could be relevant to studies varying rewards and punishments (e.g., Müller and Crott or Stephenson). One might distinguish between *distributive* and *procedural justice* after the fashion of Homans (1976). In the case of extremely unequal contributions in a reward allocation task, the equality principle might be considered unjust in terms of *distributive justice,* but it may well be appropriate when seen as a problem of *procedural justice.* Perhaps that is why actual reward allocation on the average falls roughly between the contribution principle and equality principle. After all, Homans has suggested that the essential problem in justice is, besides finding the appropriate justice principle, deciding on the dimensions for comparing the contributions and rewards of different individuals and groups (Homans, 1976, p. 37).

REFERENCES

Austin, W., E. Walster, and M.K. Utne. Equity and the law. In L. Berkowitz (Ed.), *Advances in experimental social psychology,* 1976, *9,* 163-190.

Crott, H.W., R.R. Lumpp, and R. Wildermuth. Der Einsatz von Belohnungen und Bestrafungen in einer Verhandlungssituation. In H. Brandstätter and H. Schuler (Eds.), *Entscheidungsprozesse in Gruppen.* Bern: Huber, 1976, 147-162.

Deutsch, M. *The Resolution of Conflict.* New Haven: Yale University Press, 1973.

Fitch, G. One thousand studies do not a theory make. *Contemporary Psychology,* 1976, *21,* 265-266.

Homans, G.C. Commentary. In L. Berkowitz (Ed.), *Advances in Experimental Social Psychology*, 1976, *9,* 231-244.

Nemeth, C. Bargaining and reciprocity. *Psychological Bulletin,* 1970, *74,* 297-308.

Rubin, J.Z., and B.R. Brown. *The Social Psychology of Bargaining and Negotiation.* New York: Academic Press, 1975.

11

BARGAINING AND NEGOTIATION:
THE CHARACTER OF EXPERIMENTAL STUDIES

Ian E. Morley

INTRODUCTION

"It goes without saying that, in order to be able to deal with negotiation either conceptually or experimentally, we must simplify it." (Bartos 1970, p. 46).

The laboratory study of "bargaining" and "negotiation" probably dates from Hoffman, Festinger, and Lawrence's (1954) paper, "Tendencies toward Group Comparability in Competitive Bargaining." The precise date is, of course, unimportant. Let it suffice to say that, by now, the literature is voluminous. To obtain a general picture of the "state of the art" it is, therefore, necessary to identify and evaluate the major laboratory *paradigms* which have been used. (By a paradigm I mean "a range of experimental procedures with something significant in common" [Dulany, 1974, p. 44]).

In general, laboratory studies may be identified as one of the seven types shown below:

(1) Abstract games of a matrix type, such as the "Prisoner's Dilemma", deriving from the work of Deutsch (1958) and Scodel et al. (1959). Games of this sort remain extremely popular and over 300 Prisoner's Dilemma

games have been conducted within the last ten years (Rubin and Brown, 1976). The interested reader is referred to reviews by Rapoport and Orwant (1962); Gallo and McClintock (1965); Rapoport and Chammah (1965, 1966); Rapoport (1968); Terhune (1968, 1970); Wyer (1969); Swingle (1970a); Oskamp (1971); Nemeth (1972); McClintock (1972); Wrightsman, O'Connor, and Baker (1972); and Apfelbaum (1974).

(2) Abstract games of a mechanical or electromechanical type, deriving from the work of Deutsch and Krauss (1960) using the Acme-Bolt trucking game. Other examples are provided by Shure, Meeker, and Hansford (1965); Swingle (1967); and Sermat (1970). For general review material the reader is referred to Swingle (1970a, 1970b) and Deutsch (1973).

(3) Pachisi (or Parcheesi) board studies of coalition formation, deriving from the work of Vinacke and Arkoff (1957). Such studies are less common than they used to be. Reviews have been published by Gamson (1964); Caplow (1968); Vinacke (1969); and Rubin and Brown (1975, pp. 64-80). Other studies of coalition formation do exist (e.g., Gamson, 1961) but will not be considered in this paper.

(4) Abstract games of a distribution type, deriving from Kelley's (1966) "classroom study of the dilemmas in interpersonal negotiations" (e.g., Morgan and Sawyer, 1967; Fischer, 1970; Benton and Druckman, 1974; Froman and Cohen, 1969). A detailed review of this material has been provided by Morley and Stephenson (1977).

(5) Realistic games of economic exchange, deriving from Siegel and Fouraker's (1960, 1964) studies of bilateral monopoly. Reviews of this literature have appeared in Katonah (1962); Kelley and Schenitzki (1972); and Morley and Stephenson (1977).

(6) Role-playing debates, deriving from Campbell's (1960) paper on the effects of partisan commitment (Note 1) and from Manheim's (1960) test of the hypothesis (from Williams, 1947) that the greater the differentiation between groups the greater the likelihood of conflict between them. Other examples are provided by Crow (1963); Evan and MacDougall (1967); Morley and Stephenson (1969, 1970a); and Frey and Adams (1972). Studies of this sort are becoming increasingly common and have been reviewed in Morley and Stephenson (1977).

(7) Substitute debates, used by McGrath and his associates to study negotiation between members of student groups (Julian and McGrath, Note 2; McGrath and Julian, 1963; Vidmar and McGrath, Note 5), and by Stephenson, Skinner, and Brotherton (1976) to investigate the effects of attitudinal commitment and preparation for negotiation.

If bargaining is involved whenever "the ability of one participant to gain his ends is dependent to an important degree on the choices or decisions that the other participants will make" (Schelling, 1968, p. 5), negotiation may be defined as a subclass of bargaining: i.e., as bargaining which explicitly involves a process of bid and counterbid. Consequently, it may be argued that paradigms (1) and (2) involve tacit bargaining and that paradigms (3) and (4) involve explicit bargaining (i.e., negotiation). From this point of view it is possible to say that bargaining and negotiation have been studied extensively (see Swingle, 1970a; Smith, 1974; Deutsch, 1973; Wrightsman, O'Connor, and Baker, 1972; Rubin and Brown, 1975); from another point of view it is not. If negotiation is defined as a process of joint decision-making involving verbal communication about the issues involved, bargaining may be regarded as a subclass of negotiation: i.e., negotiation in which participants search for agreement by discussing how to manage disputes between them. It may then be argued that paradigms (1) to (3) involve a form of strategic decision-making other than bargaining (Nemeth, 1972; Morley and Stephenson, 1977), and that paradigms (4) to (7) involve bargaining, defined as negotiation for agreement. From this point of view the reader will be unable to find anything like the same volume of literature ready at hand (Morley, 1976; McGrath, 1966).

But differences between the paradigms involve rather more than differences in definition. If the research is to be evaluated properly it is necessary to show how the paradigms arise, and to indicate which aspects of bargaining and/or negotiation they are trying to reproduce. In other words (using more technical language) what is required is an account which treats experimental studies as gaming simulations of real-life tasks. The term *gaming* indicates that the study of subjects engaged in laboratory tasks has been substituted for the study of decision makers at work, and that the games subjects play are games of strategy. The term *simulation* emphasizes that, while the different paradigms involve different procedures and different experimental materials, *each arises as a response to the same basic set of questions.*

The object of the exercise is to provide a simple laboratory analogue of a more complex real-life task (Bartos, 1970; see also Guetzkow, 1962, 1968; Hermann, 1967; Coplin, 1966). By simulation, I mean "the process of selecting and generating a set of properties which represent, in part or whole, the essential properties of a setting for social action" (Wager and Palola, 1964, p. 418). Consequently, the experimenter must deal with three sorts of problem: first, he must define the behavior he is trying to simulate; secondly, he must identify certain key components of that behavior; and finally, he must translate those components into components of a laboratory task. Different solutions to these problems lead to different paradigms. Each problem will be considered in turn.

THE GAMING SIMULATION OF BARGAINING AND NEGOTIATION

THE BEHAVIOR WHICH IS TO BE SIMULATED

Morley and Stephenson (1977) have shown that the literature on bargaining and negotiation contains a great deal of semantic confusion: different definitions have been given to the same term and different labels have been used to mark the same concept. What Fink (1968) has said of definitions of social conflict applies equally to the functions of bargaining and negotiation: "Sometimes a given pair of terms may be synonymous; in other contexts they may refer to sharply distinguished coordinate categories; and in still other contexts, the first may be a special case of the second, or vice versa" (p. 430).

Here it will be sufficient to indicate that a large number of different definitions exist; introduce the definitions supplied by Morley and Stephenson; and show why these definitions have been chosen.

Consider the following passage from P.G. Wodehouse's *Aunts Aren't Gentlemen:*

> "How much do I want, sir?"
> "Yes. Give it a name. We won't haggle."
> He pursed his lips.
> "I'm afraid," he said, having unpursed them, "I couldn't do it as cheap as I'd like, sir. . . . I'd have to make it twenty pounds."
> I was relieved. I had been expecting something higher. He, too, seemed to feel that he had erred on the side of moderation, for he immediately added:
> "Or, rather, thirty."
> "Thirty."
> "Thirty, sir."
> "Let's haggle," I said.
> But when I suggested twenty-five, a nicer looking sort of number than thirty, he shook his grey head regretfully, so we went on haggling, and he haggled better than me, so that eventually we settled on thirty-five.
> It wasn't one of my best haggling days. (pp. 100-101).

This short extract illustrates many of the defining characteristics of negotiation, as I shall use the term.

1. Negotiation involves more than just a conflict of opinion, it involves a process of *joint decision-making.*

2. Negotiators have different preferences concerning the set of actions which might be taken.

3. Negotiation situations are mixed-motive situations. As Nemeth (1972) has said, each negotiator will have "a motive for cooperation in order to reach a mutually agreeable solution and, simultaneously, a motive for competition in order to gain at the other's expense" (p. 210).

4. Negotiation allows the possibility of strategic decision-making of one sort or another. The ability of A to get what he wants depends upon the moves B will make. Each may be guided by his expectations of what the other will accept. Each may attempt to manipulate the expectations held by his opponent (Walton and McKersie, 1965; Jervis, 1970).

5. Negotiation involves *talking* about a relationship before doing any-thing about it (Kelley and Schenitzki, 1972). At one extreme this may involve a thoroughgoing discussion-to-consensus; at the other it may simply involve an exchange of bids.

Two further questions must be answered before a formal definition can be given, as Lall's (1966) discussion makes clear. Firstly, how is negotia-tion to be distinguished from enquiry, mediation, conciliation, arbitration, judicial settlement, and so on? Secondly, does negotiation necessarily involve a willingness to make concessions in order to reach agreement? Morley and Stephenson have followed Lall in excluding arbitration and other judicial processes from the domain of negotiation. However, unlike Lall, they have allowed negotiation to have different objectives (See Jensen, 1963; Iklé, 1964). In particular, they have adopted Iklé's distinc-tion between negotiation "for side effects" and negotiation "for agree-ment."

Formally, Morley and Stephenson (1977) have defined *negotiation* as: "Any form of verbal communication, direct or indirect, whereby parties to a conflict of interest discuss, without resort to arbitration or other judicial processes, the form of the joint action they might take to manage a dispute between them" (p. 26). *Bargaining* is then defined as one form of negotiation, namely *negotiation for agreement.*

In contrast, psychologists have, in general, adopted the *widest possible definition of bargaining* in which bargaining situations are simply situa-tions involving strategic interdependence of the participants. It was in this sense that Schelling was using the term when he defined bargaining as "Any activity in which each party is guided mainly by his expectations of what the other will accept" (Schelling, 1960, p. 21). Schelling, of course, wished to emphasize certain similarities between situations involving negotiation and situations involving limited war. In his own words, "The subject includes both explicit bargaining and the tacit kind in which adversaries watch and interpret each other's behavior, each aware that his own actions are being interpreted and anticipated, each acting with a view to the expectations he creates" (Schelling, 1960, p. 21).

It is, of course, perfectly legitimate (and, at times, extremely useful) to identify similarities between different classes of conflict, but it is important to realize that bargaining, in Schelling's sense, excludes two of the defining characteristics of bargaining identified above. *Any mixed-motive game of strategy will be defined as a bargaining game in Schelling's sense.* The experiments of a matrix game or electromechanical type which dominate social psychological research on bargaining are, by definition, studies of bargaining behavior, broadly defined in this way. Such studies may still be relevant to the study of bargaining in the more restricted sense in which Morley and Stephenson define it. However, they will no longer be defined as relevant, since they involve a form of strategic decision-making other than negotiation. There is not, as yet, a substantial body of laboratory research dealing with the process of negotiation for agreement, as defined in this paper (see Sawyer and Guetzkow, 1965; McGrath, 1966; Stephenson, 1971; Morley, 1976; Morley and Stephenson, 1977).

IDENTIFICATION OF THE KEY COMPONENTS OF BARGAINING BEHAVIOR

"A game is a *simple* model of the world. But to start gaming, you have to have a simple model" (M.G. Weiner, cited in Wilson, 1970, p. 113). Consequently, it is necessary to identify the essential aspects of the real-life task and to reproduce as many of these as is possible under laboratory conditions. Some essential components have already been identified. Different types of negotiation may differ in detail, but if negotiation for agreement is to be simulated at all the laboratory task must (by definition) be one in which subjects (a) perceive a conflict of interest, (b) exchange verbal communication aimed at reaching a joint decision with respect to the issues which divide them, (c) engage in (or be able to engage in) strategic decision-making, and (d) incur costs if the interaction persists too long or escalates too far.

Other important elements are suggested by a number of theoretical approaches to the study of negotiation for agreement. Broadly speaking, we may expect to find additional information identifying structural components, mediating processes, and important dependent variables. Each will be considered in turn.

(1) *Identification of structural components.* Different bargaining situations may be distinguished in different ways: according to the nature of the decision makers (e.g., McGrath, 1966; Vidmar and McGrath, Note 8; Stephenson, 1971b; Frey and Adams, 1972); the nature of the decision (Iklé, 1964; Walton and McKersie, 1965); the relationship between the decision makers and/or the parties they represent (Walton and McKersie, 1965; Dutton and Walton, 1966; Pondy, 1967; Brown and Terry, 1975);

and the nature of the organizational context or social system within which the interaction occurs (Pruitt, Note 6; Nicholson, 1970; Chalmers and Cormick, 1971).

Distinguishing different bargaining situations according to the nature of the decision makers involved amounts to distinguishing between formal negotiation (or collective bargaining), which involves representatives of groups, and informal negotiation (or interpersonal bargaining), which does not. (Notice that this distinction is not quite the same as McGrath's. McGrath's 1966 definition of informal negotiation relaxes both the requirement that negotiators be representatives and the requirement that they intend to resolve the differences between them.) There are several reasons for believing this distinction to be psychologically important. As Frey and Adams (1972) have said: "A conflict situation between groups (via boundary-role occupants) has a number of significant added factors not found in simple dyadic bargaining" (p. 332). In extreme cases "the spokesmen, whose job is . . . to negotiate a non-zero-sum conflict between their groups, find themselves virtually in a zero-sum conflict between the demands of their constituency and the demands of the outside group's spokesman. In a sense, then, the conflict becomes a conflict within a conflict" (Frey and Adams, 1972, p. 332).

McGrath and his associates have taken a more extreme view (McGrath and Julian, Note 4; Vidmar and McGrath, Note 7, Note 8, 1970; McGrath, 1966; Vidmar, 1971). Their "tri-polar" model of negotiation has emphasized that, in formal negotiation situations, each participant is subjected to three conflicting sets of forces. *R-forces* are those directed toward the position the negotiator is to represent; *A-forces* are those directed toward the position of the opposing party (i.e., toward reaching agreement); and *C-forces* are directed toward the position of the "broader organization or social system in which all parties participate" (McGrath, 1966, p. 110).

Like Campbell (Note 1), McGrath and his associates have seen partisan commitment as detrimental to negotiation success. More precisely, R-forces are said to arise when *attitudinal identification with a reference group is linked with a role-obligation to represent that group in negotiation* (Vidmar and McGrath, Note 8; Vidmar, 1971; McGrath, 1966). Apparently, "When a representational role is not explicit, R-forces do not exist" (Vidmar and McGrath, Note 8, p. 4). In operational terms, this amounts to saying that "the attitudinal measures used as indicants of R-, A-, and C-forces are efficacious in predicting performance only in conjunction with representational role structures" (Vidmar and McGrath, Note 8, p. 44). In other words, McGrath and his associates have argued that attitudinal commitment impairs performance in formal, but not informal, negotiation situations.

The details of McGrath's position are not important here. No doubt it can be argued that measures of R-, A-, and C-forces are likely to predict task success in any negotiation group, whether members are representatives or not (Morley and Stephenson, 1977). The point to be made here is, rather, that McGrath emphasized the differences between formal and informal types of negotiation at a time when most other researchers were emphasizing the similarities. It is now impossible to ignore such differences, and it is important to distinguish between paradigms which attempt to simulate formal negotiation situations and paradigms which do not.

If a laboratory task is to simulate a formal negotiation situation at all, it must (at minimum) include the presence of an explicit role structure in which each participant represents a party, usually excluded from the ongoing verbal exchange. It may, of course, be desirable to build other features of organizations into the laboratory setting, but these will not be discussed at present. For a more extended treatment the reader is directed to Zelditch and Hopkins (1961), Guetzkow and Bowes (1957), Weick (1967), and Wager and Palola (1964).

(2) *Mediating processes.* It is clear that representatives of groups face problems of *intraorganizational bargaining* which individuals do not (Oppenheim and Bayley, 1970; Walton and McKersie, 1965). In some cases the result may be, as Blake and Mouton (1961c) have claimed, that "representatives act on loyalty, and are motivated to win, or at least to avoid defeat, even though a judgment which would resolve an intergroup problem is sacrificed in the process" (p. 183). In general, it is clear that the process of compromise in formal negotiation cannot be understood simply in terms of the process of compromise in informal negotiation (Druckman, Solomon, and Zechmeister, 1972; Benton and Druckman, 1974; Lamm, Note 3; Klimoski and Ash, 1974; Gruder, 1971; Gruder and Rosen, 1971; Hermann and Kogan, 1968; Frey and Adams, 1972).

When party positions are linked to a negotiator's own belief system, perceptions are particularly likely to be "selective and parochial" (Hoffman, 1968). Negotiators may, for instance, fall into the errors of "possibilistic thinking" (Frank, 1968) or perceive more substantive conflict than actually exists (Blake and Mouton, 1961a, 1961b, 1962; Walker, 1962; Niemela, Honka-Hallila, and Jarvikosi, 1969). Blake and Mouton (1962) have reported one summary, by management, of a set of union proposals, which listed 62 areas of disagreement but failed to list 182 cases of agreement. Problems of this type are likely to be especially important when negotiators face severe problems of information overload (Frank, 1968; Janis, 1972). Presumably, different paradigms will allow such problems to appear to the extent that they (a) include negotiators who have partisan commitments to the positions involved, and (b) require participants to handle increasing amounts of information.

It is also important to consider changes in the process of negotiation which occur with time. So far, I have emphasized the differences between formal and informal brands of negotiation. But there are, of course, some similarities. According to Pruitt (Note 6) and Walton and McKersie (1965) negotiators often find themselves in a mutual and "progressively deepening *concession dilemma*" (Pruitt, Note 6, p. 16). At any given time, a negotiator may consider three options: whether to make a concession; whether only to indicate flexibility; or whether further to commit himself to his present position. If he makes a concession he suffers both position loss and *image loss;* if he chooses not to concede he may become committed to an untenable position or risk antagonizing his opponent (Pruitt, Note 6, pp. 9-11). Pruitt has argued that, as time goes by, arguments both for and against making a concession become more convincing, so that negotiators may fail to resolve their respective dilemmas even when they have compatible minimum goals.

This sort of analysis is important because it can be argued that the concession dilemmas have the reward structures of certain matrix games, such as Prisoner's Dilemma (Pruitt, Note 6; Sawyer and Guetzkow, 1965) or Chicken (Walton and McKersie, 1965). Certain abstract simulations of bargaining behavior attempt to translate the concession dilemma into laboratory terms.

While formal negotiation involves processes of intraorganizational bargaining which informal negotiation does not, both allow possibilities for *integrative bargaining* and *attitudinal structuring* (Walton and McKersie, 1965). Processes of integrative bargaining may be especially important in the present context since different paradigms may or may not allow such "problem-solving" strategies to occur.

(3) *Dependent variables.* Walton and McKersie's (1965) analysis of collective bargaining has been widely used to characterize the process of negotiation for agreement. In their view, "certain points on the total conceivable spectrum of outcomes attain unique distinction and prominence in the thinking of the negotiator and provide a guide to his decisions" (Walton and McKersie, 1965, p. 25). The framework they employ has clear implications for the design of laboratory tasks. If the task is to simulate a formal negotiation situation subjects should be assigned resistance points and target points, so that they are aware of the range of outcomes defined as acceptable by the organizations they are to represent. For that matter, if the task is to simulate an informal negotiation situation subjects should be assigned minimum necessary shares which they must

exceed if an agreement is to be worth their while (Kelley, Beckman, and Fischer, 1967).

One further implication of Walton and McKersie's analysis is that the subjectively expected utility of a given concession is not the same for all points within the settlement range. In one example they have shown that, to a negotiator with a resistance point of ten cents, a concession from fifteen cents to eleven may mean more than a concession from thirty cents to fifteen cents. As Morley and Stephenson (1969, 1970a, 1977) have shown, it may be important to recognize such nonlinearity in the scale of outcomes when conducting laboratory research.

Further discussion of the evaluation of outcomes will be deferred until later.

LABORATORY ANALOGUES OF NEGOTIATION TASKS

Seven types of game have been put forward as laboratory paradigms for the experimental study of bargaining (identified in the introduction to this paper). Morley and Stephenson (1977) have put forward only four of these as paradigms for the study of negotiation for agreement. There is no agreed terminology for referring to games of each type and Morley and Stephenson have labelled them distribution games, games of economic exchange, role-playing debates, and substitute debates.

The essential features of each type of game are summarized in Table 11-1, showing the type of simulation which is involved, the communication possibilities which are allowed, and the identification of different bargaining situations in different ways. Table 11-1 also shows the essential features of the matrix game paradigm which, it is argued, does not simulate the process of negotiation for agreement at all (Morley, 1976; Morley and Stephenson, 1977).

Since many of the arguments used against the matrix game paradigm also apply to the use of mechanical or electromechanical games (e.g., they involve "individual determination of action" rather than "joint determination of action"; Daniels, 1967; Morley and Stephenson, 1977) the two paradigms will not be given a separate treatment in this paper.

Studies of coalition formation of the Pachisi board type will be excluded from this paper. A few words of explanation may be in order. Briefly, Pachisi is a game for three or more players in which each moves a marker n squares toward a goal after appropriate throws of a die. The value of n is determined by multiplying the number of the die by a value of resource strength randomly assigned to each participant. In some games each player moves after every throw of the die (e.g., Vinacke and Arkoff, 1957); in others, each player moves only on his own throw (e.g., Willis, 1962). Each game ends when one player (or one coalition) reaches the

TABLE 11-1
Essential features of five types of game*

Type of game	Experimental paradigms for the study of negotiation				Experimental paradigm for other forms of strategic decision-making
	Distribution game	Game of economic exchange	Role-playing debate	Substitute debate	Matrix game
1. Type of simulation	Abstract	Realistic	Realistic	Realistic	Abstract
2. Communication possibilities	Restricted	Restricted	Unrestricted	Unrestricted	Extremely restricted
3. Amount of information about other's profits	Typically incomplete	Typically incomplete	Typically incomplete	Typically incomplete	Complete
4. Sequence of choice	Sequential	Sequential	Sequential	Sequential	Simultaneous
5. Identification of different bargaining situations	According to characteristics of profit tables and "scenario"	According to characteristics of profit tables and "scenario"	According to characteristics of profit tables and "scenario"	According to characteristics of profit tables and "scenario"	According to characteristics of pay-off matrix

Adapted from Morley and Stephenson 1977.

final square on the path. Usually the winner receives 100 points, and subjects play a number of games against the same opponents. In some cases the distribution of resource strengths is changed on each play of the game; in some cases it is not.

The psychological interest of the game occurs because subjects have an option to pool their resources and move a single counter (according to the rule that the resource strength of the coalition equals the sum of the resource strengths of the individuals in it). To form a coalition subjects must first agree how to divide the prize and it is at this point that the possibilities for "bargaining" arise.

Several points should, perhaps, be made about games of this sort.

1. The major focus of research has concerned the relationship between the resource strengths of the players and the frequency with which coalitions are formed. In other words, research has generally dealt with the choice of a "bargaining" partner, rather than the process of bid and counterbid involved in the verbal exchange.

2. Subjects attempt to build up points over a number of plays of the game. In other words, the game simulates a situation in which subjects build up resources rather than a situation in which subjects attempt to manage an issue which divides them.

3. Each play of the game involves "competitive bargaining", i.e., the object of the exercise is to exclude members of the group at the table from the bargaining relationships established at the table.

4. Subjects are not assigned minimum necessary shares.

5. Considering the n plays of the game as a whole, the situation has zero-sum rather than non-zero-sum characteristics. One is not surprised to read that "Infinite elaboration is possible in the game and that there are many variant forms such as *Monopoly* and *Careers*" (Caplow, 1968, p. 21).

The "bargaining" involved is not the bargaining identified as negotiation for agreement.

Each of the other paradigms will now be considered in turn. As we shall see, many laboratory studies do little more than include the defining characteristics of a given negotiation task. For a more detailed presentation the reader is referred to Morley and Stephenson (1977, Chap. 3).

Abstract games of a matrix, mechanical, or electromechanical type. Consider the two-person two-choice versions of matrix games such as Prisoner's Dilemma or Chicken. The possibility arises that Prisoner's Dilemma/Chicken provide "abstract formulations" (Rapoport, 1963) of the concession dilemma identified by Walton and McKersie (1965) and Pruitt (1969). The paradigm arises as soon as the "cooperative" (C) response is identified with the option *concede* and the "competitive" (D) response is identified with the option *not concede*. Sometimes such games are played only once (e.g., Deutsch, 1958); usually they are played a number of times against the same opponent (e.g., Rapoport and Chammah, 1965). Some games allow possibilities for preplay communication of one sort or another.

1. *Prisoner's Dilemma/Chicken played only once.* Does a single play of the game adequately represent the situation in which negotiators are wondering whether to concede, to indicate flexibility, or further to commit themselves to their current position? Unfortunately it does not. Indications of the C/D choices made might be taken to show subjects' dispositions to react when certain sorts of concession dilemma arise. But subjects playing matrix games make their choices simultaneously and know that their payoffs will be determined simply by the combination of choices which obtain. Once the game has been played the "negotiation" is over. Such games do not, in my opinion, simulate the problems posed by the concession dilemmas which obtain in ongoing negotiations. (I do not wish to deny that game matrices may be useful analytical devices, but I do want to maintain that the matrix cannot be translated into a laboratory situation which also captures the essentials of the real-life task.)

2. *Prisoner's Dilemma/Chicken played n times.* One major focus of research has been to identify sequences of play which increase the probability of obtaining a stable pattern of interaction characterized by a series of mutually rewarding CC responses. But making a series of CC responses is not at all like making a series of concessions in the movement toward agreement (Nemeth, 1972; Morley and Stephenson, 1977). As Morley and Stephenson (1977) have pointed out, Prisoner's Dilemma/Chicken *do not simulate bargaining situations, even very minimal ones, because such games are not exercises in joint decision-making at all.* To borrow Daniels' (1967) terminology, we can say that while Prisoner's Dilemma/Chicken involve "joint determination of outcomes" (i.e., payment is contingent upon combinations of choices) it does not involve "joint determination of action." There is, therefore, no joint decision which has to be made.

3. *Games with preplay communication.* Preplay communication may allow subjects to state which choice they intend to make, tentatively to agree how to coordinate their choices, or deliver threats (e.g. Deutsch, 1958; Thibaut and Faucheux, 1965; Murdoch, 1967; Horai and Tedeschi, 1969; Schlenker, Bonoma, Tedeschi, and Pirnick, 1970). But this does not alter the basic logic of the game. Negotiation is not pregame communication of this sort; what is required is a paradigm in which negotiation *is* the game (Morley and Stephenson, 1970b).

Similar comments would apply to mechanical or electromechanical derivatives of the Acme-Bolt trucking game (Deutsch and Krauss, 1962; Krauss and Deutsch, 1966).

Abstract games of a distribution game (DG) type. Typically, distribution games provide abstract formulations of an informal negotiation task. Subjects are given minimum necessary share (MNS) values and asked to negotiate the division of a specified number of points or a given sum of money. Those who succeed in obtaining outcomes above their MNS values are paid accordingly. Some experiments involve a single play of a game (e.g., Morgan and Sawyer, 1967); some involve repeated play of the same type of game with the same opponent (e.g., Kelley et al., 1967); and some involve repeated play of the same type of game with different opponents (e.g., Kelley, 1966). In some cases contracts may increase in value after a sequence of agreements has been reached (Kelley et al., 1970), but in general they do not.

Two features of distribution games may limit the generality of any results obtained by their use. First, very considerable time pressures may be involved. In one experiment Kelley et al. (1970) set a deadline of ninety seconds per game, and time pressures of this order are not uncommon. Consequently, subjects may care more about reaching an agreement than about what sort of agreement is reached. They will probably exchange very few communications and learn very little about the MNS values of their opponents (Kelley et al., 1967). Secondly, distribution games involve communication of a rather restricted sort. Often communication amounts to no more than an exchange of bids. In principle it is limited to moves such as bidding, threatening, exaggerating one's MNS value, appealing to common interests, and offering to trade concessions on different plays of the game. *There is nothing else to argue about.* As Morgan and Sawyer (1967) have pointed out, distribution games simulate situations in which communication focuses primarily upon *outcomes;* they do not simulate situations which also contain the potential for disagreement over *inputs.*

The game of economic exchange (GEE) paradigm. Games of economic exchange provide "realistic simulations" (Rapoport, 1963) of a variety of trading situations. They provide the same sorts of communication possibilities as distribution games. Perhaps the best known examples are those in which a single (unique) buyer confronts a single (unique) seller, simulating the market situation known as bilateral monopoly (e.g., Siegel and Fouraker, 1960; Kelley and Schenitzki, 1972). In these cases, subjects are given profit tables and asked to agree upon a price/quantity combination at which goods are to be exchanged. The generality of results obtained using games of this sort may also be limited by factors such as excessive time pressure, and focus on outcomes to the exclusion of inputs.

The role-playing debate (RPD) paradigm. Role-playing debates are intended to provide realistic simulations of formal negotiation tasks involving disagreements over inputs as well as disagreement over outcomes. (The term "debate" is intended only to emphasize the sorts of communication possibilities which are involved). Subjects are required to *learn* the details of a particular dispute (from materials provided) and to behave *as if* they were representing a party to that dispute. Some studies use hypothetical issues but ask subjects to represent experimental groups (e.g., Johnson, 1967; Johnson and Dustin, 1970); others give subjects extended experience in laboratory groups and study the negotiation of disputes between competing groups (e.g., Blake and Mouton, 1961c). The materials provided may describe different sorts of dispute, ranging from disputes between union and management (e.g., Campbell, 1960; Morley and Stephenson, 1970b); disputes between nations (e.g., Crow, 1963); disputes about legal damages (e.g., Johnson, 1967); to disputes about urban planning (e.g., Johnson and Lewicki, 1969). In some cases subjects may be allowed to introduce issues not specified in that material (Morley and Stephenson, 1969, 1970a); usually they may not (e.g., Bass, 1966).

The substitute debate (SD) paradigm. Substitute debates are distinguished from role-playing debates by the method used to incorporate a representative role structure into the laboratory task. Members of groups *already in dispute* are asked to negotiate issues which actually divide the organizations concerned. Each subject is asked to represent his own group and is given a "position paper" (outlining and defending the organizational goals involved) to use as a guideline in the negotiation task. The intention is to substitute an encounter which occurs under laboratory conditions for one which might, in any case, have occurred elsewhere.

While the SD paradigm faces few problems of external validity (it preserves the essential aspects of the process the experimenter wishes to study) it places considerable constraints upon the nature of the subject populations which can be used. It is, in fact, extremely difficult to find subjects in sufficient numbers to conduct an experiment at all. The background material is also specific to the subject population used.

A MORE FORMAL CLASSIFICATION OF LABORATORY TASKS

In principle (at least) three types of task may be distinguished *within* each of the given paradigms, according to the structure of the issues which are involved.

1. Tasks of *Type 1* are those in which subjects negotiate a single, complex issue requiring agreement on two dimensions such as price and quantity (e.g., Siegel and Fouraker, 1960).

2. Tasks of *Type 2* are those in which subjects negotiate a single one-dimensional issue, involving (say) the exchange of a single item (e.g., Chertkoff and Conley, 1967) or the division of a given sum of money (e.g., Morgan and Sawyer, 1967).

3. Tasks of *Type 3* are those in which subjects negotiate a number of one-dimensional issues at the same time (e.g., Kelley, 1966).

Consequently, as shown in Table 11-2, laboratory tasks may be distinguished according to a 4 X 3 classification scheme which identifies both the paradigm and the type of issue involved.

This scheme is, of course, a simplification, introduced for purposes of analysis. It is possible to identify more than four paradigms and to identify more than three types of issue. It may, for instance, be desirable to pay special attention to simulation of the Inter-nation Simulation type (Guetzkow, Alger, Brody, Noel, and Snyder, 1963). But to give a general picture of the state of the art it is not desirable to use a more complicated set of categories. The present scheme is, I think, sufficiently precise to give a useful description of published research.

It is, however, important to say something more about the evaluation of outcomes in laboratory tasks. Should the description of a paradigm include a specification of the measurement procedures which are to be used? McGrath has, for instance, suggested the use of what might be called a combined merit score in experiments of an SD type (Vidmar and McGrath, Note 7; McGrath, 1966). Ideally, each settlement would be rated from zero to five (say) by officials of each organization in terms of its "acceptability" to their organization, and by neutral judges in terms of "constructiveness as an approach to the underlying issue". Each subject would then be paid according to the *product* of the average ratings made by the three sets of officials. In practice, McGrath has been forced to substitute ratings made by confederates, adopting each perspective in turn, and has used similar techniques in studies of the RPD type. Sometimes the ratings of neutral judges have been used alone.

TABLE 11-2
Formal classification of negotiation tasks

Structure of issues	Distribution game	Game of economic exchange	Role-playing debate	Substitute debate
Type 1	DG1	GEE1	RPD1	SD1
Type 2	DG2	GEE2	RPD2	SD2
Type 3	DG3	GEE3	RPD3	SD3

TABLE 11-3
Number of research papers using different experimental tasks[*]

DG2	DG3	GEE1	GEE2	RPD2	RPD3	SD2	SD3	RPD + DG3
9	4	9	8	14	21	2	1	2

Adapted from Morley and Stephenson, 1977, Figure 6.2

Negotiation may be regarded as successful when agreements are reached and when those agreements are regarded as satisfactory from a given point of view. Elsewhere, I have argued that laboratory studies should concentrate upon the quality of the settlements which are reached rather than the ease with which they are obtained (Morley, 1971). However, whilst it is easy to measure number of deadlocks, time to agreement, and so on, it is not always easy to say when an agreement is of high quality and when it is not. In fact, different measures may be appropriate in different situations.

First, consider studies of the DG and GEE variety. When the tasks are *Type 1* or *Type 3* it may be possible to measure bargaining efficiency in terms of the joint profit subjects take from the experimental situation (e.g., Johnson and Cohen, 1967; Froman and Cohen, 1969). When the tasks are of *Type 2* it may be more profitable to ask questions such as: Does one subject dominate another? Do settlements reflect principles of equality or equity? And so on.

Second, consider studies of the RPD and SD variety. Several measures of quality of agreement are available, in addition to those used by McGrath and his associates. Campbell (1960) and Bass (1966) have measured absolute and algebraic deviations from a "going rate". Evan and MacDougall (1967) have rated each item of agreement as "reflecting domination, compromise, or integration elements". Morley and Stephenson (1969, 1970a, 1977) have measured the extent to which settlements favoured the side with the stronger case using a seven-point scale designed to take account of the fact that negotiators' preferences for outcomes are likely to be nonlinear. It is not obvious which measures are to be preferred; probably a number should be used.

THE CONTENT OF LABORATORY RESEARCH

Morley and Stephenson (1977) have provided a detailed review of sixty-nine research papers dealing with laboratory studies of negotiation for agreement. Their book brings the total to seventy. Just under half of these studies have involved distribution games or games of economic exchange; just over half have involved games of the role-playing debate or substitute debate type. A more detailed breakdown is shown in Table 11-3. Table 11-4 shows the content of the studies, described in a very general terms.

THE PROCESS OF BID AND COUNTERBID

Only 50/70 reports supply *any* details of the process by which agreements are obtained; of these 30 are of the DG/GEE type. This is quite a serious limitation. For instance, six studies have investigated the relationship between the use of threat and the outcomes of laboratory negotiations (Kelley, 1965, GEE1; Hornstein, 1965, GEE1; Froman and Cohen, 1969, DG3; Fischer, 1970, DG2; Smith and Leginski, 1970, DG3; and Tjosvold, 1974, GEE2). But there are no studies of the use of threat which have used either the RPD or the SD paradigm. Even if we consider what is known about the use of threat in the context of the DG/GEE paradigms

TABLE 11-4

Content analysis of laboratory research on bargaining[*]

| | PARADIGM | | | |
	DG	GEE	RPD	SD
Intergroup relations				
Partisan commitment/R-force pressure			5	2
Introducing a mediator		1	2	
Negotiators as representatives	5		5	
Preparing for negotiation		1	4	
Personal characteristics			4	2
Cultural differences	1		2	
Considerations of equity and equality		2		
Process of bid and counterbid				
Information about profit table/minimum terms		2	2	
Level of aspiration		2		
Logrolling versus compromise	2			
Mean level of demand	3		2	
Schedules of bids		8		
Use of threat	3	3		
"Extra systemic modes" of attaining settlements	1	2		
Process of formal negotiation				
Channel of communication			7	
Strategies			5	
Processs analysis	1		4	1

[*]Entries show number of research reports which focus upon each topic; some reports appear under more than one heading.

the results are not impressive. It is not at all clear when it is productive to use a threat and when it is not. Amongst other variables which seem important in dealing with the findings are: the magnitude and precision of the power available to subjects; the range of "alternative strategies" open to them; and the type of threat ("compellence" or "deterrent") they choose to send. There are many more questions than answers.

My purpose is not to decry experimental research, but to indicate the amount of uncertainty which is involved. Many conclusions emerge as the result of long and complicated arguments, and are often, in any case, derived from a small range of negotiation tasks. It is, for instance, often reported that it pays to begin negotiation with a relatively extreme opening offer. This may be so, but so far as laboratory research is concerned, the conclusion is derived entirely from six studies of the GEE2 type (Chertkoff and Conley, 1967; Komorita and Brenner, 1968; Komorita and Barnes, 1969; Liebert, Smith, Hill, and Keiffer, 1968; Pruitt and Drews, 1969; Pruitt and Johnson, 1970). Each had subjects bargain against simulated opponents programmed to follow given schedules of bids; but the studies differed considerably in detail, and all manipulated other aspects of the program's behavior.

It is often tempting to summarize studies of this sort by saying they deal with *toughness* of bargaining behaviour. But this would be oversimple. A negotiator's behaviour may vary along dimensions such as level of initial demand, mean level of demand, number of concessions, size of concessions, and level of minimum goal. Evidence from Pruitt and Drews (1969) suggests that an independent variable which affects one of these dimensions (e.g., mean level of demand) need not affect another (e.g. level of minimum goal) in the same sort of way. Consequently, to say that A's behaviour is tougher than B's is not very helpful until the dimension (or dimensions) involved has (or have) been specified. There are (potentially) as many forms of toughness as there are dimensions of the type listed above.

Most other research on the process of bid and counterbid has dealt with the effects of toughness, defined in terms of subjects' mean levels of demand. Following Morley and Stephenson (1977) this form of toughness will be referred to as toughness $_{(l.d)}$. Bartos (1966; 1970) has studied the effects of toughness $_{(l.d)}$ in two-person groups, five-person groups, and two-team groups engaged in tasks of the DG3 or RPD3 types (each team consisted of two members who took it in turns to act as spokesman). The experiments were conducted at the University of Hawaii during the period 1960 to 1967 and data aggregated from a large number of different sources. Two findings are worthy of note in the present context.

1. Toughness $_{(l.d)}$ tended to generate softness $_{(l.d)}$ in two-person groups negotiating a DG3 task, but not in five-person groups. This finding is important because it suggests that bargaining may proceed differently in two-person and n-person cases (and presumably, n-team cases). Since the great majority of laboratory studies have involved dyadic negotiations this may place severe restrictions on the generality of the results obtained. Stephenson's paper gives further examples of the effect of size of group.

2. Considering data aggregated from all sources there was some evidence of a curvilinear (inverted U) relationship between toughness-$_{(l.d)}$ and the probability of reaching an agreement. Once again, Bartos' data are consistent with the suggestion that the precise effects obtained are mediated by the size of the group involved (Morley and Stephenson 1977).

THE PROCESS OF FORMAL NEGOTIATION

Bartos (1966) has constructed a simple mathematical model of the process of concession-making in DG3 and RPD3 tasks. Formally, Bartos assumed that a negotiator's current demand (Y) would depend upon his own previous demand (X) and upon the offers previously made by each of his opponents $(Z_1, Z_2, \ldots, Z_n)$, such that:

$$Y = a + bX + c_1 Z_1 + c_2 Z_2 + \ldots + c_n Z_n.$$

This model had greater predictive power in the case of the DG3 negotiations (accounting for 31% of the variance) than in the caseof the RPD3 negotiations (accounting for 18% of the variance). Formal negotiation involves a great deal more than a process of bid and counterbid.

A study by Frey and Adams (1972; RPD2) demonstrates two of the additional components which are involved. Subjects were assigned to management roles, and exchanged ten written communications with simulated union opponents. Each communication consisted of an offer plus a message selected from one of seventeen possibilities provided by the experimenters. Subjects' bargaining behaviour was affected by *within party* considerations ("constituent trust" versus "constituent distrust") and by *between party* considerations ("received cooperation" versus "received exploitation").

The simulated union spokesman followed the same schedule of demands in each of Frey and Adams' treatments. "Received cooperation" versus "received exploitation" was manipulated by changing the content of the messages which were sent. When union tactics were "cooperative" the messages were "conciliatory and emphasized the mutual gain which an agreement would bring about"; when union tactics were "exploitative" the messages were "demanding and threatening" and "frequently emphasized the harm that a strike would do to the company" (Frey and Adams, 1972, p. 337). Quite clearly, subjects' perceptions of the union bids depended upon the context in which they occurred, and part of that context was provided by the other messages which were sent.

While researchers have paid some attention to the problems of intra-organizational bargaining suggested by Frey and Adams' analysis they have, unfortunately, made very few attempts to analyze the messages which determine the meaning of the concessions which are made. One method is to use category systems of the sort suggested by Bales' (1950) Interaction Process Analysis. Only five laboratory studies have attempted to study the process of negotiation in this way: one has used Bales' categories (Manheim, 1960, RPD3); one has used categories derived from Bales' (Morris, 1970, RPD3); two have used categories suggested by Julian and McGrath (Note 2, SD2; McGrath and Julian 1963, SD2); and one has used a set of categories, "Conference Process Analysis," developed by Morley and Stephenson (Morley, 1974; Morley and Stephenson, 1977). The potential value of such an analysis is confirmed by a number of observational studies (e.g., Landsberger, 1955; Grace and Tandy, 1957).

A good deal of interest centers around discussions of stages in the process of negotiation (Landsberger, 1955; Douglas, 1957, 1962). Research using Conference Process Analysis is described in the chapter by Stephenson in this volume.

SOME FURTHER COMMENTS ON THE STATE OF THE ART

1. *The reliability of research findings.* Most researchers have preferred to investigate new areas rather than to repeat previous work. According to Morley and Stephenson (1977) only three studies have been replicated, and then only in part (see (a) Bass, 1966, RPD3; Druckman, 1967, RPD3; 1968, RPD3; (b) Porat, Note 5, RPD3; 1970, RPD3; (c) Siegel and Fouraker, 1960, GEE1; Kelley, 1964, GEE1; Johnson and Cohen, 1967, GEE1; Kelley and Schenitzki, 1972, GEE1).

2. *The robustness of the research findings.* Bartos (1966, 1970) has presented data aggregated from a number of sources. Otherwise, only three sets of researchers have attempted to establish the generality of findings with respect to given dependent variables by using different experimental procedures and/or different laboratory tasks (see (a) Vidmar and McGrath, Note 7, SD3; Vidmar and McGrath, Note 8, RPD3; (b) Siegel and Four-aker, 1960, GEE1; Holmes, Throop, and Strickland, 1971, GEE1; (c)

Morley and Stephenson, 1969, RPD2; 1970a, RPD2; 1977, RPD2). More research of this sort is urgently required.

So far as the generality across different subject populations is concerned it must be admitted that most research has been conducted using university students as subjects, usually American, and usually male. This may limit the generality of the findings in (at least) two respects.

Some results may apply only to unskilled, inexperienced negotiators. Karass (1970, RPD2) found that, in a legal damages case, professional negotiators rated as "skilled" and "unskilled" by management reacted to variations in "plaintiff power" (manipulated by changing the number of court decisions used as precedents, and so on) in different ways. Unskilled negotiators obtained more favorable settlements when given high power than when given equal power. Skilled negotiators were not affected in this way. Boguslaw, Davis, and Glick (1966, RPD3) also found differences between experienced and inexperienced negotiators during two pilot runs of a complex simulation, similar in character to the Inter-nation Simulation. In this case, "The simulation vehicle consisted of a socioeconomic model of the American society, a simulation of major interest groups within that society, and a set of exercise procedures enabling the simulated interest group to make decisions on given public policy issues during specific future time periods" (p. 44). Seven "experienced administrators and scientists" participated in the first run of the simulation; seven graduate students participated in the second. Subjects allocated "resource units" for or against a number of given policies, and were free to negotiate any or all of the issues as and when they chose. Experienced subjects initially allocated their resource units to fewer policies, negotiated fewer issues, but reached more agreements than inexperienced subjects.

Other results may require modification to apply to a British or European population (Porat, Note 5, RPD3; 1970, RPD3; Kelley et al., 1970, DG3).

3. *Construction of theory.* Published reports of laboratory research have been responsible for the development of very few *theoretical* ideas. In general, the reader will find lists of input-output relationships, loosely integrated into a theoretical framework provided by one or two standard sources (e.g., Sieget and Fouraker, 1960; Walton and McKersie, 1965). Notable exceptions are provided by Bartos (1966); Kelley et al. (1967); Kelley and Schenitzki (1972); and Waddington (1975).

4. *Opportunities to study integrative bargaining.* Despite the importance of integrative bargaining, few studies have allowed subjects to change the nature of the agenda items on the table. I know of no examples of the study of integrative bargaining in laboratory research.

THE APPLICATION OF LABORATORY RESEARCH

It cannot be denied that laboratory settings include some features of real-life situations and exclude others. *Indeed, they are designed to do so.* Experimenters attempt to build a *simple* laboratory situation which preserves the essential aspects of some real-life case. Thus, "The fact that an experimental situation differs in obvious ways from the real world does not *ipso facto* make it irrelevant as a possible source of valid generalizations," as Kelman (1965, p. 598) has pointed out. If we are to make the most of the material which is available a three step process is required (Kelman, 1965; Druckman, 1967; Fromkin and Streufert, 1976).

The first step is to provide a detailed analysis of both the referent system (or criterion setting: i.e., "*any* environment which is the target of generalization"; Fromkin and Streufert, 1976, p. 451) and the simulate system (or focal setting: i.e., "any data collection . . . environment"; Fromkin and Streufert, 1976, p. 451). Here, I have attempted to provide a starting point for the second of these two tasks.

The second step is to identify similarities and differences between the two settings. Here, I can do no better than quote Kelman's paper at some length. "The question of generalization from experimental studies to the real world . . . cannot be settled once and for all. There is no laboratory situation that can have universal validity. The conditions on which valid generalization depend have to be reexamined for each specific problem that an investigator is pursuing." (Kelman, 1965, p. 599).

The third step is "to determine the importance for behavior of the particular situational dimensions along which variation occurs" (Druckman, 1967, p. 550). This may involve the use of other research findings, including those obtained from the laboratory. It may also involve "guesses about some (untested or unproven) general laws of behavior" (Fromkin and Streufert, 1976, p. 452).

Two further points arise from this analysis. (1) Given that problems of generalizing the results of laboratory research are situation specific and cannot be settled once and for all, it is surprising that very few experimental studies of negotiation have derived their inspiration from data collected in the field. By and large, most laboratory studies have been suggested by other laboratory research. Studies such as that of Bonham (1971, RPD3) are, therefore, especially important. Bonham has argued that differences in issue emphasis may have contributed to the failure of disarmament negotiations, conducted largely between the United States and the Soviet Union, which took place between 1946 and 1961. Participants received extensive documentation describing the negotiations, and the experiment took the form of eleven four-hour sessions between "chief negotiators" of the United States (US), the Soviet Union (SU) and the United Kingdom (UK). Issue emphasis was manipulated by means of written instructions, and each session contained twenty minutes of written negotiations. Three sorts of comparison were made between simulation results and analyses of transcripts, provided by Jensen (1963): relative amounts of insecurity, propaganda, and hostility expressed in experimental sessions and meetings 22 to 49 of the 1955 Disarmament Subcommittee; comparisons of correlations between US and SU behaviors in experimental simulation, Disarmament Subcommittee, and major negotiations; comparisons of concession behavior in experimental sessions of simulation and major negotiations. In general, data from US negotiators was more likely to be reproduced in the simulation than data from SU negotiators. (In one case, at least, data from the SU negotiators was reversed in the simulation). In some respects the data from the simulation was more like the data from the subcommittee than the data from the major negotiations; in other respects it was more like the data from the major negotiations. (2) One way of increasing the relevance of laboratory research is to integrate it into a program of study which also involves the analysis of real cases (Kelman, 1965; Morley and Stephenson, 1977). One such program, funded by the Social Science Research Council of Great Britain, is described in Stephenson's paper.

The reader will, I hope, notice similarities between the argument given above and the argument presented in the earlier sections of my paper. If the results of social psychological research are to be generalized to real-life cases it is important to consider such arguments at the beginning rather than the end of the research enterprise. Some recent research dealing with extremity shifts will help to illustrate what I mean. Attempts to replicate the "shift-to-risk" in real committees have been remarkably unsuccessful (Fraser, 1975). This may be due to a variety of causes, but one is almost certainly the fact that committees are likely to *turn into negotiation groups* (Vidmar and McGrath, Note 8; Stephenson, 1971a). Analysis of the criterion setting would suggest that the paradigm used by Hermann and Kogan (1968, RPD3) is more appropriate than that due to Stoner, which has generally been used. Fraser's negative results are, perhaps, not too surprising when viewed from the perspective of Hermann and Kogan's research. "Delegates" tended to compromise more than leaders, especially when initial positions were highly discrepant. "Leaders," by contrast, compromised only when positions were highly similar. Otherwise, leader groups exhibited shifts-to-risk by moving to the position of one of the parties involved. "Go back to the lab," is just as good advice as "Go out into the field," but a certain amount of analysis is required first.

NOTES

1. Campbell, R.J. *Originality in group productivity, III: Partisan commitment and productive independence in a collective bargaining situation* (Conducted under contract with office of Naval Research, Nonr-495 (15) (NR 170-396)). Columbus, Ohio: The Ohio State University Research Foundation, 1960.

2. Julian, J.W., and J.E. McGrath. *The influence of leader and member behaviour on the adjustment and task effectiveness of negotiation groups* (Tech. Rep. No. 17; Office of the Surgeon General Contract DA-49-193-MD-2060). Urbana, Illinois: Group Effectiveness Research Laboratory, University of Illinois, 1963.

3. Lamm, H. *Some recent research on negotiating behaviour.* Paper presented at the European Association of Experimental Social Psychology Conference, Bielefeld, April, 1975.

4. McGrath, J.E., and J.W. Julian. *Negotiation and conflict: An experimental study* (Tech. Rep. No. 16: SGO Contract MD 2060 and UPSHS contract M-1774). Urbana, Illinois: Group Effectiveness Research Laboratory, University of Illinois, 1962.

5. Porat, A.M. *Planning and role assignment in the study of conflict resolutions: a study of two countries* (Tech. Rep. No. 28). Management Research Center of the College of Business Administration, University of Rochester, 1969.

6. Pruitt, D.G. *Indirect communication in the search for agreement in negotiation* (Indirect Communication in Negotiation Project, Working Paper II 1.). Unpublished Manuscript Center for International Conflict Studies, State University of New York at Buffalo, 1969.

7. Vidmar, N., and J.E. McGrath. *Role assignment and attitudinal commitment as factors in negotiation* (Tech. Rep. No. 3; AFOSR Contract AF49 (638)-1291). Urbana, Illinois: Department of Psychology, University of Illinois, 1965.

8. Vidmar, N., and J.E. McGrath. *Role structure, leadership and negotiation effectiveness* (Tech. Rep. No. 6; AFOSR Contract AF49 (638)-1291). Urbana, Illinois: Department of Psychology, University of Illinois, 1967.

REFERENCES

Apfelbaum, E. On conflicts and bargaining. In L. Berkowitz (Ed.), *Advances in Experimental Social Psychology*, Vol. 2.

Bales, R.F. *Interaction Process Analysis; A Method for the Study of Small Groups.* Reading, Mass.: Addison-Wesley, 1950.

Bartos, O.J. Determinants and consequences of toughness. In P. Swingle (Ed.), *The Structure of Conflict.* New York: Academic Press, 1970.

– – –. Concession-making in experimental negotiations. In J. Berger, M. Zelditch, Jr., and B. Anderson (Eds.), *Sociological Theories in Progress*, Vol. 1. Boston: Houghton-Mifflin, 1966.

Bass, B.M. Effects on the subsequent performance of negotiators of studying issues or planning strategies alone or in groups. *Psychological Monographs: General & Applied*, 1966, *80* (6 Whole No. 614).

Benton, A.A., and D. Druckman. Constituents' bargaining orientation and intergroup negotiations. *Journal of Applied Social Psychology,* 1974, *4,* 141-150.

Blake, R.R., and S. Mouton. The intergroup dynamics of win-lose conflict and problem-solving collaboration in union-management relations. In M. Sherif (Ed.), *Intergroup Relations and Leadership.* New York: Wiley, 1962.

———. Comprehension of own and outgroup positions under intergroup competition. *Journal of Conflict Resolution,* 1961, *3,* 304-310. (a)

———. Competition, communication and conformity. In I.A. Berg and B.M. Bass (Eds.), *Conformity and Deviation.* New York: Harper & Row, 1961. (b)

———. Loyalty of representatives to ingroup positions during intergroup conflict. *Sociometry,* 1961, *24,* 177-184. (c)

Boguslaw, R., R.H. Davis, and E.B. Glick. A simulation vehicle for studying national policy formulation in a less armed world. *Behavioural Science,* 1966, *11,* 43-61.

Bonham, M.G. Simulating international disarmament negotiations. *Journal of Conflict Resolution,* 1971, *15,* 299-315.

Caplow, T.A. *Two Against One: Coalitions in Triads.* Englewood Cliffs, N.J.: Prentice Hall, 1968.

Chalmers, W.E., and G.W. Cormick (Eds.). *Racial conflict and negotiations: perspectives and first case studies.* Ann Arbor: Institute of Labor & Industrial Relations, The University of Michigan - Wayne State University and the National Center for Dispute Settlement of the American Arbitration Association, 1971.

Chertkoff, J.M., and M. Conley. Opening offer and frequency of concession as bargaining strategies. *Journal of Personality and Social Psychology,* 1967, *7,* 181-185.

Coplin, W. International simulation and contemporary theories of international relations. *Am. Political Science Review,* 1966, *60,* 562-578.

Crow, W.J. A study of strategic doctrines using the internation simulation. *Journal of Conflict Resolution,* 1963, *7,* 580-589.

Daniels, V. Communication, incentive, and structural variables in interpersonal exchange and negotiation. *Journal of Experimental Social Psychology,* 1967, *4,* 367-383.

Deutsch, M. *The Resolution of Conflict: Constructive and Destructive Processes.* New Haven and London: Yale University Press, 1973.

———. Trust and suspicion. *Journal of Conflict Resolution,* 1958, *2,* 265-279.

Deutsch, M., and R.M. Krauss. Studies of interpersonal bargaining. *Journal of Conflict Resolution,* 1962, *6,* 57-76.

———. The effects of threat upon interpersonal bargaining. *Journal of Abnormal and Social Psychology,* 1960, *61,* 181-189.

Douglas, A. *Industrial peacemaking.* New York: Columbia University Press, 1962.

———. The peaceful settlement of industrial and inter-group disputes. *Journal of Conflict Resolution,* 1957, *1,* 57-76.

Druckman, D. The influence of the situation in interparty conflict. *Journal of Conflict Resolution,* 1971, *15,* 522-554.

———. Prenegotiation experience and dyadic conflict resolution in a bargaining situation. *Journal of Experimental Social Psychology,* 1968, *4,* 367-383.

———. Dogmatism, pre-negotiation experience, and simulated group representation as determinants of dyadic behaviour in a bargaining situation. *Journal of Personality and Social Psychology,* 1967, *6,* 279-290.

Druckman, D., D. Solomon, and Zechmeister. Effects of representational role obligations on the process of children's distribution of resources. *Sociometry,* 1972, *35,* 387-410.

Dulany, D.E. On the support of cognitive theory in opposition to behaviour theory; A methodological problem. In W.B. Weimer and D.S. Palermo (Eds.), *Cognition and the Symbolic Processes.* Hillsdale, N.J.: Lawrence Erlbaum Associates, 1974.

Dutton, J.E., and R.E. Walton. Interdepartmental conflict and cooperation: two contrasting studies. *Human Organization,* 1966, *25,* 207-220.

Evan, W.M., and J.A. MacDougall. Interorganizational conflict: A labor-management bargaining experiment. *Journal of Conflict Resolution,* 1967, *11,* 398-413.

Fink, C.F. Some conceptual difficulties in the theory of social conflict. *Journal of Conflict Resolution,* 1968, *12,* 412-461.

Fischer, C.S. The effect of threats in an incomplete information game. *Sociometry,* 1970, *32,* 301-314.

Frank, J.D. *Sanity and survival.* London: Barrie & Rockliff, The Cresset Press, 1968.

Fraser, C. *Determinants of individual and group decisions involving risk* (Final Report, Social Science Research Council Grant HR. 542). British Lending Library, 1975.

Frey, R.L., Jr., and J.S. Adams. The negotiator's dilemma: Simultaneous in-group and out-group conflict. *Journal of Experimental Social Psychology,* 1972, *8,* 331-346.

Froman, L.A., Jr., and M.D. Cohen. Threats and bargaining efficiency. *Behavioural Science,* 1969, *14,* 147-153.

Fromkin, H.L., and S. Streufert. Laboratory experimentation. In M.D. Dunette (Ed.), *Handbook of industrial and organizational psychology.* Chicago: Rand McNally, 1976.

Gallo, P.S., Jr., and C.G. McClintock. Cooperative and competitive behaviour in mixed-motive games. *Journal of Conflict Resolution,* 1965, *9,* 68-78.

Gamson, W.A. Experimental studies of coalition formation. In L. Berkowitz (Ed.), *Advances in experimental social psychology,* Vol. 1. New York: Academic Press, 1964.

———. An experimental test of a theory of coalition formation. *American Sociological Review,* 1961, *26,* 565-573.

Grace, H.A., and M.J. Tandy. Delegate communication as an index of group tension. *Journal of Social Psychology,* 1957, *45,* 93-97.

Gruder, C.L. Relations with opponent and partner in mixed-motice bargaining. *Journal of Conflict Resolution,* 1971, *15,* 403-415.

Gruder, C.L., and N. Rosen. Effects of intragroup relations on intergroup bargaining. *International Journal of Group Tensions,* 1971, *1,* 301-317.

Guetzkow, H. Some correspondences between simulation and "realities" in international relations. In M.A. Kaplan (Ed.), *New Approaches to International Relations.* New York: St. Martin's Press, 1968.

———. (Ed.) *Simulation in Social Science: Readings.* Englewood Cliffs, N.J.: Prentice Hall, 1962.

Guetzkow, H., and A.E. Bowes. The development of organizations in a laboratory. *Management Science,* 1957, *3,* 380-402.

Guetzkow, H., C.F. Alger, R.A. Brody, C. Noel, and R.C. Snyder. *Simulation in International Relations: Developments for Research and Teaching.* Englewood Cliffs, N.J.: Prentice Hall, 1963.

Hermann, C.F. Validation problems in games and simulations with special reference to models of international politics. *Behavioural Science,* 1967, *12,* 216-231.

Hermann, M.G., and N. Kogan. Negotiation in leader and delegate groups. *Journal of Conflict Resolution,* 1968, *12,* 332-344.

Hoffman, P.J., L. Festinger, and D.H. Lawrence. Tendencies toward group comparability in competitive bargaining. In R.M. Thrall, C.H. Coombs, and R.L. Davis (Eds.), *Decision Processes*. New York: Wiley, 1954.

Hoffman, S. Perception, reality and the Franco-American conflict. In J.C. Farrell and A.P. Smith (Eds.), *Image and Reality in World Politics*. New York: Columbia University Press, 1968.

Holmes, J.G., W.F. Throop, and L.H. Strickland. The effects of prenegotiation expectations on the distributive bargaining process. *Journal of Experimental Social Psychology*, 1971, 7, 582-599.

Horai, J., and J.T. Tedeschi. The effects of credibility and magnitude of punishment upon compliance to threats. *Journal of Personality and Social Psychology*, 1969, 12, 164-169.

Hornstein, H.A. The effects of different magnitudes of threats upon interpersonal bargaining. *Journal of Experimental Social Psychology*, 1965, 1, 282-293.

Iklé, F.C. *How nations negotiate*. New York: Harper & Row, 1964.

Janis, I.L. *Victims of Groupthink: Psychological Study of Foreign-Policy Decisions and Fiascos*. Boston: Houghton-Mifflin, 1972.

Jensen, L. Soviet-American bargaining behaviour in the postwar disarmament negotiations. *Journal of Conflict Resolution*, 1963, 7, 522-541.

Jervis, A.S. *The Logic of Images in International Relations*. Princeton: Princeton University Press, 1970.

Johnson, D.W. Use of role-reversal in intergroup competition. *Journal of Personality and Social Psychology*, 1967, 7, 135-141.

Johnson, D.W., and R. Duston. The initiation of cooperation through role-reversal. *Journal of Social Psychology*, 1970, 82, 193-203.

Johnson, D.W., and R. Dustin. The initiation of cooperation through role-reversal. *Applied Behavioural Science*, 1969, 5, 9-24.

Johnson, H.L., and A.M. Cohen. Experiments in behavioural economics: Siegel and Fouraker revisited. *Behavioural Science*, 1967, 12, 353-372.

Karass, C.L. *The negotiating game*. New York & Cleveland: World, 1970.

Katonah, G. Review of S. Siegel and L.E. Fouraker, "Experiments in Bilateral Monopoly." *Contemporary Psychology*, 1962, 7, 535-572.

Kelley, H.H. A classroom study of the dilemmas in interpersonal negotiations. In Archibald (Ed.), *Strategic interaction and conflict*. Berkeley: Institute of International Studies, University of California, 1966.

———. Experimental studies of threats in interpersonal negotiations. *Journal of Conflict Resolution*, 1965, 9, 79-105.

———. Interaction process and the attainment of maximum joint profit. In S. Messick and A.H. Brayfield (Eds.), *Decision and Choice*. New York: McGraw-Hill, 1964.

Kelley, H.H., L.L. Beckman, and C.S. Fischer. Negotiating the division of a reward under incomplete information. *Journal of Experimental Social Psychology*, 1967, 3, 361-398.

Kelley, H.H., and D.P. Schenitzki. Bargaining. In C.G. McClintock (Ed.), *Experimental Social Psychology*. New York: Holt, Rinehart and Winston, 1972.

Kelley, H.H., G.H. Shure, M. Deutsch, C. Faucheux, J.T. Lanzetta, S. Moscovici, J.M. Nuttin, Jr., J.M. Rabbie, and J.W. Thibaut. A comparative experimental study of negotiation behaviour. *Journal of Personality and Social Psychology*, 1970, 16, 411-438.

Kelman, H.C. Social psychological approaches to the study of international relations: the question of relevance. In H.C. Kelman (Ed.), *International Behaviour: A Social Psychological Analysis*. New York: Holt, Rinehart and Winston, 1965.

Klimoski, R.J., and R.A. Ash. Accountability and negotiator behaviour. *Organizational Behaviour and Human Performance*, 1974, *11*, 409-425.

Komorita, S.S., and M. Barnes. Effects of pressures to reach agreement in bargaining. *Journal of Personality and Social Psychology*, 1969, *13*, 245-252.

Komorita, S.S., and R. Brenner. Bargaining and concession-making under bilateral monopoly. *Journal of Personality and Social Psychology*, 1968, *9*, 15-20.

Krauss, R.M., and M. Deutsch. Communication in interpersonal bargaining. *Journal of Personality and Social Psychology*, 1962, *4*, 572-577.

Lall, A.S. *Modern International Negotiation: Principles and Practice.* New York: Columbia University Press, 1966.

Landsberger, H.A. Interaction process analysis of mediation of labour management disputes. *Journal of Abnormal and Social Psychology*, 1955, *57*, 552-558.

Liebert, R.M., W.P. Smith, J.H. Hill, and M. Keiffer. The effects of information and magnitude of initial offer on interpersonal negotiation. *Journal of Experimental Social Psychology*, 1968, *4*, 431-441.

Manheim, H.C. Intergroup interaction as related to status and leadership differences between groups. *Sociometry*, 1960, *23*, 415-427.

McClintock, C.G. Game behaviour and social motivation in interpersonal settings. In C.G. McClintock (Ed.), *Experimental Social Psychology*. New York: Holt, Rinehart and Winston, 1972.

McGrath, J.E. A social psychological approach to the study of negotiation. In R. Bowers (Ed.), *Studies on Behaviour in Organizations: A Research Symposium.* Athens: University of Georgia Press, 1966.

McGrath, J.E., and J.W. Julian. Interaction process and task outcomes in experimentally created negotiation groups. *Journal of Psychological Studies*, 1963, *14*, 117-138.

Morgan, W.R., and J. Sawyer. Bargaining, expectations and the preferences for equality over equity. *Journal of Personality and Social Psychology*, 1967, *6*, 139-149.

Morley, I.E. Experimental studies of negotiation groups—the "state of the art." Revised version of a paper in P.B. Warr (Chair), *Psychology and Industrial Relations.* Symposium presented at the Annual Conference of the British Psychological Society, University of Nottingham, 1975; revised 1976.

———. Social interaction in experimental negotiations. Unpublished doctoral dissertation, University of Nottingham, 1974.

———. Formality in experimental negotiations. In G.M. Stephenson (Chair), *Negotiating Behaviour.* Symposium presented to British Psychology Society, Social Psychology Section Annual Conference, University of Durham, 1971.

Morley, I.E. and G.M. Stephenson. *The Social Psychology of Bargaining.* London: George Allen and Unwin, 1977.

———. Formality in experimental negotiations: a validation study. *British Journal of Psychology*, 1970, 61, 383-384. (a)

———. Strength of case, communication systems, and the outcomes of simulated negotiations: some social psychological aspects of bargaining. *Industrial Relations Journal*, 1970, *1*, 19-29. (b)

———. Interpersonal and interparty exchange; a laboratory simulation of an industrial negotiation at the plant level. *British Journal of Psychology*, 1969, *60*, 543-545.

Morris, C.G. Changes in group interaction during problem-solving. *Journal of Social Psychology*, 1970, *81*, 157-165.

Murdoch, P. The development of contractual norms in a dyad. *Journal of Personality and Social Psychology,* 1967, 6, 206-211.

Nemeth, C. A critical analysis of research utilizing the Prisoner's Dilemma paradigm for the study of bargaining. In L. Berkowitz (Ed.), *Advances in Experimental Social Psychology,* Vol. 6. New York: Academic Press, 1972.

Nicholson, M. *Conflict Analysis.* London: The English Universities Press, 1970.

Niemela, P., S. Honka-Hallila, and A. Jarvikosi. A study in intergroup perception stereotype. *Journal of Peace Research,* 1969, 6, 57-64.

Oppenheim, A.N., and J.C.R. Bayley. Productivity and conflict. *Proceedings of the International Peace Research Association, 3rd General Conference.* Essen, Netherlands: Van Gorcum & Co., N.V., 1970.

Oskamp, S. Factors affecting cooperation in a Prisoner's Dilemma game. *Journal of Conflict Resolution,* 1971, 15, 225-259.

Pondy, L.R. Organizational conflict: concepts and models. *Administrative Science Quarterly,* 1967, 12, 296-320.

Porat, A.M. Cross-cultural differences in resolving union-management conflict through negotiations. *Journal of Applied Psychology,* 1970, 54, 441-451.

Pruitt, D.G., and L. Drews. The effects of time pressure, time elapsed, and the opponent's concession rate on behaviour in negotiation. *Journal of Experimental Social Psychology,* 1969, 5, 43-60.

Pruitt, D.G., and D.F. Johnson. Mediation as an aid to face-saving in negotiation. *Journal of Personality and Social Psychology,* 1970, 14, 239-246.

Rapoport, A. Editor's introduction. In A. Rapoport (Ed.), *Clausewitz on War.* Harmondsworth: Penguin Books, 1968.

———. Formal games as probing tools for investigating behaviour motivated by trust and suspicion. *Journal of Conflict Resolution,* 1963, 7, 570-579.

Rapoport, A., and A.M. Chammah. The game of chicken. *American Behavioral Scientist,* 1966, 10, 10-14, 23-28.

———. *Prisoner's Dilemma: A Study in Conflict and Cooperation.* Ann Arbor: The University of Michigan Press, 1965.

Rapoport, A., and C. Orwant. Experimental games: a review. *Behavioural Science,* 1962, 7, 1-37.

Rubin, J.Z., and B.R. Brown. *The Social Psychology of Bargaining and Negotiation.* New York: Academic Press, 1975.

Sawyer, J., and H. Guetzkow. Bargaining and negotiation in international relations. In H.C. Kelman (Ed.), *International Behaviour and Social Psychological Analysis.* New York: Holt, Rinehart and Winston, 1965.

Schelling, T.C. *The Strategy of Conflict.* Oxford: Oxford University Press, 1968 (Originally published, New York & Harvard University Press, 1960).

Schlenker, B.R., T. Bonoma, J.T. Tedeschi, and W.P. Pivnick. Compliance to threats as a function of the wording of the threat and the exploitativeness of the threatener. *Sociometry,* 1970, 33, 394-408.

Sermat, V. Is game behaviour related to behaviour in other interpersonal situations? *Journal of Personality and Social Psychology,* 1970, 16, 92-109.

Shure, G.H., R.J. Meeker, and E.A. Hansford. The effectiveness of pacifist strategies in bargaining games. *Journal of Conflict Resolution,* 1965, 9, 106-117.

Siegel, S., and L.E. Fouraker. *Bargaining and Group Decision Making.* New York: McGraw-Hill, 1960.

Smith, P.B. *Groups within organizations.* New York: Harper & Row, 1974.

Smith, W.P., and W.A. Leginski. Magnitude and precision of punitive power in bargaining strategy. *Journal of Experimental Social Psychology,* 1970, 6, 57-76.

Stephenson, G.M. The experimental study of negotiating. In G.M. Stephenson (Chair), *Negotiating Behaviour.* Symposium presented to Psychological Society, Social Psychology Section Annual Conference, University of Durham, 1971. (a)

––––. Inter-group relations and negotiating behaviour. In P.B. Warr (Ed.), *Psychology at Work.* Harmondsworth: Penguin Books, 1971. (b)

Stephenson, G.M., M. Skinner, and C.J. Brotherton. Group participation and inter-group relations: An experimental study of negotiation groups. *European Journal of Social Psychology,* 1976, *6,* 51-70.

Swingle, P.G. (Ed.) *The Structure of Conflict.* New York: Academic Press, 1970. (a)

––––. Dangerous games. In P. Swingle (Ed.), *The Structure of Conflict.* New York: Academic Press, 1970. (b)

––––. The effects of win-lose difference upon cooperative responding in a "dangerous" game. *Journal of Conflict Resolution,* 1967, *11,* 214-222.

Terhune, K.W. The effects of personality in cooperation and conflict. In P. Swingle (Ed.), *The Structure of Conflict.* New York: Academic Press, 1970.

––. Motives situation and interpersonal conflict within Prisoner's Dilemma. *Journal of Personality & Social Psychology,* 1968, 8 (3), Part 2 (Monograph Supplement).

Thibaut, J.W., and C. Faucheux. The development of contractural norms in a bargaining situation under two types of stress. *Journal of Experimental Social Psychology,* 1965, *1,* 89-102.

Tjosvold, D. Threat as a low power person's strategy in bargaining: social face and tangible outcomes. *International Journal of Group Tensions,* 1974, *4,* 494-510.

Vidmar, N. Effects of representational roles and mediators on negotiation effectiveness. *Journal of Personality and Social Psychology,* 1971, *17,* 48-58.

Vidmar, N., and J.E. McGrath. Forces affecting success in negotiation groups. *Behavioural Science,* 1970, *14,* 154-163.

Vinacke, W.E. Variables in experimental games: toward a field theory. *Psychological Bulletin,* 1969, *71,* 293-318.

Vinacke, W.E., and A. Arkoff. An experimental study of coalitions in the triad. *American Sociological Review,* 1957, *22,* 406-414.

Waddington, J. Social decision schemes and two-person bargaining. *Behavioural Science,* 1975, *20,* 157-165.

Wager, L.W., and E.G. Palola. The miniature replica model and its use in laboratory experiments of complex organizations. *Social Forces,* 1964, *42,* 418-429.

Walker, K. Executives' and union leaders' perceptions of each others attitudes to industrial relations: The influence of stereotypes. *Human Relations,* 1962, *15,* 183-195.

Walton, R.E., and R.B. McKersie. *A Behavioral Theory of Labor Negotiations: An Analysis of a Social Interaction System.* New York: McGraw Hill, 1965.

Weick, K.E. Organizations in the laboratory. In V.H. Vroom (Ed.), *Methods of Organizational Research.* Pittsburgh: University of Pittsburgh Press, 1967.

Williams, R.J., Jr. *The Reduction of Intergroup Tensions.* New York: Social Science Research Council, 1947.

Willis, R.H. Coalitions in the tetrad. *Sociometry,* 1962, *25,* 358-376.

Wilson, A. *War Gaming.* Harmondsworth: Penguin Books Ltd., 1970.

Wodehouse, P.G. *Aunts Aren't Gentlemen.* London: Barrie & Jenkins, 1974.

Wrightsman, L.S., J. O'Connor, and N.J. Baker (Eds.). *Cooperation and Competition: Readings on Mixed-Motive Games.* Belmont, California: Brooks/Cole, 1972.

Wyer, R.S. Prediction of behaviour in two-person games. *Journal of Personality and Social Psychology,* 1969, *11,* 222-238.

Zelditch, M., Jr., and K. Hopkins. Laboratory experiments with organizations. In A.
    Etzioni (Ed.), *Complex Organizations: A Sociological Reader.* New York: Holt,
    Rinehart and Winston, 1961.

12

INTERPARTY AND INTERPERSONAL EXCHANGE IN NEGOTIATION GROUPS

Geoffrey M. Stephenson

NEGOTIATION GROUPS

By negotiation group, I refer to those occasions when representatives of two (or more) parties meet to discuss how an issue which divides the groups shall be resolved. Meetings between individuals acting each on his own behalf would be excluded by this definition. Industrial "collective bargaining" between representatives of managements and unions most clearly fits the definition.

The negotiation group has been neglected by social psychologists, although its potential contribution to our understanding of decision-making in small groups is considerable. Perhaps investigators have feared its sheer complexity. Walton and McKersie (1965) discerned no less than four major subprocesses in collective bargaining: distributive bargaining, integrative bargaining, intraorganizational bargaining and attitudinal structuring. Each of these subprocesses was said by the authors to generate its own alternative strategies and related tactics. Although an influential work, Walton and McKersie's analysis of the complexity of the dilemmas facing the representative of parties to a negotiation has probably discouraged potential researchers. The difficulties of adequately describing interactions which at any one moment have such various implications is daunting. A negotiator has to compete, he has to cooperate, he has to ingratiate, and he has to lead. His behavior at any one time may bear on all these goals, and hence, cannot be parcelled out and attributed neatly to one or the other "subprocess". Adequate description, not to say theoretical explanation, is a forbidding challenge.

The complexity arises principally from the ramifications of the negotiator's representative role. The negotiator cannot merely compete with his adversaries for the largest slice of the cake. Loyalties and friendships from the past and considerations of future relationships, with respect both to his own and also opposing group members, ensure that no simple set of rules, or straightforward choice of strategies, will determine the outcome. However, although the negotiator's position is a particularly painful one, it is not unique. We all act as representatives in our everyday transactions with our fellows, although the variety of our affiliations, to different work, family, and social groups may enable us to preserve an aura of rational debate and objective self-interest. We represent groups impulsively and irresponsibly, whereas the negotiator's performances are scheduled and formally assessed. Despite this difference, there is sufficient resemblance between the negotiator's formal representation and everyday social responsibility for us to hope that the concepts employed when describing the former may be more generally applicable. In particular the study of negotiation groups should have implications for our understanding of behavior in organizational committees and decision-making groups, whose composition is often such that the participants are willy-nilly converted into representatives of competing factions within the organization as a whole. Decision-making groups in business and academic life are frequently more aptly termed negotiation than they are problem-solving groups.

NEGOTIATION AND GROUP POLARIZATION

Mere group discussion frequently assumes the character of negotiations. For example a recent study (Stephenson and Brotherton, 1975) shows how the structure and outcome of group discussion may be influenced by competitive intergroup processes. The results suggest that these may, indeed, underlie the polarizing effect of small group debate on opinions towards issues discussed by the group. In this study, groups of coal mining supervisors discussed a variety of issues pertaining to their supervisory role. These issues took the form of key items from a role-perception questionnaire which the supervisors had completed individually some days before the experimental sessions. Such items as: "Let those I supervise set their

Figure 12-1

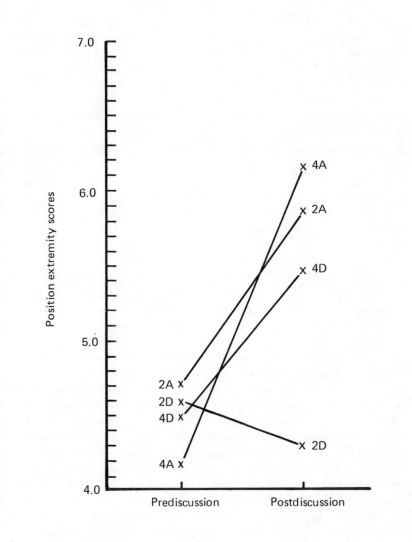

Position extremity scores in four experimental conditions at prediscussion and postdiscussion times. 4A, Four-person Agreed condition, 4D, four-person Divided condition; 2A, two-person Agreed condition; 2D, two-person Divided condition.

own workspace"; "Carry out orders even when I consider them unreasonable" and "Keep the men under me informed about what is happening in the colliery" were employed. Groups consisted of either four or two persons who were either *divided* or *agreed* on all the items they discussed together. In the *divided* two-person groups, the individuals had adopted positions on opposite sides of an issue, and in the *divided* four-person groups, two were opposed to another pair. In the *agreed* conditions all subjects had adopted positions on the same side of an issue. One principal finding showed that the polarizing effect in *divided* groups hinged on group size. Figure 12-1 portrays extremity scores for individual opinions before and after group discussion. Extremity was measured in terms of deviation from the neutral point in whatever direction. It will be seen that the two-person *divided* group members became, if anything, rather *less* polarized, or extreme, as a result of discussion than they were before they talked together. Four-person *divided* groups on the other hand became more extreme, as did both sets of *agreed* groups, ($p < .01$ for Group Size, and $p < 0.25$ for Attitude Position, i.e., 'agreed' or 'divided'). There was, however, a critical difference in the *manner* by which the *agreed* groups and the four-person *divided* group achieved their increased extremity, as Figure 12-2 indicates. Figure 12-2 gives the results for social *progression*. This term refers to the tendency to move further from neutral in the direction indicated by the initial opinion. Ratio scores were employed to take into account the available distance in terms of scale points in each direction. The results showed that the *divided* groups both progressed *negatively,* in contrast with the *positive* movement of the *agreed* groups ($p < .01$), the interaction between Group Size and Attitude Position also being statistically significant ($p < .05$). Taken in conjunction with the results for polarization it is evident that in two-person groups disagreement leads to compromise, with both parties moving towards one another, whereas in four-person groups one party or side is victorious over the other: two persons agree in the middle of the scale, four persons come to agreement at the extremes. Moscovici and Zavalloni (1969) noted the tendency for groups characterized initially by disagreement, to polarize extremely, and suggested that this represented some kind of defensive group reaction. Our results suggest that the dynamics of *inter*group conflict may best explain this tendency of divided groups to move towards extreme positions, for the same process does *not* occur in divided dyads. More recently Rabbie (1976) has shown that in Prisoner's Dilemma games the behavior of dyads competing, one pair with another, is strikingly different from that of competing individuals, in particular, by being more competitive.

Figure 12-2

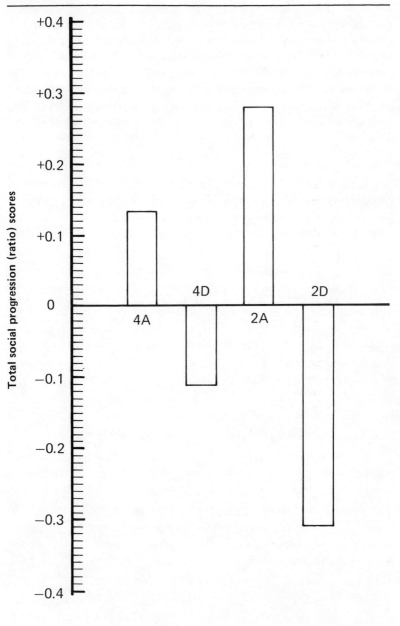

Total social progression (ratio) scores in four experimental conditions.

Individual and intergroup conflicts are resolved by different means, and our results indicate that *polarized* agreement is a product of intergroup conflict, whereas *compromise* is the product of individual conflict. Here it is useful to introduce the distinction between "interpersonal" and "interparty" exchange. Intergroup conflict, as in negotiation groups, detracts from an exchange of individual opinions, and generally reduces the salience of interpersonal considerations. Desire to be an effective representative favours interparty exchange, and concern for group interests renders interpersonal considerations of less consequence than in individual conflict or debate. The following section elaborates the distinction between interpersonal and interparty processes of exchange.

INTERPERSONAL AND INTERPARTY EXCHANGE IN NEGOTIATION GROUPS

Previous psychological approaches to negotiation groups have emphasized either the interpersonal or intergroup aspects, but have not successfully integrated the two. For example, the problem-solving approach of Bales and his followers in the Human Relations tradition emphasises the need for mutual understanding and consideration on the part of individual negotiators. From this view, given an agreeable disposition on the part of individuals, a successful outcome is an inevitable consequence of their meeting together. By way of contrast, the intergroup relations approach stresses the difficulties of obtaining agreement whatever the initial disposition of the protagonists. Loyal members of competing groups will adopt incompatible positions, reflecting the conflicts of interest between the groups. Moreover, they will view the facts, the arguments and the people involved in a way which prejudices them in favour of their own, and against the other group's proposals. In this case disagreement is the inevitable consequence of a meeting of representatives.

These two approaches epitomize "the negotiator's dilemma": that by interpersonal cooperation agreement may be achieved which betrays cherished group interests; but that by loyally defending his own party's interests the negotiator fails in his job of securing agreement. It is evident that in practice, experienced industrial negotiators successfully resolve this dilemma. It is proposed in this paper that the manner in which it is resolved can be explained only by taking into account the balance and distribution of interpersonal and interparty processes of exchange in negotiation groups.

Although it is not possible to characterize any particular action as pertaining wholly to one or the other process, it is nevertheless maintained that at any one time a negotiator may act primarily in terms of either his interparty or his interpersonal role. Hence, the relative emphasis on inter-party and interpersonal processes of exchange may vary from one negotiation to another, and from one part of a negotiation to another. The possibility of such variation has considerable implications for the way in which disputes are settled and for the quality of the settlements obtained. In support of this, I wish first to describe some experimental work which demonstrates that the *formality of the situation* may affect the balance between interpersonal and interparty exchange and, hence, the outcome of the negotiation.

FORMALITY, STRENGTH OF CASE, AND THE OUTCOME OF EXPERIMENTAL NEGOTIATIONS

Morley and Stephenson (1969, 1970) asked undergraduate student dyads to role-play a management-union dispute. The background to an industrial dispute was described in some detail, and the subjects, allocated randomly to the role of either the Personnel Officer, or the Chief Shop Steward were required to reach agreement within thirty minutes. The background information prescribed what Walton and McKersie (1965) term a "negative settlement range" in which the respective "resistance points" or minimally acceptable outcomes did not overlap. Subjects negotiated either *face to face*, or from separate rooms using an audio microphone/headphone system (the *Telephone* condition). This was the first manipulation of *formality*. The second manipulation of formality determined the freedom to interrupt. In a *Constrained* condition one subject could not speak until the other indicated that he had finished speaking for the time being. In the *Free* condition, normal interaction was permitted. Both these manipulations of formality varied the extent to which the participants were able spontaneously to convey their thoughts and feelings one to the other, and we expected that compared with the Face-to-face and Free conditions, both the Constrained and Telephone conditions would be more likely to strengthen the interparty orientation of the negotiators at the expense of interpersonal exchange. To test this hypothesis we systematically varied the relative strength of the management case and that of the union. The background material was so constructed that in one instance the management had the strongest position and the best arguments, whilst in the other instance, the union side had the stronger case. Hence, in terms of interparty exchange, one side always had the advantage. We reasoned that the side with the stronger case would more readily establish its advantage in the formal conditions, where interparty exchange could be expected to influence the outcome more than in the less formal conditions. For example, negotiators face-to-face might not be as prepared to exploit their strength than when interacting by telephone, because the implications of so doing for their opposite number would be more readily apparent. Put simply, in the face-to-face condition the negotiator representing the party with the stronger case would be more likely to feel sorry for his opponent, and, hence, not exploit his advantage, than when in the Telephone condition. The results supported this hypothesis. Figure 12-3 portrays the results for the Telephone condition. In the Telephone, as against the Face-to-face, condition we found, employing the Mann-Whitney U Test, that significantly $(p < .01)$ more victories went to the side with the stronger case. In addition, the side with the stronger case was significantly $(p < .01)$ more likely to win in the Constrained than in the Free condition of interaction, as Figure 12-4 indicates. Figure 12-5 shows a marked difference $(p < .01)$ between the most formal and least formal conditions. These experiments clearly indicated that formality, as defined, may be a highly important factor determining the outcome of negotiations between representatives of competing parties, and in our view, the important effect of formality was to alter the balance between interpersonal and interparty exchange in the relationship between the negotiators.

Short (1974) and Morley (Morley, 1974; Morley and Stephenson, 1977) have variously replicated these findings, and a recent experiment by Stephenson and Kniveton (in press) clarifies the operation of formality in these results. Using a modification of a negotiation exercise devised, and much used, by Bass and his colleagues (e.g., Bass, 1966), Stephenson and Kniveton examined the effect of seating position on the outcome of negotiations between two-person teams of negotiators consisting of subjects assigned to roles in accordance with their attitudes towards industrial relations, as measured using a reliable, validated test. Morley and Stephenson had reasoned that the principal difference between the Telephone and Face-to-face conditions lay in the different opportunities for nonverbal interactions between the participants. However, physical separation may also have been important. Stephenson and Kniveton manipulated nonverbal communication (visual interaction) within a face-to-face condition by establishing "Opposite" and "Mixed" seating positions. In the opposite condition visual interaction between the sides was facilitated, as compared with the mixed condition, for in the Opposite condition, the teams sat confronting one another across a table, whereas in the Mixed condition,

Figure 12-3

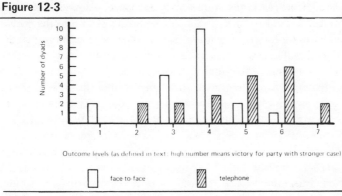

Number of dyads achieving different outcomes in telephone and face-to-face negotiations.

Figure 12-4

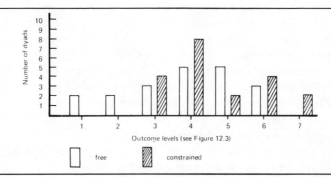

Number of dyads achieving different outcomes in constrained and free negotiations.

Figure 12-5

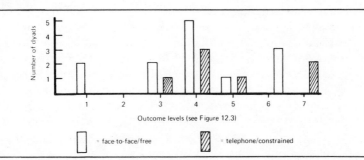

Outcomes in the most formal (telephone/constrained) and least formal (face-to-face/free) conditions

the members of the two teams were seated alternately next to one another around the table. We expected that in the Opposite condition the greater salience of visual interaction (and, hence, interpersonal exchange) would detract from an outcome in accordance with strength of case.

It was shown independently, in terms of scores on factors newly derived from semantic differential scale judgments, that the union case was highly significantly more "good" and "potent" ($p < .001$), and that the union "deserved" to and "would" win ($p < .01$). Results were analysed in terms of "deviation from the going-rate" (the average of earnings in comparable firms as detailed in the handout). Table 12-1 (a) shows that whereas in the Opposite condition management tended to win, in the "Mixed" condition the "stronger" case of the union was usually victorious ($p < .05$ two-tailed test). The same trend is true of the results when time penalties (which affect both sides) are included. The results strongly confirm the importance of formality in relation to the relative position strength of the parties, and suggest that the frequently obsessive concern negotiators show when organizing their seating arrangements is not misplaced. Pruitt and Lewis (1976) report that when eye contact between two bargainers is prevented (by placing a screen between them) their behavior is more integrative (cooperative) and less distributive (competitive). To the extent that cooperation may be regarded as a more appropriate and reasonable tactic than competition (in his experimental situation), his

TABLE 12-1

Deviation from the "going-rate" in 24 four-person negotiation groups in "opposite" and "mixed" conditions

	Opposite (n = 12 four-person groups)	Mixed (n = 12 four-person groups)	p value of diff.[*]
(a) *Without time penalties*			
Mean management "profit" or "loss"	+ £1,395	− £6,020	
			$p < .05$
Mean union "profit" or "loss"	− £1,395	+ £6,020	
(b) *Including time penalties*			
Mean management "profit" or "loss"	− £ 479	− £6,479	$p < .05$
Mean union " "profit" or "loss"	− £3,187	+ £5,604	$p < .05$

[*]Employing two-tailed Mann-Whitney U test.

result is not inconsistent with the analysis we have given. In the more formal conditions we would expect behavior to be more reasonably based, and less likely to be directed by (irrelevant) interpersonal factors.

We have assumed, in the interpretation of these various results, that the *interparty* orientation of the negotiators is strengthened in the more formal conditions, and I wish now to present some evidence which corroborates that view.

FORMALITY, ROLE IDENTIFIABILITY, AND PROCESSES OF EXCHANGE

Negotiators themselves are frequently aware that the extent to which they are acting *as representatives* varies from time to time. I have suggested that this tendency towards interparty exchange varies according to the formality of the situation and underlies the experimental findings which indicate that the party with the stronger case does better the more formal the situation in which the interaction occurs. The extent to which negotiators act as representatives may be assessed objectively in a number of ways. The most fruitful we have used may be termed *role identifiability*. Role identifiability has been measured (following Douglas, 1962) by asking judges to assess the management or union role of speakers, using only an unlabelled transcript. Randomly selected passages of transcript are given to judges without any indication of the identity of the speakers. The judges are then asked to say whether or not a particular speaker comes from the management or the union side. Results employing this technique show clearly that *formality increases the identifiability of negotiators in experimental negotiations.* Communicating by telephone rather than face-to-face, sitting opposite not side-by-side, and being unable to interrupt, all increase the identifiability of the speakers. (Morley and Stephenson, 1977; Stephenson, Kniveton, and Morley, in press). This result for medium of communication has been demonstrated using the original transcripts from Morley and Stephenson's experiments. It has also been replicated using transcripts from Stephenson, Ayling, and Rutter (1976) whose experimental conditions differed somewhat from those of Morley and Stephenson. Whereas Morley and Stephenson employed a simulation game, and asked subjects to role-play a management-union dispute, Stephenson, Ayling, and Rutter merely had subjects discuss items from a management-union questionnaire. However, subjects were selected on the basis of their overall score on this questionnaire, such that pro-management subjects were always discussing items on which they disagreed with pro-union

TABLE 12-2

Role identifiability of speakers in two experimental situations

Errors of Role Identifiability in (a) Morley and Stephenson 1969,
1970 and (b) experiments by Stephenson, Ayling and Rutter,
portrayed as percentage of number of speeches
(average of twenty judges)

(a)	Face-to-Face		Telephone	
	Free	*Constrained*	*Free*	*Constrained*
	25.27	32.68	20.69	19.91

(b)	Face-to-Face	Telephone
	40.8	33.6

TABLE 12-3

Means of conference process analysis categories[*]

	Means		
	Face-to-Face	*Telephone*	*p value*
(a) Depersonalization			
Blame for opponent	2.00	2.17	N/S
Praise for opponent	0.92	0.25	< .05
'Self' references	7.58	7.25	N/S
'Party' references	7.67	11.17	< .05
'Rejects' (disagreement)	0.67	1.08	N/S
(b) Other effects of medium			
Outcome	1.75	1.25	N/S
Offers of information	48.56	55.53	< .05
'Union' offers of information about opponent's party	1.60	3.10	< .025
	Management	*Union*	*p value*
(c) Management-Union differences			
Own party	2.07	7.51	< .001
Opponent's party	8.26	2.57	< .001
Criticize opponent	1.69	0.56	< .01
Praise opponent	0.50	0.22	< .01
Praise own/both sides	0.19	0.62	< .025
Criticize own/both sides	0.24	0.58	< .025

[*]Figures represent the mean percentage of all units allocated to CPA categories,
averaged across the management-union variable.

subjects. The subjects' predispositions were clearly more evident in the Telephone than in the Face-to-face conditions, as Table 12-2 (b) indicates. The results show the role identifiability scores of twenty judges rating Telephone and Face-to-face unlabelled transcripts, and indicate the superiority of performance in the Telephone condition ($p < .01$ employing repeated measures analysis of variance). Table 12-2 (a) gives the results of a similar analysis on Morley and Stephenson's early data, and indicates a similar trend for the Telephone versus Face-to-face comparison ($p < .001$). These data strongly endorse our interpretation of the experimental findings. Formality favours the stronger side because the interparty orientation of the negotiators is strengthened at the expense of interpersonal exchange.

Additional evidence comes from analyses using a specially devised category system for behavior in negotiations (Conference Process Analysis, see Morley and Stephenson, 1977). They show a greater concern with the exchange of information about respective party positions in the more formal conditions. For example, in the experiment by Stephenson, Ayling, and Rutter, it was found by analysis of variance (Table 12-3) that there was significantly ($p < .05$) less praise for opponent, more references to own party, ($p < .05$) and more offers of information generally ($p < .05$), and especially about opponent's party ($p < .025$) in the Telephone than in the Face-to-face conditions.

THE ANALYSIS OF REAL NEGOTIATIONS

The experimental evidence we have considered so far testifies to the importance of the *balance* between interparty and interpersonal processes in negotiation groups. Certain strategic implications may be said to follow from the results we have considered. For example, representatives of parties with the weaker case will do well to cultivate the interpersonal aspects of the relationship so that the one-sided outcome prescribed by interparty considerations will be modified out of sympathy for the other person. Representatives of the party with the stronger case should, on the contrary, if they wish to obtain an appropriate outcome, keep the negotiation firmly on a formal footing. However, the experimental negotiations in question were of short duration and, hence, unduly concentrated in comparison with real negotiations. In experimental negotiations the representatives, if they are to reach agreement in the time made available, must of necessity launch into a concession-making process which ordinarily might occur much later in the total process. This fact alone imposes real restrictions on the extent to which an examination of experimental negoti-

ations may inform us about the strategies employed in practice by negotiators as they seek to resolve their dilemma. Industrial negotiations are
frequently protracted affairs, covering many sessions each of two or three
hours duration. In such circumstances it is possible for representatives of
groups in conflict to vary their behavior strategically over time along the
interpersonal/interparty dimension in the interests of success. Hence, in
real negotiations it is likely that an examination of the *distribution* of
interpersonal and interparty emphases over time will yield valuable information about the way in which negotiators reconcile the demands of their
party with the requirement that agreement be reached.

There are good reasons to suppose that at different stages of negotiation, representatives may wish to stress either the interpersonal or interparty aspect of their role. In particular, there are reasons to suppose that
in the early stages of negotiation the demands imposed by his position as
representative will be uppermost in the mind of the negotiator. Primarily,
the negotiator must establish his credentials and his effectiveness as a
representative. Flanked by his fellow group members he will be anxious to
demonstrate his essential loyalty to the group and their present demands.
The expectations of the membership (for the shop steward) or of the
board (for the management representatives) will be particularly present in
his mind as negotiations open and unfold in the early stages. Nothing can
easily be given away; intransigence is the order of the day. However, we
may expect that such an approach may serve valuable additional interests.
Although negotiation has been described as a "dialogue of the deaf" it is
nevertheless essential that each party's case is effectively and fully expressed if a settlement which is genuinely satisfactory to both sides is to be
achieved. Each side needs to become aware of the detailed merits of the
opposition's case if either side is to be persuaded of the need to concede,
reconsider, or think afresh. Ann Douglas (1962) describes this first stage of
negotiation as being concerned with "establishing the bargaining range." It
serves to establish the limits within which parties may be expected to do
business with one another. The information it provides about the opposition's priorities aids effective strategic planning for the rest of the negotiation. It indicates where, in particular, difficulties in obtaining agreement
may be expected to occur, and hence, where efforts need to be concentrated to integrate the two positions in subsequent stages. So important do
negotiators regard this initial exchange of information that Douglas maintains that effective negotiators positively pine for a stiff opposition against
whom they may pit their wits with verve and aggression.

I have now observed and recorded a number of real negotiations, and
analyses in terms of both role identifiability and process categories point
to the value of the idea that negotiation is in practice organized into stages

which reflect different degrees of concentration upon interparty or inter-personal exchange. Apart from Douglas's findings, we have support now for the proposition that in wage negotiations at plant level, the opening stages of negotiation are characterized by a period of *interparty exchange* in which: (a) negotiators present their side's case fully and aggressively; (b) negotiators criticize both the opposition's case and individual members of the opposition; and (c) there is little or no movement towards the opposition; rather, negotiators warm to their own theme and resolve on deadlock. In a number of wage negotiations we have observed and re-corded, three bargaining sessions on three separate days were required before agreement was reached. We have analyzed in detail the interactions and the role identifiability of negotiators throughout the different ses-sions. By way of illustration we may refer to the results of an analysis of a three-session wage negotiation at a food processing plant. (Stephenson, Kniveton, and Morley, in press). Seven demands were initially made by the shop stewards, but none were conceded in the first session, which ended in apparent acrimony. New proposals integrating certain of the union pro-posals were made in the second session, and these formed the basis of the agreement whose implications were considered at some length in the final session. The results of this and other negotiations were analyzed by Session and Phase, employing role identifiability and C.P.A. categories as dependent measures. "Phases" were obtained by dividing each session into three equal parts according to the total number of acts the session contained. There was a significant decrease in identifiability from the first to the final session, and the incidence of different Conference Process Analysis categories showed generally that conflict diminished with time. For example, whereas "acceptance" of points made *increased* with time from one session to the next (p < .05), "rejection" *decreased* from a level of 5% of all acts to 1% in the final session (p < .05), as Figure 12-6 shows. In addition Figure 12-6 indicates a (nonsignificant) decrease in Acknowl-edgement Minus ("criticism") ((p < .1) and increase in Acknowledgement Plus ("praise") (p < .1) over the three sessions. Characteristically, *role identifiability* was high at the first meeting, and steadily declined on successive occasions. That is, judges could tell quite accurately from unlabelled transcripts which side the speakers belonged to on the first occasion, but became progressively less accurate as they dealt with material obtained in later sessions. (p < .05 employing analysis of vari-ance). Put another way, the behavior of managers and shop stewards became progressively *interchangeable* as time went on. Negotiators as they continue become progressively more agreeable one with another, and speak increasingly from a common viewpoint.

Figure 12-6

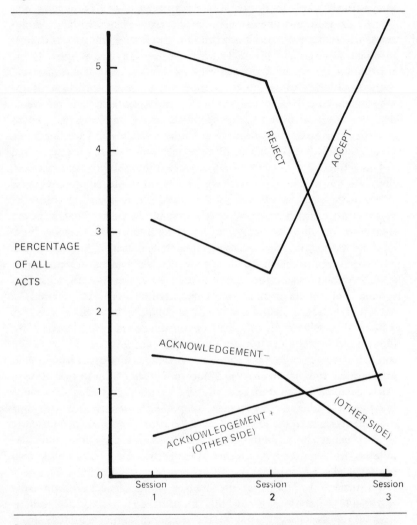

Percentage number of Acts categorized as Mode: REJECT and ACCEPT; and Resource: ACKNOWLEDGEMENT + and ACKNOWLEDGEMENT—(OTHER SIDE)

This picture of the negotiation group moving from a period of inter-party strife towards an agreeable interpersonal exchange is in stark contrast to the picture of the problem-solving group painted by Bales and his associates. In the problem-solving group negative socioemotional behavior *increases* with time as difficulties with the task are encountered. In the problem-solving group, conflict arises from coping with the task, whereas in the negotiation group conflict leads to coping with the task. Attempts to apply the problem-solving model to the practice of negotiation have led to advice which, if accepted, would contradict the process of negotiation as we see it successfully operated in practice. Psychologists have sometimes suggested that negotiators should, from the outset, seek to discern and promote areas of agreement between the two sides. Observations suggest, on the contrary, that successful negotiators initially promote conflict in order that possible solutions to the conflict may then reasonably be explored in a more agreeable manner. It should be pointed out, however, that Bales' division into stages was based on an analysis of single labora-tory sessions whereas negotiations as observed both by Douglas and ourselves were protracted. Such analyses of single sessions within a negoti-ation as we have performed suggest that we are unlikely to find a *standard* sequence for isolated sessions within a negotiation sequence. For example, Figure 12-7 depicts the results of an analysis of phases within the three sessions of the wage negotiation. The results are for incidence of the referent Other (talking explicitly about the opposition), an important category of behavior which probably underlies the role identifiability measure for which a similar interaction was apparent. While references to Other decrease overall from one session to the next ($p < .05$), the pattern is different within sessions ($p < .02$). It appears that the structure of an individual session may, reasonably enough, be determined by position in total sequence. For example, when the first session ends on a conflictful note, conflict is likely to characterize the opening phases of the next session.

Confirmation of this general pattern comes from an analysis recently completed of a three-session negotiation of an agreement on the employ-ment of temporary labor. This was carried out in a major British Chemical manufacturing company and, hence, complements and contrasts with the previous study which was conducted in a small-scale food manufacturing plant. A role identifiability study of the three meetings was carried out employing sixteen judges. There were no significant differences between judges. Figure 12-8 shows that as in other analyses, the identifiability of negotiators varied from session to session, the representatives being least identifiable in the final session (53% correct judgments as compared to 58% and 60% in the first two sessions respectively). Analysis of variance

FIGURE 12.7

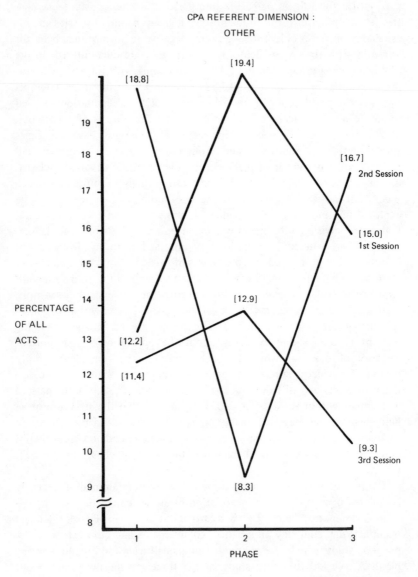

CPA REFERENT DIMENSION :
OTHER

(From three-session Wage Negotiation)

Geoffrey M. Stephenson   225

(see Table 12-4) demonstrates that the overall phases effect was comparatively weak (p < .05) indicating no strong general trend for single negotiating sessions. However, the interaction between sessions and phases was, as before, highly significant (p < .0001) as Figure 12-8 and Table 12-4

Figure 12-8

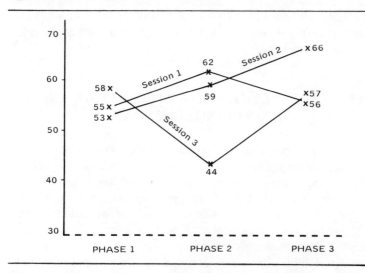

ROLE IDENTIFIABILITY OF NEGOTIATORS BY PHASES AT THREE MEETINGS TO NEGOTIATE A TEMPORARY LABOR AGREEMENT AT A MAJOR BRITISH CHEMICAL PLANT. (Stephenson, 1976)

TABLE 12-4

Analysis of variance on role identifiability scores
in sessions of negotiation of a temporary labor agreement
between managers and shop stewards

	Source	SOS	DF1	VE	F	DF2	P
A	Judges	0.5067	15	0.0338	0.775	576	n.s.
B	Meetings	0.5357	2	0.2679	6.142	30	< .01
C	Phases	0.3142	2	0.1571	4.107	30	< .05
AB		1.3084	30	0.0436	1.001	576	n.s.
AC		1.1476	30	0.0383	0.878	576	n.s.
BC		1.4603	4	0.3651	9.638	60	< 0.0001
ABC		2.2729	60	0.0379	0.869	576	n.s.

show. The first session demonstrates the characteristic rise in identifiability as the argument heats up, and this trend continues strongly with the second session where, at the close, identifiability is at its peak of 66%, before falling off in the final session. Again we may say that the position in the total negotiation crucially determines the structure of an individual session, in a more or less predictable way. In the three-meeting cases we have considered, there appears to be a "crescendo of conflict" which overlaps the first and second sessions, and which imparts a distinctive character to each meeting.

EFFECTIVE NEGOTIATION–SPECULATION AND CONCLUDING COMMENTS

It seems that negotiators learn to separate their interparty and interpersonal roles somewhat in time. Their interparty orientation is uppermost in the early stages, and an interpersonal orientation takes over as we see the bargainers make increasingly less partisan statements in the later stages. Can we say more precisely what is served by this separation of interpersonal and interparty roles in time? As we have suggested, the first stage of interparty debate serves to demonstrate a negotiator's credentials as an effective representative, and it ensures that each side is put fully in the picture about the extent of disagreement. More than this, however, the first stage may be said to determine in a general sense what the outcome of the negotiation shall be. In the various negotiations we have observed, the bargainers have battled hard until it has been decided, not in detail but in general terms, which side shall be the ultimate victor, and to what extent. At the conclusion of this first stage it will be at least implicitly determined whose position is strongest and who will be obliged to concede most in the subsequent stages. At this point the first (distributive) battle is done, and in subsequent debate it is the task of the negotiators to forge an (integrative) agreement which accurately reflects the outcome of that first stage. In this task both sides will collaborate in creating an agreement which may be presented without loss of face by representatives from both parties to their respective principals. They may readily cooperate in this task at an interpersonal level because their job as a representative is essentially over.

The increasing difficulty judges have in distinguishing between negotiators stems partly from the reduction in criticism of each side by the other, and from an increasing tendency to make proposals for the group which transcend party advantage. C.P.A. analyses reveal a considerable increase in the number of proposals for joint action in later bargaining sessions. This reaches its climax in the final phase when suggestions for drafting and presenting the agreement are being made. Although somewhat speculative, the evidence we have from an analysis of real-life industrial negotiations suggests a three-stage process in which the separation of interparty and interpersonal roles plays a crucial part. A first period of *Interparty Exchange* is characterized by *hard distributive bargaining*, the conclusion of which is an *implicit agreement* as to which side has the advantage and to what extent. A second stage of *Interpersonal Exchange* is characterized by *problem-solving behavior* designed to find an acceptable set of *detailed proposals* which will fulfill the criteria established in the first phase. In the third phase of *Group Decision-Making*, proposals for *implementing* proposals are agreed upon and a detailed *explicit agreement* is determined.

This description derives from observations of real negotiations. It is presented as a model of the way experienced negotiators in practice set about reaching agreement. Inasmuch as our observations are of the behavior of skilled practitioners of the art of negotiation, they may be said to have a certain prescriptive authority such that one may reasonably teach would-be negotiators the techniques required to progress through the stages. But its practical value is not all. Sustaining, and perhaps integrating, group and individual interests is a skill required by all to some degree, and one which the negotiator, by virtue of his task, must master. To explain the negotiator's successful performance we have suggested that the distribution and timing of interpersonal and interparty processes of exchange is fundamental. For a long time there has been in social psychology a divide between sociological explanations based on concepts of social role and psychological explanations based on assumptions of individual interest and choice. Psychologists have tended to examine experimental situations in which opportunities for the exercise of customary roles are limited, whereas sociologists have paid attention to public behavior in which individual differences are of less interest than the shared expectation of the actors. In negotiations, the participant has both to fulfil social expectations and to exercise his individual judgment and interpersonal skills. I would repeat the hope that the results of these studies will help us understand other situations in which individuals are obliged to reconcile individual and group interests, for such situations contribute largely to the domain of social psychology.

REFERENCES

Bass, B.M. Effects on the subsequent performance of negotiators of studying issues or planning strategies alone or in groups. *Psychological Monographs: General and*

Applied, 1966, *80,* (Whole No. 614), 1-31.

Douglas, A. *Industrial Peacemaking.* New York: Columbia University Press, 1962.

Morley, I.E. Social Interaction in Experimental Negotiations. Ph.D. Thesis, University of Nottingham, 1974.

Morley, I.E., and G.M. Stephenson. *The Social Psychology of Bargaining.* London: Allen and Unwin, 1977.

———. Formality in experimental negotiations: A validation study. *British Journal of Psychology,* 1970, *61,* 383-384.

———. Interpersonal and interparty exchange: A laboratory simulation of an industrial negotiation at the plant level. *British Journal of Psychology,* 1969, *60,* 543-545.

Moscovici, S., and M. Zavalloni. The group as a polarizer of attitudes. *Journal of Personality and Social Psychology,* 1969, *12,* 125-135.

Pruitt, D.G., and S.A. Lewis. The dynamics of integrative bargaining. Paper read at the XXIst International Congress of Psychology, Paris, 1976.

Rabbie, J.M., and Lieuwe. Competitive and defensive orientations in interpersonal and intergroup conflict. Paper read at the XXIst International Congress of Psychology, Paris, 1976.

Short, J.A. Effects of medium of communication on experimental negotiations. *Human Relations,* 1974, *277,* 225-234.

Stephenson, G.M., K. Ayling, and D.R. Rutter. The role of visual communication in social exchange. *British Journal of Social and Clinical Psychology,* 1976, *15,* 113-120.

Stephenson, G.M., and B.K. Kniveton. Interpersonal and interparty exchange: An experimental study of the effect of seating position on the outcome of negotiations between teams representing parties in dispute. In press.

Stephenson, G.M., B.K. Kniveton, and I.E. Morley. Interaction analysis of an industrial wage negotiation. *British Journal of Occupational Psychology,* in press.

Walton, R.E., and R.B. McKersie. *A Behavioral Theory of Labor Negotiations: An Analysis of a Social Interaction System.* New York: McGraw-Hill, 1965.

13

INTERMEMBER RELATIONS AND REWARD ALLOCATION: THEORETICAL CONSIDERATIONS OF AFFECTS[1]

Gerold Mikula and Thomas Schwinger

I. INTRODUCTION

Once upon a time there was a rich old man who left his property to two heirs when he died. The two heirs tried and tried but they could not reach an agreement about dividing up the riches. So, after a long and unsuccessful dispute they consulted a wise man—perhaps a social psychologist. The wise man told the first one "You may *divide* the riches into two parts in any way you desire", and to the second one he said "And you may *choose* the part you desire". This fairy tale demonstrates to us that joint ownership may cause allocation problems and it also shows one perhaps rather unusual solution to such a problem. In this paper we shall not concern ourselves with the solutions suggested by wise men, even if they are social psychologists. Rather, we shall concentrate our discussion on the question of how group members possessing something in common solve the allocation problem.

Let us first look at the reasons why joint ownership may come about. Besides the already mentioned inheritance, other gifts made to group members, as well as finding something in common (e.g., money), may lead to joint ownership. Finally, joint ownership may result from the joint work of group members—whether the acquired goods in common are the product of the work itself or something received in return for the work, such as wages or rewards. If group members are working together on a task and subsequently acquire something in common (which we shall call a "reward" in accordance with exchange theories) the allocation problem occupies an especially important position (see Kelley and Thibaut, 1969). This is the case because the way in which group rewards are allocated has a strong impact on group productivity, group structure, socioemotional intermember relations within the group, and members' satisfaction with their group. Some studies have shown, for instance, that the reward structure of a group influences whether the interests of the partners are congruent (which leads to cooperation), whether they are incongruent (which leads to competition), or whether a mixed motive situation arises, with partly congruent and partly incongruent interests (Deutsch, 1949; Smith, 1959; Zander and Wolfe, 1964). This correspondence of the partners' interests has an impact on the group members' mutual trust and on their willingness to support one another, so that the group productivity as well as the socioemotional intermember relations depend on the reward structure of the group. Further, the reward allocation may influence the status structure and the resulting status differences may, subsequently, bring about problems in the socioemotional area (see Bales, 1955; Strodtbeck, Simon, and Hawkins, 1965; Wiggins, 1966) as well as communicational problems (Hurwitz, Zander, and Hymovitch, 1968; Kelley, 1951), which, in turn, may impair the group productivity. Finally, the reward allocation influences the members' satisfaction in and with their groups, which has important consequences on their motivation, on their engagement in group activities, and on the continuation of their group membership (see Thibaut and Kelley, 1959).

The aforementioned group characteristics and group processes, which are interrelated with one another in a very complex way, both influence and are, in turn, influenced by the reward allocation. We shall, however, concentrate our discussion here on the interdependence of the reward allocation and the socioemotional intermember relations in the group.

REWARD ALLOCATION AS A POTENTIALLY DANGEROUS CONFLICT

What is it that makes reward allocation a problem? In the end, it seems to be the finiteness of the available goods. If the quantity of a group reward is sufficient to satisfy the wishes and needs of all participants, then everyone can take as much as he wants or needs without jeopardizing the satisfaction of any of his partners' needs. In this case, no allocation problem exists. If, however, the quantity of the reward in common is not sufficient to simultaneously satisfy the needs of all partners—as is frequently the case—a conflict arises between the partners' interests. This conflict may become increasingly dangerous to the group existence the more valuable the reward is for the group members.[3] Provided that the partners are interested in the continuation of the group existence, they will avoid violent solutions to the allocation problem which jeopardizes the group existence, and will try to find a solution which is acceptable to all of them, even if it does not fully satisfy all the individual wishes and needs. What are the possibilities of finding such a solution? As Pruitt (1972) has pointed out, there are two different procedures for solving interpersonal conflicts of interests by the group members themselves. The first consists in bargaining while the second consists in the application of a widely recognized norm. Of course these two procedures are not fully distinct. On the one hand, the arguments in the bargaining process may be supported by reference to a specific norm. On the other hand, the application of a norm may be preceded by a discussion or by bargaining about the appropriateness of norms. Nevertheless it seems that the distinction between bargaining and norm application as two possible procedures for a solution of an interest conflict is a useful one.

For several reasons bargaining may be a costly procedure involving many disadvantages: it takes a lot of time and it may be risky, because its results are unknown and insecure. Further, the usual bargaining tactics, such as deceptions and threats, may lead to distrust and consequently stress the intermember relations. Finally, a bargaining solution seems not to be a very stable solution. This is the case, firstly, because it is achieved virtually by informal influence; and, secondly, because the result of bargaining consists necessarily of a compromise between the partners, which applies only for the single situation in question. A normative solution, on the other hand, seems less costly and more stable than a bargaining solution. This is the case because the employment of a norm is accompanied by a consonant interpretation of the situation by all group members which may lead to increased group cohesiveness (see Bonacich, 1972; Kelley and Thibaut, 1969); further, the informal influence is substituted by a subordination to an impersonal authority (Thibaut and Kelley, 1959). Finally, conforming to internalized norms which are anchored in larger value systems will be experienced by the group members as intrinsically rewarding. Therefore we can conclude that the group members will try to employ a norm rather than to start a bargaining process. To avoid misunderstandings we have to make clear more explicitly our point of view: we state here that the employment of a norm will be preferred over a bargaining process because it includes fewer threats to the group's existence and to the group climate. This does not mean, however, that all problems must be solved through the employment of a normative solution. Sometimes it may not be fully clear which norm should be employed or how to carry out a chosen norm. In such situations bargaining about the norm will take place.

What are the norms which seem appropriate as means to a solution of the interpersonal conflict of interests? In connection with an allocation problem the *norms of distributive justice* seem to be most important. These norms not only guide the allocation behavior of the members of small groups, but also prevail in larger social systems and are learned and internalized by the members of a society during their early socialization (see Walster, Berscheid, and Walster, 1973; Kohlberg, 1963; Piaget, 1954; Staub, 1972). They are applied whenever a dangerous conflict of interests threatens to arise as a result of the impossibility of sufficiently and simultaneously satisfying all the participants' wishes and needs. In this sense, justice may be interpreted as compensation for the complete satisfaction of the group members' wishes and needs. One may not feel fully satisfied with a just solution, therefore, but one is not allowed to express one's dissatisfaction with it (see Mikula, 1973b, p. 18).

WHAT DOES "JUSTICE" MEAN?

Perelman (1963, p. 16), a philosopher of law, defines formal or abstract justice "as a principle of action in accordance with which beings of one and the same essential category must be treated in the same way." Because this formulation leaves the way in which the beings should be categorized undecided, it can be used to call any action whatsoever a just one.[4] Among the various possible categorizations discussed by Perelman, the following four seem especially relevant in connection with reward allocation: "to each the same thing," "to each according to his needs," "to each according to his work," and "to each according to his merits."

Probably influenced by the far-reaching significance of the performance principle in industrial societies, most social psychologists who are concerned with the problem of justice have called a social relationship a just one if the ratios of the inputs and outcomes of the participants in a relationship are equal, i.e., if all participants are receiving equal relative outcomes from the relationship (see Adams, 1965; Blau, 1964; Gamson, 1964; Homans, 1961; Walster et al., 1973). Inputs are defined in this context as those contributions a person brings into an exchange and for which he expects a just return; outcomes are defined as those positive and negative consequences a person gets from his participation in an exchange. According to this conception of justice, the "beings," as Perelman says, are thus categorized according to their work and merits, which are combined and treated as inputs. One of the most stimulating psychological justice theories—the *equity theory*—was formulated first by Adams (1965). His ideas were strongly influenced by the concepts of "distributive justice" as proposed by Homans (1961) and "relative deprivation" as it was proposed by Stouffer et al. (1949). In its original form Adams' approach was a theoretical model of reactions to states of inequity and cognitive dissonance in work situations. Such states result if the individual proportions of the inputs (like performance, effort, abilities, and seniority) and outcomes (like wages, approval) of persons having an exchange relationship with one another or with a third party are not identical.[5] The aim of Adams' model was primarily to predict the reactions, or more specifically the direction and the extent of changes in the work quality and quantity, of workers paid inequitably.

Some years later Walster, Berscheid, and Walster (1973) elaborated Adams' model to a general theory of social behavior in which social actions are analyzed as reactions to inequity, or as means to reach or maintain a state of equity, in such diverse interactions as industrial relations, exploiter-victim relationships, philanthropists-recipient relationships, intimate relationships and the like (see also Walster, Utne, and Traupman, 1977).

In this unidimensional justice approach, as it is primarily proposed in the elaboration of the equity theory by Walster et al., it is assumed that all other justice principles, such as the equality and the need principle, are only special forms of the more general equity principle, which can be easily reduced to this general principle of justice. This is really possible in certain cases if some additional assumptions are made. Imagine, for instance, that members of a group divide a joint reward according to the equality principle, despite the fact that the group members have made different contributions to the reward attainment. If one wants to interpret such an allocation as a result of an equity motivation, it is necessary to make additional assumptions, e.g., that the individual contributions are weighted in such a way that equal contributions finally result. Another possibility would be to assume that those individuals who contributed more than others get rewards other than the allocated one, so that the proportions of the total outcomes and inputs are the same for all participants (see Mikula and Uray, 1973). For other situations, e.g., for those in which the need principle prevails, the additional assumptions which are necessary to sustain the unidimensional justice approach for explaining the observed actions are so complicated, that the predictions which could be derived from the equity theory are rather weak.

Therefore, it seems to be more useful to take a multi-dimensional approach to the phenomenon of justice. We assume that several different justice principles are operating besides the equity or contribution principle, as we shall call it in this paper, and that these different principles operate under different specific conditions. In our opinion, the following two empirical results, in particular, support the necessity of assuming the operation of several different justice principles. First, in developmental studies of children's reward allocation behavior it has been found that the acquisition of the equality principle as an allocation rule clearly precedes the acquisition of the equity principle (Lerner, 1974, Mikula, 1972c). Secondly, in many other studies it has been observed that group members who made different-sized contributions to the reward attainment proposed different allocations in one and the same situation. (For a more extensive discussion of this point see Part III of this chapter.) Similar arguments have been made by other authors, too (Lerner, 1974; Leventhal, 1976a, b; Sampson, 1969, 1975).

In connection with reward allocations, the *contribution principle* (as a combination of Perelman's work principle and merit principle), the *equality principle,* and the *need principle* seem to be most important, although other justice principles may also operate.

II. THE GROUP MEMBERS' CHOICE OF A JUSTICE PRINCIPLE

The following discussion is concerned with the group members' choice of an allocation mode for a given situation. According to our previous considerations our discussion of the specific conditions leading to certain choices begins with the assumption that the group members will try to employ one of the three justice principles which we have mentioned as most relevant for the reward allocation. We do not want to present a stringent theoretical model for group decisions concerning the distribution of rewards in this paper. Rather, we want to make clear our general line of reasoning. Therefore we shall simplify the matter in some respects: First, we shall concentrate our discussion on the impact the affective inter-member relations have on the allocation decisions. Secondly, we shall assume throughout this chapter that all group members have the same aims and intentions and the same power in their group. Undoubtedly, this will very seldom be the case. Much more often the group members will differ in their power position, with the more powerful persons more successful in accomplishing their goals (see Walster and Walster, 1975).

Finally, we shall deal here only with the choice of a justice principle and not with the decision as to how the chosen principle may be implemented. Obviously, this is also an important restriction because in many group situations there will be more disagreement about how to carry out a given justice principle than about the principle to be chosen. Since it is the primary purpose of our paper to demonstrate how one must proceed in the derivation of predictions concerning the choice of a justice principle, if one starts with a multidimensional concept of justice, it seems legitimate to simplify the matter in this way.

GROUPS WITH SPECIFIC RULES

In some groups it may be the case that the participants have already established a certain allocation rule which can be called upon when needed. Such a group-specific rule may exist as an explicit formal contract between the partners, e.g., a contract concerning the distribution of the earnings of a rock band, consisting of the musicians, the manager, and the "roadies." In other groups no formal contract may exist, but it may have become a habit, over a period of time, to distribute group rewards in a certain way. If, for instance, it is the custom in a certain commune to distribute food and other resources equally among the partners, then even such special things as *cannabis india* should be distributed equally among them. Similarly, in industrial organizations in which the performance principle is the main justice principle, not only the wages but also the extra paid overtime hours, in which more than one worker is interested, may be distributed according to the same principle. Finally, in a husband-wife relationship, in which the need principle operates, the husband may not claim the purchase of a new suit whenever his wife buys a new dress.

To summarize, we state here that in some groups an allocation rule may (explicitly or implicitly) already exist, such that there is no problem with allocation because it can be simply carried out according to the existing rule. For such groups, of course, we are not in the position of being able to predict the allocation mode, without a knowledge of their specific rules. We may assume, however, that the situation-specific determinants of the allocation rule choice, which we shall discuss below, will also have determined the establishment of the group-specific rules. If we know the typical situational circumstances and characteristics of such a group, we can therefore assume that the existing group-specific allocation rule will correspond to these circumstances.

Groups which did not develop a group-specific allocation rule in the past will be heavily influenced in their choice by the normative justice principles prevailing in their superordinated social system. Furthermore, the choice will be influenced by whether or not the group members anticipate further interactions with one another beyond the present situation.

GROUPS ANTICIPATING NO FURTHER INTERACTIONS

Those groups which anticipate no further interactions of the partners beyond the present situation (i.e., the group situation will be terminated after the reward allocation) will choose that allocation rule which conforms to the justice principles prevailing in the superordinated social system for those situations which are similar to the present group situation. Such a solution to the allocation problem provides both intrinsic and extrinsic rewards to the group members in the form of self-satisfaction and social approval, because it conforms to a social norm (see Nord, 1969). Further, it involves no obligations for the participants because of its situational appropriateness. In those groups, however, in which the participants anticipate further interactions, the consequences which result from the rule application for the social relations between the group members will have great influence on the choice, in addition to the situational adequacy and the norm conformity of the rule. Let us first look, however, at the so-called situationally appropriate solutions. Under what conditions can we say that an allocation rule is appropriate for a given situation? We believe that certain situations exist in which, because of normative agreements in our society, a certain justice principle is deemed more appropriate than another one.[6] But, what are the typical situations for the different principles and what presuppositions are necessary for the employment of each of these principles?

The *contribution principle* states that each person of a given group should get a share of the reward according to the size of the contributions he has made toward the attainment of the reward. The typical situation for this principle occurs when the reward held in common has been achieved by the independent work of the group members without any interdependency of the contribution principle it is necessary to require that the contributions each participant makes can be easily assessed and associated with him.

The *equality principle* states that each member of the group should get an equal share of the reward. This principle may occur in several different situations. The first and most important situation arises in groups with strong solidarity in which the commonness and the similarity of the group members are the outstanding characteristics of their relationship. This can be the case, for instance, when the persons involved in the relationship are in more or less perfect unity with other persons (e.g. a friendship), secondly because they compete with another group, and finally because they are exposed to a common external danger. Other situations, to which the equality principle seems appropriate, are working situations in which the reward is achieved by cooperative and interdependent work, such that the individual contributions of the partners can neither be assessed nor associated with a single person; and finally, situations in which the reward consists in a gift or in finding something rather than being achieved by work. The last two situations mentioned differ in some respect from the first one in that the equality principle is presumably the only one used since no prerequisites are necessary for its employment while the prerequisites necessary for the application of the contribution principle are lacking.

The *need principle* states that each group member should get a share of the reward according to his needs. The typical situation for this principle occurs if some group members have very strong reward needs, and if they are entirely dependent on the group for satisfying these needs. The prerequisite for the employment of the need principle is exact information about the intensity of the group members' needs.

Now, we assume that given a group situation which is clearly and unequivocally structured in one of the above-mentioned ways, that the reward allocation in groups anticipating no further interactions is carried out according to the respective justice principle. The less clearly structured a situation is,[7] the more difficult it becomes to make a prediction, because the final choice will then depend upon the specific circumstances and the specific group characteristics (e.g., the power distribution).[8]

GROUPS ANTICIPATING FURTHER INTERACTIONS

In contrast to those group situations in which the group members do not anticipate further interactions beyond the reward allocation, there are many groups whose participants have to expect further contact with one another. This may be the case either because their association is a non-voluntary one (such as the association of pupils in a school class, of soldiers belonging to the same military unit, or even the association of the members of a family) or because the participants voluntarily want to continue the relationship (e.g., friends, club members). In such groups the way in which the application of the different rules influences and shapes the existing social relationships becomes important, in addition to norm conformity and the situational appropriateness of a particular allocation rule. We assume that the group members are aware of and consider the consequences resulting from each of the justice principles and finally choose that one, which corresponds to the partners' intention. Therefore, we shall now look a little closer at these consequences. As it was mentioned above we shall discuss here only the socioemotional or affective consequences of the various allocation rules. The consequences of allocation upon group productivity are discussed by Leventhal (1976a).

Generally speaking, the employment of an allocation rule can either improve the existing affective relationships, impair them, or leave them uninfluenced. Which of these consequences are attained will depend, at least in part, on the nature of the existing affective intermember relations. Therefore, we shall distinguish three kinds of relations: positive, neutral and negative. We define positive relationships as those in which the group members have positive affective intermember relations or want to shape their relations in a positive manner. Neutral relationships are those with neither distinctly positive nor distinctly negative affective intermember relations, provided the partners want to maintain this state; this means that the partners do not want to enter into obligations nor do they wish to shape their relationship in either a positive or a negative way. Finally, we call those relationships negative in which the group members have negative affective intermember relations and want to terminate their interaction.

Since voluntary relationships with negative affective bonds will rarely exist, most of the so-called negative relationships with anticipated further contact will exist on a nonvoluntary basis. Because such relationships cannot be terminated whenever the group members wish to do so, the primary intentions of the participants of negative relationships will be to satisfy their own needs as much as possible, to avoid obligations, and, if it does not seem dangerous, to harm all or some of their partners. In connection with the last point, we must take into consideration that even in so-called negative relations, purely egoistic or selfish actions will rarely be observed, because of the internalization of moral values and norms.

Having defined these three kinds of relationships, we shall now consider what consequences will result from an application of each of the three justice principles, and in which of the above-mentioned relationships these consequences will be attained. To simplify the matter, we assume throughout the following discussion that the above-mentioned intentions are the same for all group members. If this is not the case, it is impossible to predict the final solution without knowing the specific power-structure of the given group.

Contribution principle. If the contributions of the partners are different in size, an allocation according to such a distribution stresses the differences existing between the group members, and may lead to status inequality both because of the different sized rewards and the emphasis laid on the differences among contributions (see Cohen, 1974; Sampson, 1969). This may impair the affective intermember relations in the group (Bales, 1955; Strodtbeck et al., 1965; Wiggins, 1966) and support the development of competitive orientations among the partners. For these reasons we believe that allocations according to the contribution principle will tend to be avoided in groups with positive interpersonal relations. For those group members who are not interested in maintaining or improving their positive relations there will be no reluctance towards such allocations.

Equality principle. Application of the equality principle leads to relatively equal expectations among group members in terms of their reward shares, and emphasizes the existing similarities between the partners. This consequently results in an interpretation of the group situation as a cooperative one, and will maintain or improve positive affective relations between the partners. Therefore, we can assume that members of positive groups will favor this allocation rule, whereas participants of neutral or negative groups will avoid it.

Need principle. The employment of the need principle may have both beneficial and detrimental consequences for the socioemotional relations in a group. On the one hand, it demonstrates that a prosocial orientation and a responsiveness for the partner's welfare prevails in the group and may, therefore, improve the quality of the intermember relations. On the other hand, it leads to status inequality because it emphasizes the neediness and the dependency of some group members. Further, it may lead to feelings of obligation in the needy persons to reciprocate the received benefits. All these last-mentioned consequences may impair the affective relations. Some other facts suggest, however, that the need principle is more likely to be used in groups with positive socioemotional relations: first of all, its employment involves a prosocial orientation (for an exception see equality principle discussion below) which is very unlikely to exist in negative relationships. Secondly, for its employment it is necessary, as discussed above, that the group members have exact information concerning each other's needs. The disclosure of such intimate information presupposes, in general, a great deal of mutual trust between partners, because it can be easily used to exert behavior control (Thibaut and Kelley, 1959). Therefore, we can conclude that the existence of the prerequisites necessary for the employment of the need principle is much more likely to exist in positive than in negative or neutral relationships.

We have suggested above that group members who anticipate further interactions with one another consider, in their choice of an allocation rule, the social consequences of the justice rules in *addition* to the situational appropriateness and the norm conformity of each one. Until now, we have discussed, first, the typical situations for the employment of the different justice principles, and then the social consequences resulting from these principles without combining these two determinants with one another. Therefore, it is now our task to simultaneously consider the two determinants of the choice of an allocation rule. This time we shall start with the *need principle.* After having discussed the necessary prerequisites and the consequences of the need principle we concluded that it would be employed primarily in positive groups. But, because it may also have detrimental consequences for the intermember relations, it will be applied, even in positive groups, only in situations for which it is appropriate, i.e., if some group members have especially strong needs for the reward and are fully dependent on the group in the satisfaction of these needs.

Among partners with negative affective relations, the need principle will be applied only in some special cases if the necessary information is present and if the reward is not too valuable. Here the need principle may be used to emphasize the neediness and dependency of single group members, thus increasing the status differences and at the same time serving to humiliate them. This tactic, which, of course, works only if the needy persons agree with it in order to satisfy their needs or if they are too powerless to resist its employment, will be most effective in situations in which the application of the contribution or the equality principle seems appropriate. Altogether, we can conclude that the need principle will be employed in groups with positive intermember relations only if it is appropriate, whereas it is employed in groups with negative affective bonds only if it is inappropriate. Finally, in neutral social relationships, the prerequisites for the need principle will usually be lacking, but even if they are present, its employment will tend to be avoided, since the resulting obligations would burden the relationships.

Since the *equality principle* has no prerequisites, it can be employed in positive as well as in neutral and negative groups. Among partners with negative affective bonds, it will be applied only in situations for which it is appropriate and in which the prerequisites for the employment of the contribution principle are lacking because of its possible relation-improving consequences. If the participants of negative groups have made different-sized contributions to the reward attainment and the contribution principle seems to be the appropriate solution, the equality principle can be used by those group members who made the larger contributions in order to oblige or humiliate those partners with smaller contributions and thus increase status differences.

In groups with positive intermember relations the equality principle will be employed, first of all, if it seems appropriate for the specific situation. Frequently, it will also be employed, however, in situations typical for the contribution principle. This will be the case if the group members wish to avoid those social problems which might arise from the employment of the contribution principle, which accentuates the differences between the partners. In such cases, the group members will deny the relevancy of the existing contribution differences and will emphasize instead their commonness and those other dimensions in which similarities may exist among them.[9] Another argument supporting the equality principle, which may be valid in long-term relationships, consists of the notion that the contributional differences will be balanced over time, such that the equality principle, which is much easier to employ, will, in the long run, lead to the same result as the contribution principle.

Finally, participants in groups with neutral affective bonds will employ the equality principle only if it is appropriate given the situation.

The *contribution principle* can be employed in groups with positive intermember relations, as well as in groups with neutral or negative relations, if the necessary conditions are fulfilled. As we have just seen, however, in positive groups the contribution principle will frequently be avoided and replaced by the equality principle, even if it would seem to be the adequate solution. Nevertheless, the contribution principle may sometimes be applied among partners having very good affective relations (e.g., friends) without stressing the positive intermember relations, if the respective situation can be interpreted as an irrelevant, or exceptional, one and if there are sufficient other situations in which the partners are equal or similar to one another.[10] In groups with negative affective intermember relations, the contribution principle can be employed without any undesired consequences whenever the partners have made different-sized contributions to the reward attainment. Because those group members who made larger contributions will not be willing to forego their advantages, and those with smaller contributions will not want to be obliged by a concession made by their partners, an allocation according to the contribution principle will be the solution most frequently reached in negative groups, whether it seems fully appropriate or not (we shall return to this point later in this chapter).

Finally, if the affective relations among group members are neutral, they will choose the contribution principle only in those situations in which it is appropriate and, therefore, not stressful to the relations in any way.

We can conclude our discussion about the allocations utilized by group members anticipating further contact with one another with the following statements: in groups with positive intermember relations the equality principle will predominate, except in those situations which are typical for the employment of the need principle. In groups with neutral intermember relations, that justice principle will always be chosen which seems most appropriate for the given situation; hence, the allocations of neutral groups anticipating further interactions resemble those carried out by groups anticipating no further contact. Groups with negative intermember relations will choose the contribution principle whenever the necessary preconditions are fulfilled. If they are not fulfilled, the equality principle will be employed. Finally, in some special cases some group members will suggest employing the need principle or the equality principle, even though the contribution principle would be more appropriate, in order to humiliate their partners. Whether or not these suggestions will be accepted will depend on the neediness and power of these partners.

Concerning the relative weights which the situational appropriateness of a justice principle and the social consequences resulting from its employment will have in the group members' choice of an allocation rule, we propose that the consequences will assume greater importance as the situation becomes more ambiguously structured. This leads to the prediction that in unclearly structured situations the equality principle will be employed most frequently in positive groups, while the contribution principle will be the one used in neutral and negative groups, provided the necessary preconditions are fulfilled.

III. THE POLITENESS RITUAL: FUNCTIONS AND CONSEQUENCES

In this section we shall describe a special interaction pattern which has been frequently observed in studies concentrating on the reward allocations utilized by *single* members of dyadic groups, rather than on the allocation decisions made by the group members together (Leventhal, 1976a; Leventhal and Lane, 1970; Mikula, 1972a, b, d, 1973, 1974a, b, c; Mikula and Schwinger, 1973; Mikula and Uray, 1973; Schwinger, 1975; Shapiro, 1975; Uray, 1976). We have called this interaction pattern the *politeness ritual* (Mikula, 1975) and wish to discuss it here, because we are convinced that it has a great influence on the final solution reached in groups, having an allocation problem, at least in two-person groups. The above cited studies have shown that, in situations in which the employment of the contribution principle seemed appropriate, group members whose contributions to the reward attainment were different in size chose different allocations, if they felt fully responsible for the final reward allocation: those having contributed more than their partners employed the equality principle, whereas those having contributed less chose the contribution principle. These two allocation modes have in common the fact that the allocator chose that allocation rule which resulted in a larger share for the partner than the respective other rule. We interpret such allocation behavior as being guided by norms other than the justice norm, namely by general norms of modesty, politeness and responsibility.

Mikula (1974b) assumes that one reason why such norms will be especially efficient in the individual reward allocation behavior lies in the fact that in the experimental situation the allocator's partner is fully dependent on the allocator for his share of the reward. This fact activates the norm of responsibility (Berkowitz, 1972). The politeness ritual also fulfills some other functions. With such a behavioral act the allocator demonstrates his modesty and recognizes his partner's contribution. An allocator having contributed less than his partner who distributes the reward according to the contribution principle appreciates his partner's (larger) contribution and undervalues his own (poor) contribution; an allocator having contributed more than his partner does something similar when he employs the equality principle. He appreciates his partner's (poor) work and devalues his own (good) contribution.[11] By demonstrating his modesty and generosity in such a way, an allocator may gain social approval and status (see Blau, 1964) from his partner (as well as from the experimenter!) and he can oblige the partner to reciprocate the generosity with gratitude or with any other gift (see Walster et al., 1973).

Because of the functions which the politeness ritual may fulfill in social interactions, we can assume that it will occur primarily in groups with positive intermember relations. For several reasons, however, it may also occur between partners who do not want to shape their relationship in a positive manner, especially if their relationship will continue after the reward allocation. The first reason may be that the norms of being polite and modest in social encounters are internalized so strongly that it seems difficult to "forget" them, even in an interaction with a disliked partner. Furthermore, we can assume that most persons would not like being sanctioned or criticized for an impolite or selfish act, even by a disliked partner. Finally, as we have shown, a generous and accommodating behavior can also be used to oblige one's partner to reciprocations and to increase existing status differences.

We shall now concentrate our discussion on the question of how the allocation problem is solved in groups in which the politeness ritual has been triggered by the allocations suggested by the single group members. This seems to us to be an important question, for if all partners in a relationship wish to demonstrate their politeness and modesty, their intentions will conflict with one another and this subsequent conflict may sometimes be difficult to solve.[12] The resolution of the conflict resulting from the politeness ritual will partly depend on the socioemotional relations existing between the partners. In line with our earlier arguments concerning groups anticipating further interactions, we can assume that partners with positive affective relations will finally agree to employ the equality principle in most cases because of its positive consequences for the partners' relationship. For groups with negative intermember relations it is somewhat more difficult to make a prediction. Generally speaking, we would assume that the contribution principle will prevail as the final solution: The person who contributed less than his disliked partner will not be willing to be obliged by the generosity of his partner and will therefore insist on his suggestion to choose the contribution principle. The person who made the larger contribution may have suggested the equality principle only because he was afraid of being taken for selfish and would not really be willing to forego his advantages resulting from his larger contribution. Therefore, he may agree with his partner's suggestion.

Sometimes, however, negative groups may also end up with the equality principle. A group member who contributed less and who is primarily interested in getting a large share of the reward and has suggested the contribution principle for the same reasons as his partner suggested the equality principle (precisely because he was afraid of being taken for selfish) can quickly withdraw his offer after having heard the partner's suggestion and agree on the employment of the equality principle. These considerations demonstrate that a polite behavioral act can be used very easily as a negotiation tactic to impel one's opponent to a concession in a bargaining situation.[13] Because the final solution will depend in part on the negotiation skills and on the speed with which one reacts to the partner's suggestions (see Schwinger, 1975), it seems difficult to make an unequivocal prediction concerning the final solution in negative groups which have started their bargaining with the politeness ritual.

IV. SOME EMPIRICAL DATA

In the last part of the chapter we shall analyze some empirical data concerning the choice of an allocation rule, in light of our theoretical considerations elaborated above. Unfortunately, no studies exist so far which are directly derived from our approach. Therefore, we must content ourselves with a discussion of a few studies on dyadic groups which were conducted primarily from another theoretical context. The results of these studies can therefore provide, at best, only tentative support for our predictions. Another shortcoming results from the fact that no studies exist concerning the need principle. This is the case, presumably, because it is very difficult to create an adequate situation for its employment in the laboratory. Finally, we must mention that in all investigations discussed here, the situation of the reward attainment was structured in such a way that according to our classification it was typical for the employment of the contribution principle: the reward was achieved by the independent work of the group members, whose contributions were different in size and could be easily assessed and associated with the proper person.

First, we shall review some studies supporting our assumption that the anticipation of future interactions influences the choice of an allocation rule. In the first of these studies (Mikula, 1974b), the group members had to reach an agreement regarding the final allocation after having first suggested an allocation independent of one another. In this investigation we studied two different samples of subjects. One sample consisted of students, who did not have any further contact with one another beyond the reward allocation. The subjects of the second sample were soldiers belonging to the same military unit, and hence had contact with one another before, as well as after, their participating on the experiment. Although a statistical comparison between the data stemming from the two different samples was avoided, certain obvious differences between the results of the two samples seem remarkable in the present context. Whereas the members of the dyads having no further contact preferred the contribution principle as the final solution (which was the situationally appropriate one), those having further contact with one another preferred the equality principle. These different preferences are quite in line with our predictions derived earlier in this paper. However, they can provide support for our theoretical framework only if they are replicated in another study in which the anticipation of further interactions varies within the same sample of subjects.

Such a study, in fact, already exists: in an experiment which concentrated on the reward allocations executed by *single* members of dyadic groups, rather than on allocation decisions made by the group members together, Shapiro (1975) compared the allocations carried out by group members who differed in their anticipation of further contact. In one condition the allocator had no contact whatsoever with his partner before and after the reward allocation. In the other he anticipated an interaction after the reward allocation. The results showed that, those allocators anticipating no further contact chose, predominantly, the situationally appropriate contribution principle. In the dyads anticipating further interactions, the results are somewhat more complex: allocators who had made a larger contribution to the reward attainment than their partners allocated the reward mainly according to the equality principle, whereas those who had made a smaller contribution chose the contribution principle. This pattern of individually executed allocations is exactly what we have called the politeness ritual. If we assume that those subjects who anticipated further interactions with their partners wanted to demonstrate their politeness, modesty, and generosity in order to shape the ongoing relationship in a positive manner, then the obtained results fit very well in our theoretical framework. It is also easy to understand, then, why the politeness ritual was observed only a few times in the other experimental condition: because those subjects had been informed that their partners, with whom they had to share the reward, had participated in the task several days previously, so that they could never meet and receive reciprocations for their gifts by social approval.

The final two studies, which we shall discuss here (Mikula and Schwinger, 1973; Mikula, 1974b) investigated how the choice of an allocation rule is influenced by the quality of the affective relations existing between the group members. Both investigations are based on data stemming from the previously described sample of soldiers belonging to the same military unit. The first of these investigations (Mikula and Schwinger, 1973) concentrated on the allocations suggested by the *single* members of the dyads who believed they were fully responsible for the final allocation. The subjects were placed into groups with positive, neutral, and negative affective relations, respectively, as measured by means of a previously given sociometric test. The results indicated that, regardless of the existing affective relations, the politeness ritual clearly prevailed; that is, allocators who contributed more than their partners frequently suggested the equality principle, whereas those who contributed less nearly always suggested the contribution principle.

This general prevalence of the politeness ritual may have been caused by the fact that the subjects belonged to the same military unit and thus had to anticipate further interactions. Besides this, however, it was found that those subjects who made a larger contribution and who were paired with a liked partner, suggested the equality principle more frequently than those with a disliked partner. The allocations suggested by the persons who made smaller contributions were not influenced by the existing affective relations. This final result is in accordance with other similar studies and shows, as Mikula (1975 p. 7) has pointed out, "that the range of norms and allocation rules applicable for persons having contributed less to the reward attainment is seemingly much more restricted than that for superior group members. In the experimental situation the amount of the group reward depended directly on the . . . amount of work of both partners. An inferior group member therefore cannot neglect the existing difference between his own and his partner's performance, because this would seem like a disavowal of the partner's superiority, which would violate general norms of being modest and polite in social encounters."

In the second of our investigations (Mikula, 1974b), we analyzed the allocation rules finally chosen by *both* group members *together*. Here the results show that partners with positive affective relations preferred the equality principle over the contribution principle. In groups with negative affective intermember relations, both principles were chosen equally frequently as the final solution; which demonstrates very well that no unequivocal prediction is possible concerning the final solution in negative groups who start their bargaining with the politeness ritual. On the whole, we can conclude that the results of both investigations fit quite well into our theoretical framework and shows how the final choice of an allocation rule is influenced by the affective intermember relations in the group.

NOTES

1. The research reported in this manuscript was supported in part by the research grant 1454 from the Fonds zur Förderung der wissenschaftlichen Forschung.

2. We are indebted to Nancy Lyon for her help with the English translation.

3. The disastrous consequences which may result from reward allocation problems are well known from various descriptions in literature, mythology, and history. So, one could say, e.g., that the central theme of the Iliad is the consequences of a disagreement between Achilles and Agamemnon concerning the "allocation" of a booty, the lovely Briseis. Boccacio describes in his Decamerone a band of robbers who kill one another to the last man in a quarrel about the distribution of stolen jewels. Finally Marxian political scientists interpret revolutions, in part, as consequences of controversies about the distributions of gross national product.

4. The supporters of slavery, for instance, when confronted with human rights advocates, have argued that slaves are either *inferior* men or that they are not even human.

5. Imagine, for instance, the case of a senior worker, doing a hard job, who observes that his very recently hired colleague who has an easier job earns as much money as himself.

6. There may exist, of course, great differences in these typical situations between social systems embedded in different cultures. Since, however, it is our primary goal to demonstrate only our line of argumentation, we shall not take up these differences.

7. As an example of an unclearly structured situation, imagine a cooperative working arrangement among friends in which the partners' contributions can be assessed. Another case of an unclearly structured situation would exist if the participants of a working group know that some of the members have much stronger needs for the attained reward than others.

8. Because an allocation according to the equality principle is the simplest to execute (it is a "prominent solution" in the sense of Schelling, 1960), and has no necessary prerequisites, it is likely to be frequently chosen by groups as a solution in an unclearly structured situation.

9. Because it is up to the group members to define and weight the dimensions which should be taken as a basis for computing the deservingness (Leventhal, 1976b) of each member, the definition of the relevant dimensions and the weighting of the contributions can easily be done in such a way that the contribution principle and the equality principle coincide. With this argumentation we are in strong contrast to such equity theorists as Walster et al. (1973). Whereas these authors would interpret such an equal allocation as a special case of the equity principle, we are convinced that the group members *first* decide to employ the equality principle and *then* rationalize their choice by an appropriate interpretation of the situation.

10. Typical contribution situations may become dangerous, however, for the relationship between friends, regardless of which justice principle is employed, if contribution differences exist and if they are always to the advantage of the same person over a longer period of time. If the contribution principle is applied all the time, the existing and emphasized differences between the partners will stress their relationship; if the equality principle is always employed, the permanent renunciation of the superior partner and the increasing obligations of the inferior partner will serve to do the same.

11. It seems interesting to note that Feather and Simon (1971) have observed a similar strategy in quite another context, that is in attributing the causes of success and failure in social work settings: those persons who had done better than their partners attributed their own (good) and their partner's (poor) performance to such external causes as chance factors, whereas those persons who had done worse attributed their own (poor) and their partner's (good) performance to such internal causes as ability and trying.

A similar case is given in situations in which a high status and a low status person wish to exchange compliments: whereas the low status person will stress the existing difference between him and his partner, the high status person will undervalue it.

12. The problems which may arise from such a mutual exchange of polite behavioral acts can be demonstrated best by the well-known "door-game," as we call it. Imagine two persons of equal status approaching a door way. In such a situation it frequently occurs that each of them wants to demonstrate his politeness and his recognition of his partner by allowing him to enter first. This, however, may result in a long exchange of mutual deferences, until one of the two persons takes the initiative and either enters the doorway first or pushes the other one through it.

13. This is best illustrated perhaps by the following anecdote: two gentlemen having dinner together in a restaurant are served two fish of markedly different size. After each gentleman repeatedly offered the larger fish to the other, the first gentleman takes it into his plate. The other is enraged: "Don't you know that it is poor manners to take the larger serving for oneself?" "Which fish would *you* have taken?" "I would have taken the smaller one of course!" the other replies. "Fine, you got what you wanted."

REFERENCES

Adams, J.S. Inequity in social exchange. In L. Berkowitz (Ed.),, *Advances in Experimental Social Psychology.* New York: Academic Press, 1965.

Bales, R.F. Adaptive and integrative changes as sources of strain in social systems. In A.P. Hare, E.F. Borgatta, and R.F. Bales (Eds.), *Small Groups: Studies in Social Interaction.* New York: Knopf, 1955.

Berkowitz, L. Social norms, feelings, and other factors affecting helping behavior and altruism. In L. Berkowitz (Ed.), *Advances in Experimental Social Psychology.* New York: Academic Press, 1972.

Blau, P.M. *Exchange and Power in Social Life.* New York: Wiley, 1964.

Bonacich, P. Norms and cohesion as adaptive responses to potential conflict: An experimental study. *Sociometry,* 1972, *35,* 357-375.

Cohen, R.L. Mastery and justice in laboratory dyads: A revision and extension of equity theory. *Journal of Personality and Social Psychology*, 1974, *29*, 464-474.

Deutsch, M. An experimental study of the effects of cooperation and competition upon group processes. *Human Relations*, 1949, *2*, 199-232.

Feather, N.T., and G.S. Simon. Attribution of responsibility and valence of outcomes in relation to initial confidence and success and failure of self and other. *Journal of Personality and Social Psychology*, 1971, *18*, 173-188.

Famson, W.A. Experimental studies in coalition formation. In L. Berkowitz (Ed.), *Advances in Experimental Social Psychology*. New York: Academic Press, 1964.

Homans, G.C. *Social Behavior: Its Elementary Forms*. London: Routledge and Kegan Paul, 1961.

Hurwitz, J.R., A.F. Zander, and B. Hymovitch. Some effects of power on the relations among group members. In D. Cartwright and A. Zander (Eds.), *Group Dynamics: Research and Theory*. New York: Harper & Row, 1968.

Kelley, H.H. Communication in experimentally created hierarchies. *Human Relations*, 1951, *4*, 39-56.

Kelley, H.H., and J. Thibaut. Group problem solving. In G. Lindzey and E. Aronson (Eds.), *The Handbook of Social Psychology*. Reading: Addison-Wesley, 1968[2].

Kohlberg, L. The development of children's orientation toward moral order. I. Sequence in the development of moral thought. *Vita Humana*, 1963, *6*, 11-33.

Lerner, M. The justice motive: "Equity" and "parity" among children. *Journal of Personality and Social Psychology*, 1974, *29*, 539-550.

Leventhal, G. The distribution of rewards and resources in groups and organizations. In L. Berkowitz and E. Walster (Eds.), *Advances in Experimental Social Psychology*. New York: Academic Press, 1976. (a)

–––. Fairness in social relationships. In J. Thibaut, J.T. Spence, and R.C. Carson (Eds.), *Contemporary Topics in Social Psychology*. Morristown, N.J.: General Learning Press, 1976. (b)

Leventhal, G. and D.W. Lance. Sex, age, and equity behavior. *Journal of Personality and Social Psychology*, 1970, *15*, 312-316.

Mikula, G. Studies on reward allocation in dyadic groups. Berichte aus dem Institut für Psychologie der Universität Graz, 1975.

–––. Nationality, performance, and sex as determinants of reward allocation. *Journal of Personality and Social Psychology*, 1974, *29*, 435-440. (a)

–––. Individuelle Entscheidungen und Gruppenentscheidungen über die Aufteilung gemeinsam erzielter Gewinne: Eine Untersuchung zum Einfluss der sozialen Verantwortung. *Psychologische Beiträge* 1974, *16*, 338-364. (b)

–––. Gewinnhöhe, Gewinnerwartung und die Aufteilung gemeinsam erzielter Gewinne. Berichte aus dem Institut für Psychologie der Universität Graz, 1974. (c)

–––. Gerechtigkeit und Zufriedenheit beider Partner als Zielsetzungen der Aufteilung eines von zwei Personen gemeinsam erzielten Gewinns. Berichte aus dem Institut für Psychologie der Universität Graz, 1973.

–––. Gewinnaufteilungsverhalten in gleichgeschlechtlichen Dyaden: Eine Vergleichsuntersuchung an österreichischen und amerikanischen Studenten. *Psychologie und Praxis*, 1972, *16*, 97-106. (a)

–––. Gewinnaufteilungsverhalten in Dyaden bei variiertem Leistungsverhältnis. *Zeitschrift für Sozialpsychologie*, 1972, *3*, 126-133. (b)

–––. Die Entwicklung des Gewinnaufteilungsverhaltens bei Kindern und Jugendlichen. Eine Untersuchung an 5-, 7-, 9- und 11 jahrigen. *Zeitschrift für Entwicklungspsychologie und Pädagogische Psychologie*, 1972, *4*, 151-164. (c)

– – –. Die Berücksichtigung der Leistungskompetenz bei der Gewinnaufteilung. Eine Untersuchung an geschlechtsheterogenen Dyaden. *Psychologische Beiträge*, 1972, *14*, 283-291. (d)

Mikula, G., and T. Schwinger. Sympathie zum Partner und Bedürfnis nach sozialer Anerkennung als Determinanten der Aufteilung gemeinsam erzielter Gewinne. *Psychologische Beiträge*, 1973, *15*, 396-407.

Mikula, G., and H. Uray. Die Vernachlässigung individueller Leistungen bei der Lohnaufteilung in Sozialsituationen. *Zeitschrift für Sozialpsychologie*, 1973, *4*, 136-144.

Nord, W.R. Social exchange theory: An integrative approach to social conformity. *Psychological Bulletin*, 1969, *71*, 174-208.

Perelman, C. *The Idea of Justice and the Problem of Argument.* London: Routledge & Kegan Paul, 1963.

Piaget, J. *Das moralische Urteil beim Kinde.* Zürich: Rascher, 1954.

Pruitt, D.G. Methods for resolving differences of interest: A theoretical analysis. *Journal of Social Issues*, 1972, *28*, 133-154.

Sampson, E.E. On Justice as equality. *Journal of Social Issues*, 1975, *31*, 45-64.

– – –. Studies in status congruence. In L. Berkowitz (Ed.), *Advances in Experimental Social Psychology*. New York: Academic Press, 1969.

Schelling, T.C. Bargaining, communication, and limited war. *Journal of Conflict Resolution*, 1957, *1*, 19-38.

Schwinger, T. Zur Entstehung gruppenspezifischer Normen der Gewinnaufteilung. Phil. Diss., Graz, 1975.

Shapiro, E.G. Effects of future interaction on reward allocation in dyads: Equity or equality. *Journal of Personality and Social Psychology*, 1975, *31*, 873-880.

Smith, E.E. Individual versus group goal conflict. *Journal of Abnormal and Social Psychology*, 1959, *58*, 134-137.

Staub, E. Instigations to goodness: The role of social norms and interpersonal influence. *Journal of Social Issues*, 1972, *28*, 131-150.

Stouffer, S.A., E.A. Suchman, C.G. DeVinney, S.A. Starr, and R.M. Williams, Jr. *The American Soldier: Adjustment during Army Life.* Vol. 1. Princeton, New York: Princeton University Press, 1949.

Strodtbeck, F.L., R.J. Simon, and C. Hawkins. Social status in jury deliberations. In I.D. Steiner and M. Fishbein (Eds.), *Current Studies in Social Psychology*. New York: Holt, Rinehart and Winston, 1965.

Thibaut, J., and H.H. Kelley. *The Social Psychology of Groups.* New York: Wiley, 1959.

Uray, H. Leistungsverursachung, Verantworthungszuschreibung und Gewinnaufteilung. *Zeitschrift für Sozialpsychologie*, 1976, *7*, 69-80.

Walster, E., E. Berscheid, and G.W. Walster. New directions in equity research. *Journal of Personality and Social Psychology*, 1973, *25*, 151-176.

Walster, E., M.K. Utne, and J. Traupman. Equity Theorie und intime Beziehungen. In G. Mikula and W. Stroebe (Eds.), *Sympathie, Freundschaft und Ehe: Psychologische Grundlagen zwischenmenschlicher Beziehungen.* Bern: Huber, 1977.

Walster, E., and G.W. Walster. Equity and social justice. *Journal of Social Issues*, 1975, *31*, 21-43.

Wiggins, J.A. Status differentiation, external consequences, and alternative reward distributions. *Sociometry*, 1966, *29*, 89-103.

Zander, A., and D. Wolfe. Administrative rewards and coordination among committee members. *Administrative Science Quarterly*, 1964, *9*, 50-69.

14

BEHAVIOR ORIENTATION IN BARGAINING: THE DYNAMICS OF DYADS[1]

Günter Müller and Helmut Crott

INTRODUCTION

Work by Deutsch and Krauss (1960) and Messick and McClintock (1968) have contributed to the awakening research interest in the motivational explanation of interpersonal conflict behavior. Since those studies, McClintock (1972), Griesinger and Livingston (1973), MacGrimmon and Messick (1976) and others have attempted to systematize the field. According to Crott (1972) and Walster et al. (1973), situational variations in *bargaining behavior* might be explained on the assumption of three motivational components: (a) the individualistic motivation, maximizing one's own gain; (b) the social motivation, following a prevailing norm of reward allocation; and (c) the competitive motivation, following relative gain orientation. In this system, it is implicitly presumed that motivational orientation is established by the characteristics of the conflict situation. The models of motivational structure contain no statements on orientation changes during interaction itself and none on conditions under which they might occur.

Thus, statements on the dynamics of motives during bargaining cannot be derived from these statically formulated motivational concepts. However, Deutsch and Krauss (1960) concluded from empirical findings that a

competitive orientation during bargaining sessions, in which the participants have the possibility of penalizing each other, increases continuously.
As Deutsch and Krauss have observed, the possibility of penalizing induces
the subjects to employ the penalty. This results in reprisals by the
penalized person and triggers off a "seesaw" effect that leads to a high
degree of mutual aggressiveness. This tendency should be greater when
monetary gain possibilities are low than when they are high, as Gallo
(1966) has pointed out.

It has been concluded from these results by several authors that
competitive tendencies are promoted by the existence of the possibility of
penalizing and are restricted by the prospect of high gains. With high gain
possibilities a motivation oriented towards gain maximization should have
the upper hand. There should be no barrier for competitive tendencies
when monetary incentives are low, at least not when differences in the
probability of winning and the power to penalize exist (Crott 1974).

These hypotheses were derived from the overt behavior of subjects
(decisions and agreements) in conflict situations like the Prisoner's
Dilemma Game, the Trucking Game, the Bargaining Game, or other
paradigms of conflict. However, the situation from the perspective of the
subjects has not been examined. The following study was designed to
assess whether subjects have a different awareness of the situation depending on the varying features of monetary incentives, and whether the
bargaining process shows motivational dynamics that correspond to the
conception of Deutsch and Krauss (1960). In addition, the bargaining
experience of the participants was also varied. It is likely, according to a
study by Crott and Müller (1976) that orientation towards gain maximization increases with bargaining experience. As one consequence of the
dominating individualistic orientation, experienced subjects should impose
fewer penalties, especially when penalty use is costly for themselves.
Having a deeper insight into the dynamics of the conflict situation,
experienced subjects recognize that imposing penalties reduces their own
profit and moreover leads to counterattacks by the partner (which again
reduces their own outcome).

The study of dynamic motivational aspects of behavior in a bargaining
situation is problematical. In experiments with the Prisoner's Dilemma
Game it is easy to restrict the number of times the game is played. For this
reason the length of interaction can be determined by the experimenter. In
the case of a Bargaining Game it makes no sense to define a fixed number
of exchange offers to be made. Even a limited number of exchange offers
would severely disturb the decision-making process. We consider it better
to let the subjects bargain without limitations and to interview them

during the interaction about motive-relevant points of view concerning the bargaining process.

Using this method, Druckman et al. (1972) were able to obtain information on changes of the subjects' expectations regarding their opponent's offers; likewise, Yukl (1974) obtained information on the changes of the subjects' aspiration level.

Our experiment was intended to examine the extent to which different monetary incentive conditions and conditions of experience influence and differentiate the bargaining behavior of persons according to postulated motivations, and the extent to which the behavioral orientation of the bargainers was subject to change.

EXPERIMENTAL PROCEDURE AND EVALUATION

The subjects were 112 male students from Mannheim University. Their experimental assignment was to come to an agreement on the price of an imaginary product. The bargaining range was set at 40 price alternatives between 30 and 70 German Marks (DM). Subjects were informed of the

TABLE 14-1
Table of prices and profits for bargaining participants A and B (high gains)

Price	A	B	Price	A	B
70	20.00	0.00	49	9.50	10.50
69	19.50	0.50	48	9.00	11.00
68	19.00	1.00	47	8.50	11.50
67	18.50	1.50	46	8.00	12.00
66	18.00	2.00	45	7.50	12.50
65	17.50	2.50	44	7.00	13.00
64	17.00	3.00	43	6.50	13.50
63	16.50	3.50	42	6.00	14.00
62	16.00	4.00	41	5.50	14.50
61	15.50	4.50	40	5.00	15.00
60	15.00	5.00	39	4.50	15.50
59	14.50	5.50	38	4.00	16.00
58	14.00	6.00	37	3.50	16.50
57	13.50	6.50	36	3.00	17.00
56	13.00	7.00	35	2.50	17.50
55	12.50	7.50	34	2.00	18.00
54	12.00	8.00	33	1.50	18.50
53	11.50	8.50	32	1.00	19.00
52	11.00	9.00	31	0.50	19.50
51	10.50	9.50	30	0.00	20.00
50	10.00	10.00			

gains of their bargaining partners in addition to their own gains (complete information). As Table 14-1 indicates, both bargainers had identical chances of making gains (symmetrical situation).

The amount of the monetary incentive was varied in such a way that half of the subjects could win a maximum of DM 2 (low monetary incentive), the other half a maximum of DM 20 (high monetary incentive). Subjects considered as "experienced" had taken part in an experiment with a similar "assignment" a few months before the present study. Those subjects who had not taken part in a bargaining experiment before were looked upon as "inexperienced." The grouping of dyads in which two inexperienced or two experienced subjects bargained was random. The bargaining took place in the following manner: the subjects sat in separate cubicles and made price offers that were visible on luminous dial projectors when both bargainers had set their offers. The price indicator was erased automatically after seven seconds. Thereafter, a new offer could be made, and so on. In addition, the bargainers had different response options at their disposal. With these actions they could influence their partner's pay-offs either positively (reward) or negatively (penalty). By giving a bonus under the high monetary condition the subjects credited their partners with DM 0.50. However, their own costs rose to the same amount. With an x-option, subjects reduced the partner's pay-offs by DM 0.20, with a y-option by DM 0.60 and with a z-option by DM 1.00. Their own costs were half the amount. In addition, the bargainers had the option of warning their partners. No costs were connected with this action. The increasing costs and additional gains accumulated on a meter in the cubicles, i.e., the subjects always knew the amount of their own costs and gains and those of their partner. After every five exchanged offers, a bargaining break was taken, during which half of the subjects were questioned about their impression on the past bargaining sequence. After a preliminary study, questions had been selected that showed a sufficient discrimination in the sense of the postulated motivations. The internal consistency of questions on aspects of social motivation ("cooperation" and "teamwork") resulted in a correlation of 0.86, on aspects of individualistic motivation of 0.71 ("gain orientation" and "gain maximization") and on aspects of competitive motivation of 0.83 ("competition" and "rivalry"). The subjects submitted their answers on a five-point rating scale. In order to examine a possible effect of the interview procedure on the bargaining process and result, this interview was only conducted with half of the subjects. After the fifth interview, i.e., after the twenty-fifth exchange offer, there were no further interruptions of the interaction. The bargainers had one hour to reach an agreement. The following dependent variables were chosen for analysis:

1. Number of bonuses, penalties, and the summed losses subjects inflict on their partners by using X-, Y- or Z-actions.

2. Amount of the mean demand level (arithmetic mean) in each group of five exchange offers up to the 25th trial.

3. Evaluation of the past bargaining sequence according to the three dimensions at the five indicated time-periods.

4. Level of the mean ratings (arithmetic mean) on the items of the three motive dimensions (motive attributions) at all five interview periods.

In addition, the subjects answered pre- and postexperimental questions soliciting additional information about their evaluation of the situation.

HYPOTHESES

Corresponding to the motivational considerations sketched in the introduction, we formulated the following expectations:

1(a). If the monetary incentive is low, there are more penalties imposed than if it is high.

1(b). If the monetary incentive is low, the situation is considered less individualistic (that is, less oriented towards gain maximization) than if the monetary incentive is high.

1(c). If the monetary incentive is low, interaction becomes increasingly more competitive. Thus, the subjects rate their behavior during a bargaining situation as being increasingly more oriented towards competition and rivalry. Such a trend does not appear if the monetary incentive is high.

2(a). Experienced players impose penalties less frequently than inexperienced players.

2(b). Experienced players rate the situation as more individualistic (that is, oriented towards gain maximization) than inexperienced players.

2(c). Inexperienced players bargain increasingly more competitively. As bargaining proceeds they rate their behavior as increasingly oriented towards competition and rivalry.

Hypotheses 1(c) and 2(c), which postulate an increasingly competitive tendency during bargaining between inexperienced players if the monetary incentive is low, are based on the assumption that under these conditions, as it is presumed in statements 1(a) and 2(a), penalties are imposed frequently. The imposition of penalties gives the interaction an increasingly more competitive atmosphere.

No predictions were made concerning the rating of the situation as social or concerning the shift of this rating during the bargaining process.

RESULTS

An analysis of variance of the responses to questions on preliminary experimental gain orientation and on the amount of gain possibilities confirmed the success of experimental manipulation. Experienced subjects were significantly more gain oriented than inexperienced subjects ($F = 14.97$, df = 1,96, $p < 0.01$). Participants who bargained for low gains rated the gain possibilities significantly lower than subjects with high gains ($F = 95.56$, df = 1,96, $p < 0.01$).

The employment of sanctions corresponded to our expectations. If monetary incentive was low, penalties were imposed more frequently than if they were high (sign test, $p < 0.10$). However, rewards were also more frequently given ($p < 0.10$). In experienced groups the subjects imposed penalties more frequently than in inexperienced groups (sign test, $p < 0.05$).

The assumption indicated in Hypotheses 1(a) and 2(a), that if monetary incentive is low and if bargaining experience is lacking, penalties were more frequently imposed, can be accepted (see Table 14-2).

The mean motive attribution did not at all differ between monetary incentive conditions, contrary to the prediction. Nor was there any substantial correlation between the number of penalties employed and the mean rating of competitiveness under the four experimental conditions.

TABLE 14-2
Mean reduction of the opponent's pay-off by the use of
X-, Y- and Z-actions
(in units of DM .10 for low gains and DM 1.00 for high gains)

	Inexperienced dyads	Experienced dyads	ϕ
Low monetary incentive	3.65	1.46	2.56
High monetary incentive	1.61	0.86	1.24
ϕ	2.63	1.16	

TABLE 14-3
Mean Kendall coefficients of trend τ

	Inexperienced dyads	Experienced dyads
Individualistic aspects	−0.26 (p < 0.01)	−0.15 (p < 0.10)
Competitive aspects	−0.16 (p < 0.05)	−0.20 (p < 0.05)
Social aspects	0.30 (p < 0.01)	0.14 (p < 0.10)

Different degrees of experience did not show the predicted effect concerning individualistic motivation, but only concerning competitive motivation (F = 5.20; df = 1,24; p < 0.05).

Hypotheses 1(b) and 2(b), which presumed more competitive motive attribution if monetary incentive was low and higher individualistic motive attribution if the players were experienced, could not be confirmed.

Trends in the motivation attributions during the bargaining process did not differ between the conditions of monetary incentive. Hypothesis 1(c), which predicted an increase of competitive tendency during bargaining if monetary incentive was low, could not be accepted.

As far as the experience variables are concerned, trends in motive attributions during the bargaining process contradicted the prediction. Ratings of competition show a decreasing tendency in both inexperienced (τ = −0.20, p < 0.05) and experienced groups (τ = −0.16, p < 0.05). Parallel to this, individualistic orientation decreases while social orientation increases as bargaining proceeds. The mean Kendall coefficients of trend (tau) are shown in Table 14-3; the corresponding trends are shown in Figure 14-1. Thus hypothesis 2(c) must be rejected, because the competitive tendency does not increase, but diminishes.

The experimental interview on motivational evaluations of the bargaining situation was only conducted with half of the subjects. The other half were not interviewed, to establish whether the interview itself had a retroactive effect on the behavior of the subjects. Neither group differed, however, in any of the dependent variables examined (number of bonuses, number of penalties, speed of concessions during the first twenty-five bargaining offers, bargaining time and number of bargaining offers, bargaining result).

DISCUSSION

The option of imposing costly penalties is often introduced with the intention of increasing the competitive character of experimental settings (Deutsch and Krauss, Froman and Cohen, 1969). Individualistic motiva-

Figure 14-1

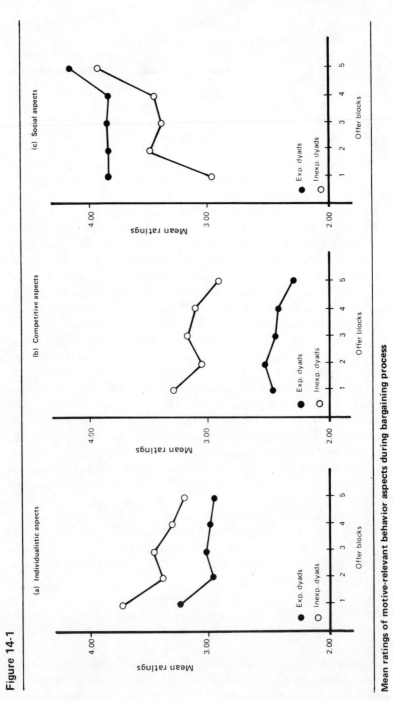

Mean ratings of motive-relevant behavior aspects during bargaining process

tion should be subject to influence by increasing of gain possibilities (Gallo, 1966, McClintock and McNeel, 1966a, 1966b).

In the present study the behavior of bargaining participants seems to indicate that the (competitive) orientation towards maximization of relative gain is less developed if monetary incentive is high than if it is low. But the fact that the bargainers also reciprocally rewarded more often when monetary incentive was low makes the motivational importance of the chosen incentive operationalization dubious. The assumption of Deutsch and Krauss (1960) that the employment of penalties causes reprisals, leading to a series of aggressions that are difficult to break, is supported by the data. The high correlation between the number of penalizing actions by two members of a bargaining group (mean $\tau = 0.60$) during the first twenty-five trials also points to this. On the other hand, this is not necessarily reflected in the average evaluations of the situation as competitive. Although if pay-offs are low, subjects penalize more often, there is no indication of a tendency to rate the situation as more competitive. Neither is the bargaining *process* rated as increasingly competitive when gains are low. On the contrary, a decrease in the competitive and individualistic orientation and an increase in the social orientation, which is typical for both conditions of experience, is observable when monetary incentive is low or high.

It is therefore presumable that the bargaining participants do not at all impose penalties as a competitive instrument. The subjects possibly want to attain a good bargaining result (not necessarily a high pay-off) even under low monetary incentive conditions. To this end they consider the sanctions as a possibility to induce the partner to comply. They employ this means more recklessly than subjects under high monetary incentive, because the associated loss to themselves is smaller. The partner reacts, however, with the same means, so that the expected result does not occur. Alternatively one could suppose that the inexperienced subjects try their response options in "playing," not anticipating any serious consequences. Anyway, once the exchange of blows has commenced, nobody wants to hold back. This interpretation is supported by the fact that experienced subjects make less frequent use of the means of imposing penalties than inexperienced subjects. The experienced bargainer recognizes that the means of imposing penalties is not suitable for attaining bargaining objectives.

It is interesting that the subjects are aware of a contrast between social orientation on the one hand and competitive and individualistic orientation on the other hand. In the same way, competitive ratings decrease, individualistic ratings also diminish and cooperative ratings increase. This holds true for both experience groups. The correlation between the rating as social and individualistic is $r = -0.46$; between individualistic and competitive, $r = 0.56$; and between social and competitive, $r = -0.72$. In earlier studies with similar experimental conditions (Crott and Müller, 1976, Crott et al., 1976), subjects had been asked the same questions *after* bargaining had been finished (postexperimental questionnaire). There, however, no substantial correlations between individualistic, competitive and social ratings were found. Postexperimental questionnaires consisting of twenty to fifty items could be summarized by three orthogonal factors—individualistic orientation, competitive orientation, and social orientation— with the six questions used in this experiment loading high on respective factors. The correlations obtained in this experiment therefore seem to indicate that this more complex structure collapses to one dimension: "individualistic/competitive versus social orientation."

Possibly the motivational ratings during the bargaining process are mainly influenced by the concession process that is dependent on an adjustment of the aspiration levels. According to Siegel and Fouraker (1960), bargaining participants revise their original aspiration levels during exchange of offers to a more realistic degree. Yukl (1974) could determine by questioning that a mutual adaption of aspiration levels does indeed result during bargaining. Price concessions are accompanied by a decrease of the aspiration level.

If the motivational rating of the bargaining process is not actually connected with the penalizing actions but only with the concession process, then the observed antagonism between the individualistic and the competitive ratings on the one hand and the social ratings on the other hand becomes plausible. The mutual adaptation of demands in a concession process, which reduces the probability of getting a very favorable pay-off, lessens also the opponent's respective success. At the same time the probability of a fair distribution of rewards (equal-split) increases, a solution with which indeed 75% of the observed interactions ended (mean price = 49.5). As far as the structure of the conflict situation (ignoring the penalizing possibilities) during concession process is concerned, individualistic and competitive tendencies should be correlated positively while individualistic/competitive and social tendencies should be correlated negatively.

It is possible to record the following results and interpretations: As Deutsch and Krauss (1960) presumed, a mutual "seesaw" effect or at least reciprocity of penalizing was indeed revealed in the employment of costly sanctions. As other studies have already shown, this is more distinctly evident if monetary incentive is low than if it is high. But this does not show up in the competitive evaluation of the situation. It is dubious, therefore, whether penalties are employed under given circumstances as a competitive device. The employment of penalties can also be interpreted as an unsuccessful attempt to induce a partner to comply or simply to explore the opponent's behavior. Also, the willingness to cooperate during bargaining is not influenced by penalizing which can be interpreted as a correlate of the concession process. With the approximation of demands, the individualistic and competitive objectives are abandoned, while the social tendency increases.

Penalizing behavior is mainly observable in inexperienced groups. This, too, supports the assumption that penalties are employed in order to induce the opponent to comply.

It would be interesting to examine how experienced bargaining participants behave toward inexperienced opponents. Further data, that have not been completely evaluated up to now, indicate that experienced subjects impose penalties in a similar way when they interact with inexperienced subjects. The latter persons usually *start* with the employment of penalties. Under these circumstances the experienced participants react by imposing penalties. Unlike all-experienced groups, the participants consider the bargaining interaction competitive, and their rating of competitiveness increases, rather than decreases, while bargaining proceeds.

NOTE

1. This study was conducted at the Sonderforschungsbereich 24 für Sozial- und Wirtschaftspsychologische Entscheidungsforschung, Universität Mannheim (FRG), financed by the Deutsche Forschungsgemeinschaft with support from the government of Baden-Württemberg.

REFERENCES

Crott, H. W. Verhandlungen als soziale Austauschprozesse. Habilitationsschrift, Universität Mannheim, 1974.
———. Der Einfluss struktureller und situativer Merkmale auf das Verhalten in Verhandlungssituationen, Teil II. *Zeitschrift für Sozialpsychologie*, 1972, *3*, 227-244.
Crott, H. W., R. R. Lumpp, and R. Wildermuth. Der Einsatz von Bestrafungen und Belohnungen in einer Verhandlungssituation. In H. Brandstätter and H. Schuler (Eds.), Entscheidungsprozesse in Gruppen. *Zeitschrift für Sozialpsychologie*, Beiheft, 1976, 2, 147-162. Bern: Huber.

Crott, H. W., and G. F. Müller. Der Einfluss des Anspruchsniveaus und der Erfahrung auf Ergebnis und Verlauf dyadischer Verhandlungen bei vollständiger Information der Verhandelnden. *Zeitschrift für experimentelle und angewandte Psychologie*, 1976, *XXIII*, 548-568.

Deutsch, M., and R. M. Krauss. The effect of threat upon interpersonal bargaining. *Journal of Abnormal and Social Psychology*, 1960, *61*, 181-189.

Druckman, D., K. Zechmeister, and D. Solomon. Determinants of bargaining behavior in a monopoly situation: Opponent's concession rate and relative defensibility. *Behavioral Science*, 1972, *17*, 514-531.

Froman, L. A., and M. Cohen, Jr. Threats and bargaining efficiency. *Behavioral Science*, 1969, *14*, 147-153.

Gallo, P. S., Jr. Effects of increased incentives upon the use of threat in bargaining. *Journal of Personality and Social Psychology*, 1966, *4*, 14-20.

Griesinger, W. D., and J. W. Livingston, Jr. Toward a model of interpersonal motivation in experimental games. *Behavioral Science*, 1973, *18*, 173-188.

Komorita, S. S., and A. R. Brenner. Bargaining and concession making under bilateral monopoly. *Journal of Personality and Social Psychology*, 1968, *9*, 15-20.

MacCrimmon, K. R., and D. M. Messick. A framework for social motives. *Behavioral Science*, 1976, *21*, 86-100.

McClintock, C. G. 1972. Social motivation: A set of propositions. *Behavioral Science*, 1972, *17*, 438-454.

McClintock, C. G., and S. P. McNeel. Reward and score feedback as determinants of cooperative and competitive behavior. *Journal of Personality and Social Psychology*, 1966a, *4*, 606-615.

– – –. Reward level and game playing behavior. *Journal of Conflict Resolution*, 1966b, *10*, 98-102.

Messick, D. M., and C. G. McClintock. Motivational bases of choice in experimental games. *Journal of Experimental Social Psychology*, 1968, *4*, 1-25.

Siegel, S., and L. E. Fouraker. *Bargaining and Group Decision Making: Experiments in Bilateral Monopoly*. New York: McGraw-Hill, 1960.

Walster, E., E. Berscheid, and G. W. Walster. New directions in equity research. *Journal of Personality and Social Psychology*, 1973, *25*, 151-176.

Yukl, G. A. Effects of situational variables and opponent concessions on a bargainer's perception, aspiration, and concessions. *Journal of Personality and Social Psychology*, 1974, *29*, 227-236.

15

SOCIAL DECISION SITUATIONS: INTEGRATION AND APPLICATION

Hermann Brandstätter and Heinz Schuler

The first chapter of this book, by Nagao, Vollrath, and Davis, points out the diversity of empirical research and theoretical reasoning on social decision or choice situations, both in origins and current status. It also makes clear how the work reported in this volume is related to similar research activities elsewhere. This final chapter looks briefly at a taxonomy of social decision situations, at research strategies facilitating theoretical integration, and at problems associated with the application of results.

Nominal classifications like "mixed-motive interaction" and "cooperative interaction" prove useful in grouping experimental literature. Real-life choice situations, however, can perhaps be described better by a set of dimensions on which the situation in question can be rated. The dimensions we wish to propose are derived from a preliminary phenomenological analysis of social decision situations. Future research must determine if they are not only intuitively plausible but also useful for theoretical differentiation and integration of the field. Five task and two social relations dimensions will be proposed.

The five task dimensions are: (a) prominence of the probabilities of events (including the probabilities of outcomes of a social decision); (b) prominence of the values of events (including the values of outcomes of a social decision); (c) prominence of the allocation of resources among the members of a group; (d) perceived verifiability of the correctness of the social decision; (e) perceived importance of the consequences of the social decision. Examples may clarify the meaning of these dimensions. A commission of experts can disagree about the efficiency of measures to curb unemployment (high prominence of probabilities of outcomes) but agree on the evaluation of unemployment as a deplorable state (low prominence of the evaluation of a state). On the other hand, a committee in charge of reforming penal law may agree on estimating the probabilities of crimes and on estimating the efficiency of preventive measures, but disagree about the ethical acceptability of the death penalty and life sentences as a measure to prevent criminal acts. In bargaining for a lower price of a commodity, the central controversy is not one of probabilities or values, but of which one of the groups will receive what portion of the benefits and bear what costs. Some choice situations have a clearly verifiable solution, whether by logical reasoning, by empirical operation or by comparison with a social norm; others lack such a verifiable solution. Finally, situations may vary in perceived importance of consequences.

Any social choice situation relates to all five dimensions, although to varying degrees. A conflict over the distribution of benefits and costs is prominent in a bargaining situation, but can also become salient in a group cooperating in the search for the correct solution to a problem—such as when competition arises for influence and prestige. The value controversy, too, can emerge from any discussion of facts and probabilities of possible outcomes. Verifiability of a social decision and importance of its consequences may vary widely within almost any kind of social choice situation.

We propose the following dimensions of social relations among members of a group: (f) perceived social dependence; (g) perceived obligations to a constituency.

The perceived social dependence is high, for example, in situations where: a group must decide under a unanimity rule, individual responses can be observed by the other group members, members of the group expect future interaction, or members of the group can reward and punish one another. Perceived social dependence is low, conversely, for a person not actively participating in a discussion when listening to it before individually deciding the issue, when not caring about friendliness or hostility of the others, or when no obligation to the group decision is experienced.

Obligations to a represented group may vary from no obligation at all to strict orders concerning the range of allowed concessions. Even if no formal delegation exists, a person in a social choice situation may feel more or less obliged to persons or groups not participating in the decision.

It will be necessary to develop procedures that allow reliable measurement of decision situations on these various dimensions. Further analysis will lead to a more satisfactory differentiation and definition of the dimensional structure. It should be useful for describing real-life as well as experimental social choice situations, and facilitate in the judgment of external validity.

Since any social decision situation may change its character in the course of interaction, the general descriptive system should be viable also in measuring those changes. More specific descriptive systems like the Interaction Process Analysis and its modifications (Bales, 1970), or the Conference Process Analysis (Morley and Stephenson, 1977) can be conceived of as rather microscopic analyses of selected classes of social choice situations. They can and should be related to the more comprehensive and less differentiated dimensions proposed here.

A brief look at some of the experiments reported in this volume suggests that the aforementioned dimensions could prove useful in theory building and hypothesis testing. For example, Verhagen's experiment is based on the assumption that in matters of value, when probabilities of events are not salient, agreement with a co-oriented peer immunizes against the influence of an expert. Depending on whether probabilities or values, or both, were salient in the various discussion experiments reviewed by Brandstätter, verbal aggressiveness of a discussant apparently was perceived differently and elicited different responses in others. When the social choice situation is characterized mainly by controversy over the distribution of benefits and costs, as in the research reported by Morley, Stephenson, Mikula and Schwinger, Müller and Crott, we have an area of research not only marked by a special name, "mixed-motive interaction," but also structured by specific theories. The verifiability of the social decision seems to be relevant for explaining the results of experiments reported by Zaleska. The importance of consequences of a social choice is the dimension on which real negotiation groups analyzed by Stephenson, and real decision committees analyzed by Rüttinger, differ from the laboratory experiments reported in this volume. Within the laboratory setting, the experiment of Müller and Crott as well as that of Lambert focus on the importance of consequences by varying the amount of money at stake.

In the studies reviewed or reported in this volume, various degrees of social dependence with specific theoretical implications have also been realized. Social dependence is high when a unanimous decision must be made as in the experiments of Lambert and Zaleska, but also in Müller and Crott's bargaining experiment and in Stephenson's real negotiation groups. On the other hand, social dependence is low in the experiments with

subjects observing a discussion and giving private ratings of their preferences, as in the experiment of von Rosenstiel and Stocker-Kreichgauer.

Furthermore, links between different types of social decision experiments could be established by defining a broad category of dependent
variables "yielding to the partner's demand," including meeting the partner's judgments of facts and values as well as meeting wishes in interpersonal allocation of resources. Virtually all experiments reported in this
volume have in common a dependent variable of "yielding to the partner's
demand," whether this demand is openly stated or inconspicuously hinted.

No doubt the proposed dimensions can be criticized for many reasons,
but few would disagree that the multiplicity of situational variables facing
experiments on social choice must be reduced to a few key concepts by
combining variables presumably functioning in a similar way. Witte (1977)
has taken an important step in that direction with stimulating ideas for
theoretical integration of small group research.

Phenomenological analysis of one's own and the other's subjective
experience may prove helpful in developing integrative concepts and
promoting theory. To find out how a person structures various social
decision situations, possibly with a quite restricted number of concepts
along with how he plans his actions within this cognitive structure, is an
important step toward understanding the social process. Thinking aloud or
the retrospective comments of group members viewing a videotape of their
earlier discussion are promising, although cumbersome, methods for analyzing subjective experience.

A great deal of experimental work seems to be lacking sensitive and
circumspect analysis of subjective experience, causing a tremendous loss of
time and effort. To strive for improvement of phenomenological analysis
(both of subjective experience and observed behavior) is probably the best
way not only to overcome the dissipation of experimental efforts, but also
to secure external validity and social relevance of laboratory experiments.

Having collected information on the perception of social choice situations by the flexible and rather unrestricted procedures of "thinking
aloud" or "playback comments," one may proceed to more precise
methods of scaling or factor analysis of perceived similarities of social
choice situations, and of deriving thereby the dimensions that people use
in their cognitive structuring of situations (see Magnusson, 1976). One
may hope that phenomenological and statistical procedures can be combined in a way that the specific strengths of the two kinds of methods
cumulate whereas their specific weaknesses neutralize each other in establishing a finally acceptable system for measuring social decision situations.

Let us consider, as a final question, what the papers in this volume, and
research on social decision processes, may contribute to better understand-

ing of behavior outside the laboratory or to improving social choice actions by improved control of conditions and consequences. Can we directly apply laboratory results and related theory to real-life social action, or must an additional link be typically constructed to connect the two realms? Or, must we even admit that, aside from the satisfaction of curiosity, little is to be expected from such research? The answer to this general question, tentative and constantly subject to revision, has to be discriminative with respect to differing contributions and scope as well as with regard to our ultimate goals. In other words, we must ask whether our efforts are aimed exclusively at a better understanding of human social behavior, or whether we also hope to improve interaction processes and their consequences.

In some respects, the "Studies in Cooperative Interaction: Cognitive Aspects" stand ready to be generalized with the least difficulty. This seems to be more often the case when the thrust of the investigation lies with individual cognition rather than with processes of interactional dynamics. Paradoxically, this happens when social psychology is minimally social. It may well be that we are coping with the most refractory field of psychology in this respect. Recall, for example, the early investigations in cognition by the "Wurzburg School" of the 1920s. There was no essential problem of generalization for the results Karl Bühler and his colleagues gained from trained subjects "thinking aloud," although even here the subjects may have been far from representative in their sophistication in psychology. There are, however, several areas in modern psychology as well where problems of external validity hardly exist.

Doise's paper may be one of the more fortunate in this regard. The results of his investigations, based on the work of Piaget, presumably hold for classroom and other interaction settings. These processes might be expected, of course, to interact in any given situation with several others, altering accordingly the exact character of experimental results.

More difficult to generalize are results from studies of variables which are changed by the very characteristics of the group; examples might be the dependency of decisional risk level on group size or of the conflict resolution process on group homogeneity. Recent reports of the search for the risky shift phenomenon in real group decisions may have been too pessimistic. Janis' (1972) analysis of the victims of groupthink show there *is* something to such phenomena, but the numerous failures to demonstrate risky shifts in actual groups indicate that real decisions must be different from decisions in the laboratory, perhaps not only in complexity but in basic structure. It does not seem unreasonable, then, to provide laboratory group decisions with better opportunities to achieve external validity by placing subjects in the roles of real decision makers, as in the reported studies with mock trials. Should these studies prove generalizable, they promise not only to be *descriptive* of real events or processes, but also to suggest an important means for studying diverse decision procedures. (For example, studies are underway at the University of Augsburg comparing certain German and U.S. trial procedures.)

More problematic is the extension beyond the laboratory of experimental results addressing persuasion processes. These are the object of various contributions in the first and second parts of this volume. Results and applications of such complex experimental procedures depend extensively on the particular operationalizations of variables. Experimental biases also may operate in such studies to an especially high degree. The introduction to Part II remarked upon the difficulty inherent in generalization from this type of study. Moreover, it may be difficult to recognize the nature of any implications for improvements in social decision processes. For example, is the finding that some sorts of friendly behavior tend to enhance influence over discussion partners to be welcomed or decried? Such effects may have advantages as well as disadvantages in practical social choice situations. However, while such research may have no obvious immediate application, as in many gaming or bargaining experiments, it should certainly contribute to a better general understanding of how group decisions occur.

There have been numerous claims of external validity for mixed-motive research results. Among the most ambitious was Deutsch's (1969, p. 1091) claim that games of conflict are relevant to war and peace. Whether such expectations are accurate is not much less questionable now than at the time they were first expressed. Therefore, critics have especially scored conflict games as unsuitable, lacking much mundane realism. Not only are theories and experimental results ideally to be linked to each other, but both in turn must be related explicitly to the questions and problems of social life which initiated the research activities.

It would not seem unfair to assess now the return on the tremendous investment of resources in experimental gaming, by systematically seeking the ecologically relevant combinations of models, hypotheses, and results that best satisfy the questions about social reality that initiated the research efforts.

To avoid an overly pessimistic view, it must be said that some of the results from studies of conflict games have withstood the test of generalizability in quite different settings, e.g., the observation that eye contact, verbal communication, and physical closeness all benefit cooperation.

Looking at the wider field of experimental bargaining and negotiation studies (as reported by Morley in this volume), many results appear which apparently generalize to real life; these seem to be the product of experimental simulations that capture the crucial characteristics of real bargaining situations. Also relevant in this connection is a study reported by Tietz (1976) in which data on student aspiration levels were collected while students were playing the part of wage negotiators with a high degree of realism. Studies comparing self-dependent behavior in bargaining with the behavior of representatives also belong to this category. By linking these data to field observations of practical policy, showing, say, that representatives of political groups tend to be more extreme than their constituency, a wide and important range of applications comes to mind.

Experiments in reward allocation look somewhat less favorable at first glance; only very small rewards are to be distributed to members, the important variable of "power" is neglected, and other restrictions make many such studies inadequate simulations of highly complex social situations. It might seem that only less global results which can be recognized in everyday interaction, like the "politeness ritual," are generalizable. While this may be true for many of these studies, the nucleus which they all share is indeed relevant for matters of importance to our social world. Adams (e.g., 1965) has claimed that equity theory makes meaningful statements about reactions to perceived social inequality and to different modes of economic resource distribution. Perhaps, one ought to view the research to date as preliminary. But, there can be no doubt that further progress in this direction belongs to the most important work psychology can perform today, because these questions are directed to some of the most important problems to be solved within the next decades.

It holds for all studies of group decision processes that a sufficient amount of external validity will only be attained by large investments of creative effort including methodology. Subjects, settings, group size, discussion topics, and many other determinants of outcomes must be varied, as well as reasonable dependent variables recognizable in the world beyond the laboratory, in order to gain results that bear at least some plausible generalizability. But, the notion of a map where the *terra incognita* is eventually charted seems to be an erroneous one; the unknown also increases as we proceed. There is another picture we consider more reasonable and, by far, more economical. It is the picture of stones thrown into a brook in sufficient number and distance from each other such that one may reach the other bank—with a certain risk but perhaps with dry feet. Part of this technique is, of course, to have at least some idea where the other bank is located.

All things considered, answers to the questions of generalizability and the applicability of results from studies of social decision processes do not seem overly optimistic; at second glance, the situation appears to be

270 DYNAMICS OF GROUP DECISIONS

markedly better. In some cases, the findings even appear to be of great social relevance. We must set about further tests.

REFERENCES

Adams, J. S. Inequity in social exchange. In L. Berkowitz (Ed.), *Advances in Experimental Social Psychology,* Vol. 2. New York: Academic, 1965.

Bales, R. F. *Personality and Interpersonal Behavior.* New York: Holt, Rinehart and Winston, 1970.

Deutsch, M. Socially relevant science: Reflections on some studies of interpersonal conflict. *American Psychologist,* 1969, *24,* 1076-1092.

Janis, I. L. *Victims of Groupthink.* Boston: Houghton Mifflin, 1972.

Magnusson, D. *Analysis of situational dimensions.* In N. S. Endler and D. Magnusson (eds.), *Interactional Psychology and Personality.* New York: Wiley, 1976.

Morley, I.E., and G. M. Stephenson. *The Social Psychology of Bargaining.* London: Allen and Unwin, 1977.

Tietz, R. Der Anspruchsausgleich in experimentellen Zwei-Personen-Verhandlungen mit verbaler Kommunikation. In H. Brandstätter and H. Schuler (Eds.), *Entscheidungsprozesse in Gruppen.* Bern: Huber, 1976.

Witte, E. H. Das Verhalten in Gruppensituationen. Ein theoretisches Konzept. Inauguraldissertation, Hamburg, 1977.

OTTOBEUREN SYMPOSIUM ON GROUP DECISION PROCESSES, 1976

The following persons participated in the Ottobeuren symposium on group decision processes in October, 1976. Those whose name is preceded by an asterisk are authors or co-authors of chapters appearing in this volume.

*Prof. Dr. Hermann Brandstätter, Universität Augsburg, Augsburg, Federal Republic of Germany.

*Prof. Dr. Helmut Crott, Universität Mannheim, Mannheim, Federal Republic of Germany.

*Prof. Dr. James Davis, University of Illinois at Urbana-Champaign, Champaign, Ill.

*Prof. Dr. Willem Doise, Université de Genève, Genève, Switzerland.

Prof. Dr. Hubert Feger and Mrs. Barbara Feger, Rheinisch-Westfälische Technische Hochschule Aachen, Aachen, Federal Republic of Germany.

Prof. Dr. Hans Hiebsch, Friedrich-Schiller-Universität, Jena, German Democratic Republic.

Prof. Dr. Gerhard Kaminski, Universität Tübingen, Tübingen, Federal Republic of Germany.

*Prof. Dr. Roger Lambert, Université Paris, Paris, France.

*Prof. Dr. Gerold Mikula, Universität Graz, Graz, Austria.

*Dr. Ian Morley, University of Warwick, Great Britain.

*Mr. Ulf Peltzer, Universität Augsburg, Augsburg, Federal Republic of Germany.

*Prof. Dr. Lutz von Rosenstiel, Universität München, München, Federal Republic of Germany.

*Dr. Bruno Rüttinger, Universität Augsburg, Augsburg, Federal Republic of Germany.

*Dr. Heinz Schuler, Universität Augsburg, Augsburg, Federal Republic of Germany.

*Dr. Geoffrey Stephenson, University of Nottingham, Nottingham, Great Britain.

*Dr. Gisela Stocker-Kreichgauer, Universität Augsburg, Augsburg, Federal Republic of Germany.

Prof. Dr. Percey Tannenbaum, University of California, Berkeley, Cal.

*Dr. Jan Verhagen, Katholieke Universiteit, Nijmegen, Netherlands.

Dr. Erich Witte, Universität Hamburg, Hamburg, Federal Republic of Germany.

*Dr. Maryla Zaleska, Université Paris, Paris, France.

*Authors of contributions contained in this volume.

ABOUT THE AUTHORS

Hermann Brandstätter, born in 1930 in Grünburg, Austria, studied psychology and philosophy at Innsbruck and Munich. He was a member of the Institute of Applied Psychology at the University of Munich from 1964 to 1970. Since then he has held a chair of psychology at the Department of Economics and Social Sciences at the University of Augsburg. His research interests have been primarily in the fields of group decision making, emotions, and organizational psychology.

Helmut W. Crott, born in 1938, studied psychology at the University of Münster (Diploma, 1964) and the University of Hamburg (Ph.D., 1967), where he remained until 1974. Since 1975 he has been professor of general and social psychology at the University of Freiburg. His current research interests are in psychology of social interaction and groups, stereotypes and prejudices, and methodological problems in social psychology.

James H. Davis received his Ph.D. from Michigan State University and is currently professor of psychology at the University of Illinois. In addition to numerous articles on small-group problem solving and group decision making, he is author of *Group Performance.* His research has primarily been concerned with formal theories of basic social processes associated with collective behavior.

Willem Doise was born in 1935 in Flanders, Belgium. He studied psychology at the Sorbonne, Paris (License, 1964; Doctorat, 1967). From 1967 to 1972 he was a research associate at the Ecole Pratique des Hautes Etudes and The Centre National de la Recherche Scientifique, Paris. Since 1972 he has been professor of experimental social psychology at the University of Geneva. During 1976-1977 he was visiting professor at the Université Libre de Bruxelles. His main research interests are intergroup relations, group discussion and polarization, social interaction and cognitive development.

Roger Lambert is director of research at the Centre National de la Recherche Scientifique. In addition, he directs a research group at the Laboratoire de Psychologie Sociale of the Université Paris, where he also supervises thesis work. His research is now mainly concerned with the experimental study of social influence and decision processes in situations of uncertainty.

Gerald Mikula, born in 1943, received his psychological training at the University of Graz. Since completing his Ph.D. in 1966, he has become professor and director of the Department of Social Psychology at the University of Graz. Reward allocation and equity, as well as interpersonal attraction, are his main research interests.

Ian E. Morley, born in 1945, received his Ph.D. in psychology from the University of Nottingham in 1971. He was assistant lecturer and lecturer at the Department of Psychology, University of Hull, until 1974. He then became lecturer in psychology at the University of Warwick. His research focuses upon the psychology of bargaining and negotiation, as well as other topics in social and industrial psychology.

Günter F. Müller was born in 1946 and studied psychology at the University of Mannheim, where he received both his Diploma (1974) and his Ph.D. (1977). Since 1974 he has been assistant professor at the Center for Economic and Social Psychological Research on Decision Making at the University of Mannheim. His research interests include intra- and intergroup processes of conflict and power and of decision making in applied settings (wage equity, leadership, labor negotiations, training of bargaining skills).

Dennis H. Nagao received his B.A. degree in 1975 from the University of Illinois, where he is currently a Ph.D. candidate in social psychology. His current research interests center on group performance, particularly the influence of task factors on the decision making processes of mock juries.

Ulf Peltzer was a member of the Institute for Psychological Methods and Mathematical Psychology at the University of Regensburg before joining the "Group Decision Processes" research group at the University of Augsburg in 1974. His publications have been in areas of industrial and social psychology. His main research interests include social interaction and formal models of group processes.

Bruno Rüttinger is a member of the Institute for Psychology at the University of Augsburg. His main research interests are group decision making, social conflict, and industrial clinical psychology.

Heinz Schuler is a member of the Institute for Psychology at the University of Augsburg, where he earned his Ph.D. In 1977 he received a Deutsche Forschungsgemeinschaft grant supporting his project on research ethics. Besides decision making and research ethics, his interests and publications focus on person perception and organizational psychology.

Thomas Schwinger, born in 1948, studied psychology at the University of Graz, receiving his Ph.D. in 1976. Since then he has held the position of assistant professor at the University of Mannheim's Center for Economic and Social Psychological Research on Decision Making.

Craig E. Spitzer is presently completing his Ph.D. in the Social Psychology Division at the University of Illinois. He received his B.S. from Syracuse University in 1974 and his M.A. from the University of Illinois in 1977. As of 1978 (September) he will be a research analyst for the Quaker Oats Company, Chicago, Illinois. His research interests have included the study of the social processes exhibited by mock juries, and the patterns of mutual social influence in dynamic task groups.

Garold Stasser received his Ph.D. in social psychology at the University of Illinois in 1977. He is presently an assistant professor of psychology at Miami University, Oxford, Ohio. Current research interests include the role of normative and informational influence in decision making groups and the effects of competition and evaluation on individual performance.

Geoffrey M. Stephenson has been reader in psychology and director of the Applied Social Psychology Research Unit at Nottingham University. In 1978 he took the chair of social psychology at the University of Kent at Canterbury. Besides his theoretical work in experimental social psychology, he has conducted research and advised in a wide range of industrial and other organizations, and has published studies on such topics as negotiation, motivation, job satisfaction. He currently holds a five-year Programme Grant from the Social Science Research Council on "Experimental Social Psychology in Organizations."

Gisela Stocker-Kreichgauer is a member of the Institute for Psychology at the University of Augsburg. She has conducted research investigation socio-emotional influences on group decision making. Her interests also include group dynamics and organizational training and development.

Jan Verhagen studied social psychology at the University of Utrecht (Holland), where he specialized in group dynamics. He is currently a member of the Department of Social Psychology at the University of Nijmegen, and he is engaged in research on the processes of power in small systems, social composition, and attitude formation and change within group relationships. His most recent theoretical interest centers on the translation of intra- and intergroup power dynamics into organizational power processes.

David A. Vollrath is a Ph.D. candidate in social psychology at the University of Illinois. He received his B.A. degree from the University of Wisconsin in 1976. His interests center on applications of psychology in legal settings, particularly involving juries, but include more general topics in group decision and memory processes as well.

Lutz von Rosenstiel, born in 1938 in Danzig (German Democratic Republic), is professor of psychology at the University of Munich and head of the Department of Industrial and Organizational Psychology. He has recently been working in the fields of motivation, organizational psychology, and consumer psychology.

Maryla Zaleska, born in Poznan, Poland, in 1947. In 1964 she obtained a Diplôme d'Etudes Supérieures at the Sorbonne University and in 1972 her doctor's degree. Her diploma was concerned with group performance and the thesis with individual and group risk-taking. She is currently at the Laboratoire de Psychologie Sociale de l'Université Paris, associated with the Centre National de la Recherche Scientifique. While her general area of interest is the study of influence and decision process in small groups, she has published papers on group problem-solving, risk-taking and on probability perception.